TURKEY'S KURDISH QUESTION

TURKEY'S KURDISH QUESTION

Henri J. Barkey and Graham E. Fuller

CARNEGIE COMMISSION ON PREVENTING DEADLY CONFLICT

CARNEGIE CORPORATION OF NEW YORK

ROWMAN & LITTLEFIELD PUBLISHERS, INC.
Lanham • Boulder • New York • Oxford

ROWMAN & LITTLEFIELD PUBLISHERS, INC.

Published in the United States of America
by Rowman & Littlefield Publishers, Inc.
4720 Boston Way, Lanham, Maryland 20706

12 Hid's Copse Road
Cumnor Hill, Oxford OX2 9JJ, England

British Library Cataloguing in Publication Information Available

Library of Congress Cataloging-in-Publication Data

Barkey, Henri J.
 Turkey's Kurdish question / Henri J. Barkey and Graham E. Fuller.
  p. cm.
 Includes bibliographical references (p.) and index.
 ISBN 0-8476-8552-7 (cloth).—ISBN 0-8476-8553-5 (pbk.)
  1. Kurds—Turkey. 2. Turkey—Ethnic relations. 3. Turkey—
Politics and government—1980– 4. Kurds—Turkey—Ethnic identity.
I. Fuller, Graham H. II. Title.
DR435.K87B37 1998
956.1'00491597—dc21   97-30696
                  CIP

ISBN 0-8476-8552-7 (cloth : alk. paper)
ISBN 0-8476-8553-5 (pbk. : alk. paper)

Printed in the United States of America

∞ ™ The paper used in this publication meets the minimum requirements of
American National Standard for Information Sciences—Permanence of Paper for
Printed Library Materials, ANSI Z39.48–1984.

ABOUT THE
Carnegie Commission on Preventing Deadly Conflict Series

Carnegie Corporation of New York established the Carnegie Commission on Preventing Deadly Conflict in May 1994 to address the threats to world peace of intergroup violence and to advance new ideas for the prevention and resolution of deadly conflict. The commission is examining the principal causes of deadly ethnic, nationalist, and religious conflicts within and between states and the circumstances that foster or deter their outbreak. Taking a long-term, worldwide view of violent conflicts that are likely to emerge, it seeks to determine the functional requirements of an effective system for preventing mass violence and to identify the ways in which such a system could be implemented. The commission is also looking at the strengths and weaknesses of various international entities in conflict prevention and considering ways in which international organizations might contribute toward developing an effective international system of nonviolent problem solving. The series grew out of the research that the commission has sponsored to answer the three fundamental questions that have guided its work: What are the problems posed by deadly conflict and why is outside help often necessary to deal with these problems? What approaches, tasks, and strategies appear most promising for preventing deadly conflict? What are the responsibilities and capacities of states, international organizations, and private and nongovernmental organizations for undertaking preventive action?

The books are published as a service to scholars, students, practitioners, and the interested public. While they have undergone peer review and have been approved for publication, the views that they express are those of the author or authors, and commission publication does not imply that those views are shared by the commission as a whole or by individual commissioners.

Published in the series:

Bridging the Gap: A Future Security Architecture for the Middle East, by Shai Feldman and Abdullah Toukan

The Price of Peace: Incentives and International Conflict Prevention, edited by David Cortright

Sustainable Peace: The Role of the UN and Regional Organizations in Preventing Conflict, by Connie Peck

Turkey's Kurdish Question, by Henri J. Barkey and Graham E. Fuller

Forthcoming:

The Ambivalence of the Sacred: Religion, Violence, and Reconciliation, by Scott Appleby

Opportunities Missed, Opportunities Seized: Preventive Diplomacy in the Post–Cold War World, edited by Bruce Jentleson

The Costs of Conflict: Prevention and Care in the Global Arena, edited by Michael E. Brown and Richard N. Rosecrance

Reports available from the commission:

David Hamburg, *Preventing Contemporary Intergroup Violence,* founding essay of the commission, April 1994.

David Hamburg, *Education for Conflict Resolution,* April 1995.

Comprehensive Disclosure of Fissionable Materials: A Suggested Initiative, June 1995.

Larry Diamond, *Promoting Democracy in the 1990s: Actors and Instruments, Issues and Imperatives,* December 1995.

Andrew J. Goodpaster, *When Diplomacy Is Not Enough: Managing Multinational Military Interventions,* July 1996.

Jane E. Holl, *Carnegie Commission on Preventing Deadly Conflict: Second Progress Report,* July 1996.

John Stremlau, *Sharpening International Sanctions: Toward a Stronger Role for the United Nations,* November 1996.

Alexander L. George and Jane E. Holl, *The Warning–Response Problem and Missed Opportunities in Preventive Diplomacy,* May 1997.

John Stremlau with Helen Zille, *A House No Longer Divided: Progress and Prospects for Democratic Peace in South Africa,* July 1997.

Nik Gowing, *Media Coverage: Help or Hindrance in Conflict Prevention,* September 1997.

Cyrus R. Vance and David A. Hamburg, *Pathfinders for Peace: A Report to the UN Secretary-General on the Role of Special Representatives and Personal Envoys,* September 1997.

Preventing Deadly Conflict: Executive Summary of the Final Report, December 1997.

Gail W. Lapidus with Svetlana Tsalik, eds., *Preventing Deadly Conflict: Strategies and Institutions,* Proceedings of a Conference in Moscow, Russia, February 1998.

Scott Feil, *Preventing Genocide: How the Early Use of Force Might Have Succeeded in Rwanda,* March 1998.

Douglas Lute, *Improving National Capacity To Respond to Complex Emergencies: The U.S. Experience,* March 1998.

Tom Gjelten, *Professionalism in War Reporting: A Correspondent's View,* March 1998.

To order *Power Sharing and International Mediation in Ethnic Conflicts* by Timothy Sisk, copublished by the commission and the United States Institute of Peace, please contact USIP Press, P.O. Box 605, Herndon, VA 22070, USA; phone: (800) 868-8064 or (703) 661-1590.

Full text or summaries of these reports are available on the commission's web site: http://www.ccpdc.org

To order a report or to be added to the commission's mailing list, contact:
Carnegie Commission on Preventing Deadly Conflict
1779 Massachusetts Avenue, NW, Suite 715
Washington, DC 20036-2103
Phone: (202) 332-7900 Fax: (202) 332-1919

Members of the Carnegie Commission on Preventing Deadly Conflict

Contents

Foreword

How to deal with Turkey's Kurds is the subject of this important and provocative book.

The "Kurdish issue" is Turkey's most difficult and painful problem, one that presents a vast moral dilemma for the country. The issue, as the authors note, feeds Turkey's continuing inflation and is the major source of human rights violations and the biggest irritant in Turkey's relations with the European Union. Its most pronounced manifestation, the war in the southeast against Kurdish insurgents, has left more than twenty thousand dead and many hundreds of thousands displaced. Despite the massive Turkish military effort and some significant gains in coping with the Kurdistan Workers' party (PKK) insurgency, the fighting continues after thirteen years, although it has not reached the major cities of Turkey as many have long predicted.

The issue has been with Turkey almost since the beginning of the republic in 1923. Atatürk stamped out serious Kurdish rebellions in the 1920s and '30s. Modern Turkey has never accepted the notion of a Kurdish ethnic minority with minority rights. Turks have readily accepted Kurds as Turks but have difficulty letting Kurds be both Kurds and Turks. In the past twenty years the issue has been transformed by a variety of factors—demographic, economic, and geopolitical. Perhaps half of Turkey's six to twelve million Kurds (estimates vary widely) have moved out of the southeast and into the western cities of Turkey and have increasingly become integrated into the growing Turkish economy. Large numbers of Kurds have emigrated to Europe, where they finance Kurdish nationalist activity, including the PKK, and promote the Kurdish cause among Western European publics. The insurgency has outside support (Syria and Iran), outside financing, and a refuge inside the internationally policed no-fly zone in Iraq. Moreover, unlike earlier Kurdish insurrections, the war with the PKK gets public attention in the United States and Western Europe, not least because the Gulf War led to a major involvement of Turkey in the predominantly Kurdish areas of northern Iraq.

As the authors correctly point out, the Turkish state has treated the Kurdish issue as if it were identical to the PKK insurrection, as if the problem would be over once the PKK was eliminated. Until very recently, the United States has mostly agreed with this position, but the European states less so. The focus of the Turkish government, except for the spasmodic interest in the economic development of the southeast, has been to wipe out the PKK's military arm.

A month before his death in April 1993, I asked President Turgut Özal, a man of insight and great intellect, the question "What would you do?" Inherent in his answer was that economic growth would ultimately resolve the problem by ending the Kurds' status as a disadvantaged minority. But his explanation had a different thrust. He pointed out that half the people of the southeast had already left, primarily for economic reasons. Private investment would not go there; it is dangerous and costly, and there are far more productive and easier opportunities elsewhere in Turkey. The only answer, Özal believed, is to install incentives to get the remaining population of the southeast to move out. Özal was not just jesting, and he was not oblivious to the difficulties. Sizable emigration and the existence of a large urban Kurdish minority in a vast Turkish sea has already significantly complicated Kurdish perspectives. In any event, no Turkish government is likely to adopt Özal's approach publicly.

This book is the authors' answer to the "What would you do?" question. It is based on extensive study, many interviews with Kurds and Turks, and a long familiarity with Turkey. It is a policy book since the mass of information and analysis is directly geared to finding a better approach to the issue. Unfortunately, no good statistical basis exists for analyzing Kurdish matters, or for generalizing about the views of Turkey's far-flung Kurdish populations. The authors have had to make important judgments on some basic concerns. They call for a solution "within current borders" that inter alia (1) effectively establishes a legal Kurdish identity, (2) radically reduces and alters the current military approach in the southeast, (3) protects rather than harasses or bans Kurdish political parties, (4) allows Kurds education in their own language, and (5) decentralizes the administration of the state. They call for a dialogue, as inclusive as possible, with Kurds of differing political views and from various backgrounds. A basic requirement, in their view, is greater democracy and openness in Turkey, a prescription that in any case would serve Turkey's ultimate interests. Such a proposal as greater government decentralization is also important for Turkey regardless of its impact on the Kurdish issue. Many of these ideas have been voiced before, but until now they have not been put together in such a comprehensive way geared to policymakers and backed up by detailed analysis. I am not sure the authors' solutions will deal with the problem, but I frankly do not have a good prescription. Many Turks will declare them unnecessary and divisive. In the unlikely event that the Turkish government were to agree on the utility of the proposed measures, carrying them out is another question. There are strong and differing views on this issue among important groups in Turkey. But the authors have done a great deal; they cannot also be implementers.

This issue requires ventilation among and between Turks and Kurds alike. While public discussion of the Kurdish issue has significantly increased in Turkey in this decade, it is a subject that is handled very tenderly; options are rarely discussed. Turks do not like to be branded as unpatriotic, nor do they want to be threatened with a trial by the state prosecutor. Many Turks in fact still believe that the United States really is trying to split Turkey and carve out a Kurdish state. My numerous denials of such a plan when I was the American ambassador in Turkey were met with a certain skepticism; I felt at times that even raising the Kurdish issue made me suspect in some quarters.

The book's greatest contribution may be its impact in Turkey. It will certainly be widely read and get attention in the media. It will be noted and discussed, and this is of real, if intangible, value and very much what the authors hope to see.

Morton Abramowitz
Washington, D.C.

Preface

A few comments about the nature of this study—what it is and what it is not: First of all, this work represents a policy study. It is designed to examine the problems for Turkish policymakers and Turkish society, as well as for Turkey's friends and allies, stemming from the unrest among the Kurdish population in Turkey. We attempt to analyze the nature of the Kurdish problem in the setting of Turkish culture, politics, and society, and to offer some tentative approaches toward a solution. The report focuses much attention on the Kurds in Turkey but is not intended to be a study of Kurdish culture and society except as it relates to the policy problem.

Our first concern in preparing this study is for the future stability and well-being of Turkey as a key American ally, and for the Turkish government's ability to deal satisfactorily with the debilitating Kurdish problem. We are concerned for the preservation of the territorial integrity of Turkey; we strongly favor a solution that can be achieved within a unified Turkish state if this is at all possible—at a time when many countries of the world are beset by devastating ethnic rebellions and separatist tendencies. We are also concerned for the loss of life suffered by Kurds and Turks as a result of the conflict.

The study is not intended to be a report on human rights in Turkey. Others have done that work. Our study looks at the human rights problem only insofar as human rights must be increasingly observed by all states that wish to be successful members of the international community; failure to observe human rights also carries a political cost for Turkey in Europe and Washington. Also, we are interested in determining how the Turkish government can work to satisfy the special material and psychological needs of the Kurds to maintain a secure existence within Turkey. If their basic needs cannot be successfully met by state policies, the integrity of Turkey as a state will be at risk. Other countries face similar problems, and we hope that that eventuality can be avoided in Turkey.

We must state at the outset that our research leads us to believe that the Kurdish conflict is in essence an ethnic problem, and not one of simple terrorism or economics—although both terrorism and economic hardship are indeed part of the current crisis. The key policy questions we raise in this study are the following:

- What are the origins of the Kurdish conflict in Turkey?
- What is the current nature of the conflict involving Kurds within Turkey?
- What do the Kurds in Turkey want?
- What are the problems that Kurdish aspirations raise for the Turkish state?
- How can Kurdish needs in Turkey be met while preserving the integrity of Turkish territory?

Both authors have spent many years professionally studying Turkey from various points of view—political, cultural, linguistic, social, economic, and foreign policy—and have spent much time in Turkey. Our interviews with well over one hundred people over a five-year period tended to focus more upon those Kurds and Turks who are concerned with the Kurdish problem. One might argue that, statistically speaking, we should have spoken with many Kurds who are not interested in the problem—to the extent they exist. But the problem the Turkish state confronts stems specifically from those Kurds that are concerned about and perhaps even active regarding the Kurdish issue. So our study is naturally influenced by those Kurds and Turks who think about the problem—the active elites who make things happen.

But it is important to point out that this study is not quantitative in approach. We did not seek to poll as many individuals as possible to find their views, nor was our interview technique designed to fill out a specific questionnaire or opinion poll. We rather sought to gain an understanding of the viewpoints, attitudes, and psychology of various and diverse Kurdish interlocutors: businessmen, intellectuals, lawyers, journalists, members of parliament, politicians, human rights activists, conservatives and liberals, "nationalists" and "assimilated." After a period of intensive interviews and discussions, we began to find considerable similarities of response from quite diverse individuals on many of the key issues of greatest concern to us. Over the course of two years we traveled often to Turkey and Europe, continuing the interviews and updating our sources. These interviews and meetings represent the bulk of our fieldwork. Indeed, we feel that our impressions from our many interviews and discussions left little ambiguity on many of the key issues, such as questions of identity, grievances, and hopes and aspirations.

We talked with a broad variety of ethnic Turks: members of nearly every political party, lawyers, human rights activists, members of parliament, businessmen, journalists, government officials—including members of intelligence organizations—academics, liberals, and conservatives. We have studied the full spectrum of Turkish daily newspapers and journals to get a feel for the range of press attitudes, to the extent the Kurdish problem is discussed; the majority of our citations in this study are from Turkish sources and from Kurds and Turks inside Turkey. We purchased as many books on the Kurdish issue published in Turkey as we could find. We especially tried to read frequently those newspapers published by Kurds in Turkey and outside. While the pro-Kurdish press is of much interest on issues of attitudes and goals, most of our press citations are from the few serious mainstream Turkish dailies. We also interviewed a number of Kurds and Kurdish leaders in several European countries, and we talked with many Kurds from Iran and Iraq in several Western countries, including the United States. We met with Kurdistan Workers' Party (Partiya Karkeren Kurdistan, or PKK) representatives in Europe as well as anti-PKK leaders.

While this study focuses on Turkey, we have tried to keep a broad comparative perspective as relates to ethnic issues generically. We have examined other ethnic issues and conflicts—in particular the Israeli-Palestinian problem, with which we are quite familiar—to find parallels. The two cases are of course quite different in many respects: Unlike the Palestinians in Israel, Kurds and Turks have lived on a basis of full legal equality in Turkey for over seventy-five years (as long as Kurds suppressed their identity); Israel seized the West Bank by military force, whereas Kurdish regions had long been part of the Ottoman Empire; major cultural, linguistic, and religious differences exist between Palestinians and Israelis, far less so between Kurds and Turks in Turkey. At the same time there are useful parallels between the two situations, such as issues of refusal to recognize distinct national identities, problems of dealing with nationalist movements that also practice terror and guerrilla warfare, the experiences with rapprochement of the two peoples, evolution of guerrilla organizations and their use of terror, and so forth. It is important to recognize that Turkey is hardly unique or alone in suffering from modern crises of an ethnic nature, and the Turkish case is far from the worst in the region.

We are well aware that the study has shortcomings. The single greatest problem is the paucity of hard data. Few Western scholars have written about the Kurds of Turkey, in comparison with the number of studies on other cultures in the Middle East. There has been very little writing at all from Turkish and Kurdish scholars in Turkey, for the simple reason that such inquiry has generally been forbidden by the state and often punishable under charges of inciting separatism or terrorism. Kurds have traditionally been reluctant to discuss their concerns as Kurds; foreigners visiting the southeast in the years since the guerrilla warfare and state of emergency have been under close scrutiny, so that private meetings with Kurds in the region are yet more difficult.

If this were a purely academic study, we would simply have had to conclude that we could not "prove" some of our key hypotheses in any way that would "convince" skeptics; indeed what constitutes "proof" is what academic debate is all about anyway. Because the most pertinent questions for policymakers are probably the most difficult to answer—that is why they are posed—we have felt compelled to answer those questions as we initially listed them. They require careful response, even if they cannot be answered definitively. We have tried in much of this work to indicate the difficulties in providing firm responses, and to give the basis of our reasoning when we feel the evidence is less than fully convincing. There perhaps is no data or evidence that would ever prove sufficient to convince those whose beliefs are already firm on this topic. We can only rest on our best judgments, based on the broad variety of information we acquired and on some considerable experience with the daunting problems of political forecasting.

Above all, we hope that this work will serve to encourage greater debate within Turkey itself, so that the Kurdish issue can be seriously treated by the many Turks and Kurds who have thought carefully about the problem, even if they have not always been able to publicize their views. If the Turkish government would permit it, Turkish and Kurdish scholars in Turkey could very quickly amass a body of data far superior to anything we present here, and debate it thoroughly in the press and academia. If this study can spark that kind of further research, marked by greater precision and increased information and understanding, then it will have been worthwhile.

We cannot presume to come in and tell either the Turkish government or the Kurds what their problem is and what to do about it. The Turkish government will move in the time and manner of its own choosing. On the other hand, this kind of effort must begin somewhere, and our chief concern is that at present there seems to be a political stalemate of long standing in the country. Indeed, this study was undertaken precisely because there are so few things written on this policy question that can help concerned Turks, Kurds, or Americans. For the Carnegie Commission on Preventing Deadly Conflict, the Kurdish case in Turkey has been one of the most important examples of ethnic violence today in a state that matters a great deal to the United States.

We have refrained from citing by name the individuals in Turkey whom we interviewed; we promised in all cases that no one would be identified, in order to overcome concerns and induce greater openness and frankness. We owe a great deal to the many individuals who spent so much time talking with us, often at great length or on several occasions, to give us deeper insight into their concerns and the nature of the problem. We would also like to take this occasion to especially thank Jane Holl at the Carnegie Commission on Preventing Deadly Conflict for having made this study possible. We thank RAND for having made its own financial contribution to the study. We also owe a debt of gratitude to Morton Abramowitz, George Harris, Heath Lowry, Serif Mardin, Stanley Roth, Eric Rouleau, and Shibley Telhami for encouraging us and reviewing and providing useful critiques of the manuscript before it was published. In addition we would like to thank Melissa Fuller, who helped us with a valuable literature review of relevant scholarly thinking on the problem of ethnic identity, separatism, and alternative forms of solution, and members of the staff of the Carnegie Commission on Preventing Deadly Conflict, especially Bob Lande, for their patience in arranging valuable critiques of the manuscript and in helping prepare the book for publication.

Introduction
Why Turkey Matters

W HY SHOULD AN EXAMINATION of the Turkish case be of interest to a broader audience concerned with conflict prevention? There are, after all, a multiplicity of countries in the world with internal frictions also meriting attention. Turkey is of particular interest because it presents a fascinating range of issues that have considerable generic applicability to conflict situations in the rest of the world.

Turkey's key internal conflict centers on the role of its large Kurdish minority—ethnically and linguistically distinct—in a state that constitutionally consists only of "citizens of Turkey"—Turks—with no ethnic distinctions drawn. Bearers of a long tradition and culture of their own for perhaps two millennia, the Kurds today are rapidly reformulating their own ethnic identity as a community and seeking its expression in legal terms in the cultural and political realm of Turkish life. In generic terms then, the Kurdish problem represents the striving of an ethnic minority to achieve legal recognition as such, and to establish legal rights deriving therefrom. Since most states in the world are multiethnic in reality, even if they are not always recognized as such, and in them minority ethnic rights are often denied, the Turkish situation is broadly representative of what most countries in the world already face, or will be facing.

The question raises difficult problems of multiculturalism—again common to much of the world. Is it desirable to seek broad "assimilation" of minorities when most members of that minority group perhaps prefer to retain their own language and culture in their own historical ethnic home-land? Is it understandable, or anachronistic, that minorities seek to pre-serve their own identity? And how much can the state impose "assimilation," particularly when it threatens the loss of distinct ethnicity and culture in the face of a larger and more dominant Turkish culture? These questions are likely to dominate the political agenda of much of the world in the next century.

Second, Turkey's Kurds represent only about 50 percent of the Kurds in the Middle East—Kurds are especially heavily represented in Iran and Iraq, and to a lesser extent in Syria. In other words, as an ethnic problem, Turkey's Kurds are not only an internal but also an international problem, in several senses. First, they are divided across international borders, like many other peoples of the world: Baluch, Punjabis, Uzbeks, Tajiks, Pash-tuns, Hungarians, Albanians, Mayas, Mongols, and many African peoples, to name just a few. The aspirations of a people in one country thus directly affect the aspirations and actions of the minority across the border. Any pretensions to ethnic unification of one of these peoples therefore not only imply separatism of territory from one country but also a massive redraw-ing of the international boundaries in the whole region in which that na-tionality resides. As a result of this threat, regional states may cooperate to ensure that a cross-boundary ethnic group is unable to exercise any resur-gent nationalism or separatism. This generic problem will confront the world more broadly in decades ahead as ethnic assertiveness inevitably grows.

States like Turkey that are faced with this kind of dilemma must there-fore either learn to develop new liberalized policies that will satisfy the cultural and political aspirations of the minority or face continual insur-gency, violence, and damage to democratic institutions and human rights, becoming unattractive as members of a new international community. How easily can this transition be negotiated?

The problem is also international in the sense that the Kurdish problem has been "exported" to Western Europe as well. Over half a million Kurds are resident there, particularly in Germany, where their political activities lead to domestic disruption and violence between Turkish and Kurdish communities. International organizations such as the European Union and the North Atlantic Treaty Organization (NATO) are affected because they are inevitably forced to take a position on the Kurdish problem in Turkey as it affects their organizations.

The difficulty of the Kurds in Turkey also raises important issues about the nature of governance in a state and its ability to solve internal ethnic conflict. Like several countries in Eastern Europe, Turkey is well along the road toward a reasonably functioning democratic order. It has had generally free elections for nearly forty years, punctuated by only three brief "correctional" military coups which—atypical of the region—fairly soon returned civilian government to power in each case. In an era in which a large number of countries in the world are on the threshold of democratic experiment, Turkey's democratic experience is of considerable importance. What is the relationship of the democratic order to the exigencies of conflict prevention and revolution? In the case of Turkey—a country with a broad and active civil society, a free press, and functioning democratic institutions—the tragedy has been that these democratic institutions have not yet been extended to the Kurdish population. The Kurdish problem has instead been relegated to the category of a "national security problem," thereby rendering most open discussion largely taboo.

How do aspiring democratic societies extend democratic discourse into the sensitive realm of security issues and domestic unrest? This problem assails many societies of the world, demonstrating first that less than fully developed democratic governance may be insufficient to manage complex aspects of internal security problems. As Turkey comes to develop a more open and liberalized policy toward its Kurdish minority, significant demands will again be placed upon its democratic institutions to facilitate the transitions from a constitutionally proclaimed homogeneous society to a formally recognized multiethnic society.

Turkey is also of special interest because it is probably the most politically advanced Muslim society of the world. Although constitutionally (and in many respects actually) a secular society, Turkey nonetheless has deep Muslim roots that affect its perceptions of minority status. Kurds, for example, were never considered a minority under Ottoman Islamic law because they too are Muslims; Islamic law recognizes only non-Muslims as officially constituting "minorities." That legacy has complicated the acceptance by most Turks today of the concept of a Muslim minority within the country. Turkey's effort to reconcile modern nationalism and contemporary norms of minority and human rights with traditional Islamic views will be of relevance to other Muslim countries that face problems of ethnic or religious minorities. In this vein, Turkey's Islamist Welfare party had an opportunity when in power to develop an "Islamic formula" whereby the

Kurds can be accommodated as an ethnically distinct group without offending Turkish nationalist instincts. It clearly was unable to provide such an alternative during its year-long tenure.

The Turkish case matters also because Turkish aspirations to gain full membership in the European Union raise questions about the kinds of societies and ethnic makeup that are compatible with European norms. Such problems confront any potential members in the EU that suffer from ethnic problems.

Finally, because of Turkey's close alliance with it, the United States faces particular challenges in helping Turkey to manage the Kurdish problem. This same challenge arose with Israel and its handling of the Palestinian problem. What types of pressures, if any, should the United States put on Turkey to move it toward a solution—out of its concern for human rights, democratic practice, and, above all, Turkey's own future viability?

For all these reasons, then, the case of the Kurds in Turkey is of interest to generalists in the fields of international relations and diplomacy. The problem is on the doorstep of the West, involving a close ally of the West and the largest ethnic group in the world without a state of its own. Can the problem be solved within the existing borders of today's Turkey? The outcome of this crisis has major implications for much of the rest of the world.

1

Origins of the Problem: The Roots of Kurdish Nationalism

THE KURDS ARE UNDERGOING a period of profound (re)awakening of their national consciousness as a people. They have, to be sure, been aware of themselves as a distinct people and community for well over a thousand years—linguistically sharply different from their Arab and Turkish neighbors and a distinct branch among diverse Iranian peoples. In the late nineteenth and twentieth centuries the Kurds of Iraq, Iran, and Turkey have at various times agitated for their local or national rights. Today, faced with a combination of dramatic domestic political changes and profound international developments, the Kurds of Turkey (as well as Iraq and Iran) have entered a new phase of national awareness. Domestic assertiveness has emerged in the context of a modern world of nation states, the spread of democratization and human rights, increased communication among all Kurds themselves, and raised political expectations. The emergence of new Kurdish political self-awareness is a political evolution largely irreversible in character: One does not readily unlearn learned ethnicity.

A Delayed National Emergence

Why have the Kurds, who constitute the largest ethnic bloc after the Arabs, Persians, and Turks in the Middle East, been relatively late in developing a modern nationalist movement? Different peoples of course experience differing patterns of nationalist growth, consistent with their geography and historical circumstances. The Kurds' delay in developing a strong nationalist movement results from several factors. Geography heads the list: As a people inhabiting a primarily mountainous region, the Kurds have been scattered and isolated from each other, with no strong central state structure like those that developed in the great plains of the Tigris and Euphrates or in the Nile valley in Egypt. Geography and a nomadic way of life for long periods strengthened the divergence of several Kurdish dialects, many of them not readily mutually comprehensible today. In political terms, for at least the past five hundred years the Kurds have been divided between Persian and Ottoman Empires; in the past seventy years they have been yet further divided among the states of Turkey, Iran, Iraq, and Syria. These political divisions, not surprisingly, seriously constrained opportunities to develop a more comprehensive national vision; at the same time, the states involved have been clearly intent upon inhibiting Kurdish nationalism within their borders.

The Kurds have also generally lived in the more isolated regions of larger empires, such as the Persian, the Arab Abbasid Caliphate in Baghdad, or the Ottoman; isolation from imperial centers slowed their development as a united and strongly self-conscious people. Isolation and an often pastoral way of life in many areas contributed to the development of a strong clan and tribal structure that perpetuated political and regional divisions.

During the time of the Ottoman Empire, the Kurds, along with other Muslims, were part of a broader Sunni Muslim core within a multiethnic empire. The empire was fully cognizant of its minorities—but it defined them in religious, not ethnic, terms. Thus the existence of sizable Christian and Jewish minorities was legally recognized. For Muslim ethnic groups, however, the concept of minority status in legal terms did not really exist: The Muslim social and religious core of the empire was made up of Turks, Arabs, and Kurds. Even if their languages and cultures differed, their religion basically did not: Sunnis were all equally Muslims and believers; ethnic and linguistic differences among them were of no legal consequence.

Kurds, as part of the Sunni community of the Ottoman Empire, were already treated as a distinct group by the sultan in the sixteenth century, when a number of independent principalities or fiefdoms (emirates) were established. Used by the sultan to ensure the stability of the borders, these emirates were autonomous in their internal affairs. In exchange for their autonomy, they provided the sultan taxes and soldiers. Although the relationship between these Kurdish lords and the sultan was not always free of trouble, the system survived into the nineteenth century.[1] Certainly Kurdish tribes and clans were well aware of their cultural and linguistic distinctiveness, but this was not an age in which "national" concepts were well formed. The autonomous Kurdish leaders were not particularly kind to their own populations either. Overall, Kurds identified with the larger Ottoman society, but, far more important, at the local level they identified with various religious orders or tribal groupings. These tribal groupings were often in conflict with each other, forming shifting patterns of alliances; indeed, the primary social cleavage lay between the tribal fighter and the sedentary cultivator.[2]

By the nineteenth century, new factors induced gradual political change in the relationship between the Kurds and the Ottoman administration: increased imperial intervention in the Kurdish regions, levies for troops, and warfare between Russia, Iran, and the Ottoman Empire that touched Kurdish areas increased challenges to the privileges of Kurdish overlords and a broader pattern of rebellion against Turkish rule throughout the empire. The empire's attempt at centralization was met with increased unrest in Kurdish areas, some of which was the result of recklessness by Kurdish chieftains intent on pursuing their own aggrandizement.[3] Among these rebellious leaders, Mir Mehmet Pasha of Rewanduz and Bedirhan Bey of Cizre are the most famous. The revolts were suppressed at the cost of many lives. There were a total of fifty various Kurdish insurrections against the Ottoman state, many involving the Kurds of today's Iraq as well.[4] These revolts, however, were not nationalistic in character and their suppression led to the strengthening of shaykhs and *tariqats* (religious orders) leaders, who would later play a significant role in fomenting new rebellions. By and large, the traditional feudal Kurdish lords in the areas, the *aghas,* perceived themselves "as Sunni Muslim subjects of a fundamentally Islamic empire and had no interest in an unpredictable Kurdish entity in which their own status may change for the worse."[5]

The changing fortunes of the empire at the end of the nineteenth century together with the nationalist stirrings of Armenians in regions also inhabited by Kurds provided some of the other reasons for Kurdish disenchantment. With his ascension to the throne in 1876, Sultan Abdulhamid II sought to solidify the base of the Ottoman state by emphasizing the

Islamic character of the empire. Among those to be co-opted were Kurdish leaders and elites. Yet, at the same time, the seeds of differentiation were also being sown by the state. Among the first instances of direct intervention and differentiation in the Kurdish region by the imperial state in Istanbul was the creation in 1891 of Kurdish officered and soldiered *Hamidiye* regiments. Designed to maintain order in the eastern provinces, these battalions were eventually used by the Ottoman state in its campaign against the Armenians. In the interim, the armed and tribally organized battalions became the source of a state-sponsored division within the Kurdish community as those Kurds benefiting from state patronage and arms would antagonize and oppress those who did not. They also represented an attempt by the state inadvertently perhaps to differentiate between Kurds and non-Kurds, including Turks.[6] The *Hamidiye,* just like the village guard system a century later, further strengthened tribal links among Kurds.[7] While there is a debate over the degree of ethnic consciousness exhibited by Kurds during the latter part of the century, from the increased political activities in Istanbul and elsewhere, it is evident that something was afoot. The empire itself was experiencing turmoil at the center: The Committee of Union and Progress had begun to agitate and conspire for a return to constitutional rule that the sultan had abrogated.

It is during this period that the first Kurdish national newspaper, *Kurdistan,* was published in 1898 by Kurdish exiles in Cairo, later transferred to Geneva and then to England. Indeed, much of the Kurdish elite went into exile in various parts of the Middle East, Turkey, and Europe.[8] With the Young Turk revolution in 1908, two contradictory tendencies appeared. On the one hand, the emphasis on Islam was replaced with secularism and constitutionalism. In the ensuing atmosphere of liberalism, "Kurdish" national activities increased when many Kurdish intellectuals who had abandoned hope in the efficacy of nationalist revolt looked to Ottoman liberal movements and constitutional reform as the best means to achieve greater national rights. Kurdish political and cultural societies burgeoned, not only in Istanbul but also in the large towns of the Kurdish southeast. The first nationalist organization, the Kurdish Society for the Rise and Progress, was formed in 1908. But the "Constantinople Spring" was soon repressed in 1910. On the other hand, while the return to constitutionalism served the more modern elements of the Kurdish elite, it did lead to an antiregime reaction among the shaykhs and religious orders. Some of them engaged in open rebellion. The Young Turk regime, finding itself besieged domestically and internationally, increasingly turned to pan-Turkism as a means of consolidating its power. In the end, when the Young Turks dragged the empire into World War I, the Kurds proved to be loyal subjects: They fought in and alongside the Ottoman armies.

The defeat of the Ottomans in 1918 and the signing of the 1920 Sèvres Treaty provided a turning point for the Kurds. The victorious allies had occupied large segments of the empire with the purpose of dismembering it. The Sèvres Treaty itself not only promised Armenians statehood out of territories carved from the Ottoman Empire but also "envisaged interim autonomy for the predominantly Kurdish areas of Turkey with a view to full independence if the inhabitants of these areas wanted this."[9] That, of course, never materialized because the Turkish nationalist movement, under the leadership of Mustafa Kemal Atatürk, revolted against the sultan and the occupying Western powers. In the process of this rebellion, Atatürk was successful in enlisting the support of the Kurds in his quest. In the beginning of the War of Independence, Kemal often invoked the equality of Turks and Kurds, the commonality of the struggle, and the brotherhood of the two peoples.[10] In his first speech to the newly gathered parliament in April 1920, Mustafa Kemal argued that the parliament was not composed of the representative of Turks, Kurds, Circassians and the Laz, but rather the representatives of a strongly unified Islamic Community. Kemal had even envisaged, according to some accounts of his speeches and conversations with journalists, that where Kurds were in a majority they would govern themselves autonomously.[11] Kemal and his rebellious forces, facing shortages of men and matériel, could not afford to alienate the Kurds: They needed Kurdish cooperation to carry out the war against the foreign invaders. The Kurds claim that they gave their support on the understanding that a common Muslim cause existed against Western interventionists, and that a future Turkish-Kurdish common multiethnic state would emerge. Still, some Kurds did revolt against Kemal: Among those revolts, that of the Koçgiri in 1920 was the most significant, as it forced Kemal to divert troops from the main theater of war to deal with what could potentially have led to a serious division within Turkish/Kurdish ranks.

The New Republic and the One-Party Era

If the Kurds expected equality in the management of the new state they were sorely disappointed, as the new regime quickly embraced everything it deemed modern, from a centralizing mission to a secular approach that was to bring it into line with contemporary values of the nation-building process of the period. The state also assumed a Turkish character through a process by which the Kemalist regime reinvented the Turkish "ethnie." Ismet Inönü, Atatürk's confidant and successor, succinctly summarized the official position in 1925: "We are frankly [n]ationalist[s] . . . and [n]ationalism is our only factor of cohesion. In the face of a Turkish majority other elements have no kind of influence. We must turkify the inhabitants of our land at any price, and we will annihilate those who oppose the Turks or 'le turquisme.' "[12]

In the 1924 constitution, the terms "citizenship" and "citizen" had been equated with Turkishness. Accordingly, the document stated that one had to be a Turk to become a member of parliament and the like. Certainly Kurds could qualify as "Turks," but only at the expense of denying their own ethnic identity. Here then the seeds for eventual Kurdish dissatisfaction were planted: In a state now officially defined as "Turkish" the Kurds were not Turks, and only by giving up their ethnicity could they be treated as Turks. It is clear that the leaders of the Kemalist regime perceived unintegrated, unturkified Kurds as both a backward element and a potential threat to the integrity of the modern state they were intent on constructing. Compounding the problem was the fact that with the rise of the shaykhs and Islamic *tariqats* in the nineteenth century, it was Islam that had assumed a major role in bringing Turks and Kurds together. But with the decision of the new regime to abandon religion as one of its unifying characteristics and with the abolishing of the Caliphate in 1924, another bond that united both communities appeared to have been severed. This also provided Kurdish shaykhs in the east, such as Shaykh Said of Palu, with the justification for rebelling against Ankara.

With the population exchanges with Greece that followed the establishment of the republic in 1923, the Kurds, de facto, became the single largest unrecognized minority with the potential to threaten the state. In fact, Kurdish resistance to the extension of Ankara's political, economic, social, and cultural role began. At times violent, this resistance has been continuous and has remained a major preoccupation of successive governments in Ankara.

The Shaykh Said rebellion was the first. Started prematurely, before the rebels had had time to gather all of their assets, the rebellion was eventually suppressed by Ankara with a great deal of force and violence; its leader and many others were tried and summarily executed by newly created special tribunals called the Independence Tribunals. These would become one of the main tools of repression in the area for years to come.[13] This rebellion had both a religious and nationalist character: It was as much a revolt against the secularist and anti-Islamic tendencies of the new regime as it was the first stirrings, albeit regionally circumscribed, of Kurdish nationalism.[14] To this day, the descendants of Shaykh Said and his associates have remained politically active within the Kurdish community and the Turkish parliament. Another casualty of the revolt was the liberal-minded prime minister Fethi Okyar, who was compelled to resign by hard-liners—led by Inönü and supported by Kemal—advocating force against the Kurds. The new government, led by Prime Minister Inönü, introduced the Law for the Maintenance of Order (Takrir-i Sükûn Kanunu), which was used to suppress other groups and muzzle the press.[15]

The Shaykh Said rebellion represents a major turning point. For some it signified a change in the regime's attitude, from one of ignoring the Kurds to a policy of violence.[16] Bernard Lewis has suggested that the rebellion gave a greater impetus to Kemal's efforts at secularization and repressing religious orders.[17] Interestingly, the Shaykh Said rebellion, which initially was clearly interpreted correctly by the Ankara government as a Kurdish and religious reaction, in later official interpretations lost its Kurdish attributes as the state officially classified it as a reactionary movement. There could be little confusion, however, regarding the 1930 Agri and 1937–38 Dersim (Tunceli) revolts. They too were limited geographically in that they did not benefit from regionwide mass participation, but they were Kurdish in nature and aspiration. Almost from the beginning, the government in Ankara decided on the eventual complete assimilation of the Kurds—by force if necessary wherever and whenever serious nationalist resistance was encountered. From the perspective of the time, the regime may not have been unrealistic in attempting to integrate the Kurds by assimilating them: There was no cohesive Kurdish leadership that exerted significant pressure, much less one that could mobilize against Ankara to pose an immediate threat. In other words, Kemal and his associates did not expect to encounter significant resistance to their project in the long run.

In their quest to build a "modern" state, the Kemalists not surprisingly decided to emulate the "homogeneous" states of the West. They were more interested in building the center at the expense of the periphery. Kurds, as a result, were relegated to the minor role of errant Turks or descendants of Turkish tribes. Expressions of Kurdish nationalist thought as well as language and culture were severely repressed.[18] This was a long way from when Kurds were often mentioned as coequal members of the new state; they had become nonentities. The news media ceased referring to them as Kurds. The government passed many laws that enabled it to exile Kurds from their traditional areas to other parts of the country, where they would be in a minority. At the same time, however, to the extent that individual Kurds did accept the "new Turkish identity," they enjoyed the full rights of citizenship. In fact, many assimilated Kurds rose through political, economic, and even military ranks to occupy important positions in Turkish society, from president and prime minister to chief of staff of the armed forces. True to the official dogma, they were accepted as bona fide Turks: No one ever questioned their loyalty or Turkishness.

The attitude of the new regime toward the Kurds would undergo a subtle change as it tried to come to grips with the new Turkish identity it was constructing. If, at the outset of the new republic, the Kurds were perceived as a threat to the unity of the remaining territories of the Ottoman Empire, with time that definition was altered as the Kemalists themselves defined Turkishness and Turkish identity. As Taha Parla demonstrates, Atatürk's conception of nationalism underwent a gradual but significant degree of change: It started off as anti-imperialist and Wilsonian in spirit, careful and peaceful in orientation.[19] But with time it assumed first a cultural and then an ethnic dimension. Still, this conception of nationalism had many inherent contradictions. Not only did it discourage interest in "Turks" living in other parts of the world, primarily Central Asia, but it also encouraged a dual understanding of Turkishness. The resulting Turkish nationalist idea was both civic and ethno-cultural in nature.[20] Its civic character made possible the rise of assimilated Kurds, while its ethno-cultural aspect formed the basis of forced assimilation and repression of those Kurds who refused to accept the "higher" Turkish identity.

But this "revolution from above" set into motion a process of change that was far too complex and disruptive to predict its end result accurately. Assimilation was only partially successful: It may have been too ambitious, as it required that Kurds give up not only their political identity but also all forms of cultural links and the language that bound them, not to mention their traditional ways of expressing piety. The suppression of language, the unavailability of books and other materiels in Kurdish, and the bans on the use of the language meant that with time Turkish became the primary language for many, and especially for those who left their traditional areas either for economic reasons or because they had been exiled by the central government. Assimilation had its limits; those limits were imposed by geography (the remoteness of the region), economics (the relative backwardness of the region making it easy for it to be economically ignored), or the lack of resources (the Turkish government's limited resources proving insufficient for the massive task it confronted in educating and integrating the Kurdish regions' inhabitants). Today the southeast and east are still filled with families unable to speak any language but Kurdish. However, the assimilationist policies of the state also had a reverse effect: They set into motion—albeit slowly—a process of constructing a new sense of Kurdish national identity.

With the disappearance of Atatürk from the scene in 1938, the regime assumed an even more static character on this issue. His "successors sought to legitimize themselves in his shadow. Reformulating or questioning some of the basic tenets of the Kemalist reforms became equated with political disloyalty."[21] Republicans under İnönü, who were not predisposed to change policy, maintained the course with even greater zeal. One event during this period would loom large in Kurdish nationalist folklore. This was the cold-blooded execution of thirty-three unarmed villagers near the Iranian border on July 28, 1943. The general in charge of the region, who ordered the massacre, Mustafa Muglali, tried to cover his tracks with the connivance of the regime. It was only with the newly constituted Democrat party, in order to embarrass the ruling Republicans and curry favor with the region's inhabitants, that the subject came up in parliament after five years of official silence. Muglali, under the overwhelming weight of the evidence, was sentenced to twenty years in prison.[22]

The Multiparty Era

With the suppression of the last of the rebellions in 1937–38, the Kurdish question in Turkey went through a transformation of sorts: While the official state ideology and the state's approach to and fear of the Kurds did not change, the failure of the localized rebellions and lack of a cohesive national leadership gave way to a period of tranquil political activity centered on the educational opportunities offered by the state's assimilationist policies. Heralded by the success of the Democrat party at the polls in

1950, the coming of multiparty politics to Turkey somewhat eased the pressure Kurds had experienced during Kemal and his successor's rule. The Democrats, though cut from the same cloth as the Kemalists, inasmuch as they represented a breakaway faction of Kemal's Republican People's party, had promised to reduce some of the more "secularist" policies of the state. During the election campaign they also promised to ease some of the "cultural restrictions in the east" and to reduce the oppressive practices of the gendarmes in the rural areas.[23] The Democrats also enlisted the leaders in the prominent families who had been exiled during the one-party rule to run on their party lists in their regions of origin.[24]

Democrats swept through most of the east and southeast. Still, they could not, and were unwilling to, engage in activities that could have encouraged the renewal of "separatist" activities. Another important outcome of the change of power in Turkey was the emergence of a commercial bourgeoisie that benefited from a less restrictive and domineering state. Kurds too were beneficiaries of this change, except that most Kurdish businessmen chose to invest, as they continue to do, in the economically more developed regions of the country, ignoring their own, more backward provinces. This further increased the difference and distance between the underdeveloped Kurdish areas and those of the western provinces, primarily Istanbul. In turn, the growing differentiation would provide one of the main reasons for the Kurds' turn to left-wing activism. The Democrat Decade (1950–1960) was also notable for the new and relative freedom of expression that allowed all, including Kurds, to articulate their grievances. The Democrats would ultimately succumb to the authoritarian tendencies of their predecessors and the civil and military elites' unease with the Democrats' perceived disregard for them. The decade culminated, from the Kurdish point of view, in one of the more significant of trials. Forty-nine prominent Kurdish intellectuals were tried for sedition, and the government formed by the military coup that overthrew the Democrats in May 1960 quickly arrested some 484 Kurds and banished 55 aghas to western provinces.

The end of the Democrat party era was momentous for another reason: It coincided with the return to Iraq of the legendary Kurdish leader Molla Mustafa Barzani, which rekindled the dormant hopes of Kurdish nationalism there. The 1960 military regime assumed an uncompromising attitude to the Kurdish question: Not only was a campaign initiated to rename Kurdish villages but, in addition, coup leader Cemal Gürsel warned that "the army would not hesitate to bombard towns and villages" in the event of unrest.[25] Yet, the coup makers of 1960 also bequeathed a liberal constitution that set the groundwork for the emergence of trade unions and student organizations. These, in the politically charged atmosphere of the 1960s, became important avenues of political organization for the Kurdish groups. The first of these was the Turkish Workers' party (Türkiye Isçi Partisi, TIP). TIP soon became enmeshed in the "Eastern Problem," as the Kurdish question has been euphemistically known. Pushed by its Kurdish members, the party in 1970 openly suggested that there was an ethnic problem in Turkey—though its analysis was heavily laden with class and leftist terminology. The mere mention of ethnicity was later used by the Constitutional Court in 1971, in the aftermath of another military coup, as the reason for closing the party down.[26]

The 1960s were turbulent times: It was a period of left-wing mobilization, and many politically active Kurds threw their lot in with the Turkish Left in search of their "national rights." They assumed that Kurds, as the inhabitants of the most underdeveloped regions of the country, would undoubtedly benefit from the liberation of the Turkish people from the "capitalist and imperialist yoke." However, frustration with the Turkish Left's less than committed attitude to the Kurds ultimately led to the creation of left-wing explicitly Kurdish groups, especially among the university youth. Already by 1965 an organization parallel to the Iraqi Kurdish Democratic party, the Democratic Party of Turkish Kurdistan, had been created. This party was a nationalist rather than a revolutionary one. The most important of the left-wing Kurdish groups was the Eastern Revolutionary Cultural Hearths (DDKO), formed in 1969. It provided the kernel for a large number of other revolutionary Kurdish groups, including the present-day Kurdistan Workers' party (Partiya Karkeren Kurdistan), or PKK, which began its operations in 1984. Critical to burgeoning left-wing nationalist Kurdish movements in the 1960s and 1970s was the impact of the generational change. The older generation, whose traditional ties limited its rebellious temptations, was replaced with one raised with all the symbols of nation and state.[27] The collapse of the Molla Mustafa Barzani's movement in Iraq following the 1975 Algiers Accord, in which the shah of Iran and, by extension, the United States withdrew their support for him, further convinced Turkish Kurds of the foolhardiness of relying on "imperialist powers" in their own struggle for liberation.

The 1980 military coup—which brought to power a junta determined to forcibly eradicate not just left- and right-wing opposition but also all activities falling beyond the "acceptable" scope of political behavior—accelerated the process of Kurdish identity formation. Harsh policies reminiscent of the 1930s—banning the use of the Kurdish language and daily humiliations of the region's population, often by state-appointed civil servants—intensified rather than discouraged latent Kurdish nationalist feelings and thus contributed to the eventual appeal of the PKK. Bülent Ulusu, commander of the naval forces and one of the architects of the 1980 coup, in an interview a year before the coup told a journalist that when the army went on maneuvers in the southeast, it was met with slogans calling for its expulsion. "The East is boiling; the communists and the Kurds are in complete cooperation there."[28]

The military unwittingly created a political vacuum by banning all existing parties and attempting to engineer a new political system. In turn, this reengineering of the political system gave rise to a period of political uncertainty, realignment, and vacillation among and within the political parties that continues to this day. While all Turkish political parties included Kurdish members, it is only in the latter part of the 1980s that any of these members ventured to raise the question of the Kurdish minority. The main vehicle for their activism was the newly (re)emerging Social Democratic People's party (Sosyal Demokrat Halkçi Parti, SHP).[29] Openly critical of the Turkish state's policy, some members of SHP expressed their criticisms at various forums. One such parliamentarian, Ibrahim Aksoy, representing Malatya, bluntly described the grievances of the Kurds at a 1989 meeting with European parliamentarians; this action provoked a furor within SHP, leading to his dismissal from the party. This event heralded a new phase in Turkish politics that eventually led to other expulsions from SHP and the creation of Kurdish political parties.[30]

By the late 1980s, the Kurdish question emerged onto the political scene with full force. Kurdish refugees fleeing from Iraqi repression and especially the chemical attacks on Halabja, and the rising levels of violence in the southeast, meant that the issue could no longer be contained. With Kurdish MPs increasingly willing to challenge the taboo on this question, the press joined the debate. Kurds were now referred to as Kurds and not as an unnamed minority or as separatists. This issue would win even greater currency with the 1991 Gulf War, which resulted in hundreds of thousands of Iraqi Kurds seeking refuge in Turkey from Saddam Hussein's murderous onslaughts. This second and much larger flight of Iraqi Kurdish refugees provided an opportunity for the mobilization of Turkish Kurds to help their brethren, and the symbolism of this mobilization was not lost on the Kurds. While there was no significant change in state policy—with the exception of the late president Turgut Özal's uncompleted search for alternative solutions—the Kurdish question came to dominate the domestic and international policy preoccupations of successive governments.

Today, the process of growing national consciousness *(bilinçlenme)* among the Kurds and the violence in the southeast—traditional violence against Kurdish self-expression, violence provoked by the PKK, and state counterviolence—have led to the alienation of the Kurds as a population in many respects. In the process, the insurgency has created enormous hardships for the people of the region; their families have been divided and moved, their way of life has been disrupted, and their means of earning income have disappeared. Violence is not the only form of expression: Turkey is teeming with political activities related to the Kurdish issue. Kurdish political activism is reflected in the workings of human rights organizations, cultural associations, political parties, self-help organizations, local administrations, and movements of different political stripes, ranging from the traditional Left to Islamic movements. Increasingly, Turks and Kurds are coming to live in their own separate psychological worlds—working jointly in society but increasingly nourishing suspicions about each other's intentions and identifying with different things. It is this growing psychological gap between Kurds and Turks that is the most dangerous feature of the Kurdish issue in Turkey today.

Notes and References

1. For greater detail on the Kurdish emirates and their relationship with the state, see David McDowall, *A Modern History of the Kurds* (London: I. B. Tauris, 1996), 21–37. Martin van Bruinessen discusses the incorporation of the Kurdish areas into the Ottoman Empire in *Agha, Shaikh and State* (London: Zed Books, 1992). On the international politics of the region, see Kemal Kirişci and Gareth M. Winrow, *Kürt Sorunu: Kökeni ve Gelisimi* (The Kurdish question: Origins and development) (Istanbul: Tarih Vakfi Yurt Yayinlari, 1997), 69–79. Kurdish authors argue that the Kurdish areas were divided up to hinder any attempts at their coalescing into a united front, and the sole expectation of them was that they remain loyal to the sultan; see Kendal, "The Kurds under the Ottoman Empire," in *A People without a Country: The Kurds and Kurdistan,* ed. Gerard Chaliand (New

York: Olive Branch Press, 1993), 14. It is also worth noting that Kurdish history is very much a hotly contested issue, not just between Turks and Kurds but also among Kurds themselves. Because the Kurds have not formed a state in the modern era, it is difficult for them to have an accepted or official "Kurdish history" or national narrative; see Gürdal Aksoy, "Kürt Tarih Yazimi'nin Tarihi" (The history of the writing of Kurdish history), *Demokrasi,* June 18, 1996.

2. See Siyamend Othman, "Kurdish Nationalism: the Instigators and the Historical Influences," 5, unpublished paper based on chapter two of the author's Ph.D. dissertation, *Contribution historique a l'étude de Parti Demokrati Kurdistan-i 'Iraq. 1946–1970,* Ecole des Hautes Etudes en Sciences Sociales, Paris, 1985.

3. McDowall, *A Modern History of the Kurds,* 41–42.

4. Kendal, "The Kurds under the Ottoman Empire," 17.

5. David McDowall, "The Kurdish Question: A Historical Review," in *The Kurds: A Contemporary Overview,* ed. Philip Kreyenbroek and Stefan Sperl (London: Routledge, 1992), 17.

6. On the *Hamidiye* regiments, see van Bruinessen, *Agha, Shaykh and State;* McDowall, *A Modern History of the Kurds;* and Osman Aytar, *Hamidiye Alaylarindan Köy Koruculuguna* (From Hamidiye regiments to village guards) (Istanbul: Medya Günesi Yayinlari, 1992).

7. Mete Tuncay, *T. C. 'nde Tek-Parti Yönetmi'nin Kurulmasi (1923–1931)* (The formation of the single-party system in the Turkish Republic) (Istanbul: Cem Yayinevi, 1992), 132n.

8. Othman, "Kurdish Nationalism," 8.

9. McDowall, "The Kurdish Question," 17.

10. Cumhur Keskin, "Türkiye'nin Kürt Politikasi ve Resmi Ideoloji" (Turkey's Kurdish policy and official ideology in Turkey's Kurdish problem), in *Türkiye'nin Kürt Sorunu,* ed. Seyfettin Gürsel et al. (Istanbul: TÜSES, 1996), 52–54.

11. Mustafa Kemal, *Eskisehir-Izmit Konusmalari (1923)* (The Eskisehir-Izmit speeches) (Ankara: Kaynak Yayinlari, 1993), 104–5; Kirişci and Winrow, 96.

12. Bilal Şimşir, *Ingiliz Belgeleriyle Türkiye'de "Kürt Sorunu" (1924–1938)* (The "Kurdish problem" in British documents) (Ankara: Türk Tarih Kurumu Basimevi, 1991), 58.

13. For more on the origins and development of the Shaykh Said rebellion, see Robert Olson, *The Emergence of Kurdish Nationalism and the Sheikh Said Rebellion, 1880–1925* (Austin: University of Texas Press, 1989).

14. The state took advantage of the revolt to dispose of other Kurdish opponents, including Sayyid Abdülkadir, the president of the Istanbul-based Kurdish Society for Rise and Progress. When led to the gallows, separately from Shaykh Said, he and some of his followers were reputed to have exclaimed, "Long Live the Kurdish Idea! Long Live Kurdistan!" Ergün Aybars, *Istiklâl Mahkemeleri* (Independence tribunals) (Vols. 1, 2) (Izmir: Ileri Kitabevi, 1995), 309.

15. Tuncay, *T. C. 'nde Tek-Parti Yönetmi'nin Kurulmasi (1923–1931), 139–43.*

16. Keskin, "Türkiye'nin Kürt Politikasi ve Resmi Ideoloji," 58.

17. Bernard Lewis, *The Emergence of Modern Turkey* (London: Oxford University Press, 1961), 261.

18. In the 1930s, for instance, people who spoke Kurdish in public were fined five kurus per word. Muhsin Kizilkaya and Halil Nebiler, *Dünden Yarina Kürtler* (Kurds: From the past to the future) (Ankara: Yurt Kitap-Yayin, 1991), 36.

19. Taha Parla, *Türkiye'de Siyasi Kültürün Resmî Kaynaklari: Kemalist Tek-Parti ve CHP'nin Alti Ok'u* (The official sources of Turkish political culture: the Kemalist single-party and the RPP's six arrows) (Istanbul: Iletisim Yayinlari, 1992), 182–83.

20. Ümit Cizre Sakallioglu, "Historicizing the Present and Problematizing the Future of the Kurdish Problem: A Critique of the TOBB Report on the Eastern Question," *New Perspectives on Turkey* 14 (Spring 1996): 6; Tanil Bora, *Milliyetçiligin Kara Bahari* (The dark springtime of nationalism) (Istanbul: Birikim Yayinlari, 1995), 74–75.

21. Henri J. Barkey and Graham E. Fuller, "Turkey's Kurdish Question: Critical Turning Points and Missed Opportunities," *Middle East Journal* 51, no. 1 (Winter 1997): 64.

22. Muglali died soon after his conviction. The Milan tribe whose members had been killed were grateful to the Democrats and, until recently, remained loyal to the Democrats and their successors in the 1960s and 1970s, the Justice party. Ironically, in recent years they have switched their allegiance to the Islamist Welfare party. Günay Aslan, *Yas Tutan Tarih 33 Kursun* (History in mourning: 33 bullets) (Istanbul: Pencere Yayinlari, 1989), 40–43.

23. Cem Erogul, *Demokrat Parti: Tarihi ve Ideolojisi* (The Democratic Party: Its history and ideology) (Ankara: Imge Kitabevi, 1990), 49.

24. Atilla Hun, *Dogu ve Güneydogu Bölgelerinde Çok Partili Sisteme Geçisten Günümüze Gelismeler* (Developments in the eastern and southeastern province since the transition to multiparty rule) (Ankara: Yenidogus Matbaasi, 1995), 15.

25. McDowall, *A Modern History of the Kurds,* 404.

26. Sadun Aren, *TIP Olayi (1961–1971)* (The TIP event) (Istanbul: Cem Yayinevi, 1993), 70–72. TIP's involvement was not just with words. In 1967, many protest meetings were organized in Kurdish areas under the name of Eastern Meetings. TIP members were active in these, something that did not escape the notice of the authorities.

27. Aytekin Yilmaz, *Etnik Ayrimcilik: Türkiye, Ingiltere, Fransa, Ispanya* (Ethnic separatism: Turkey, England, France, Spain) (Ankara: Vadi Yayinlari, 1994), 72.

28. Cüneyt Arcayürek, *Müdahalenin Ayak Sesleri, 1978–1979* (The footsteps of the intervention) (Istanbul: Bilgi Yayinevi, 1985), 272. This interview, conducted on September 6, 1979, did not see the light of day until Arcayürek published his book.

29. SHP would eventually split and reunite and rename itself in the 1990s as the Republican People's party (CHP).

30. These will be discussed in greater detail in subsequent sections.

2

Enter the PKK

THE EMERGENCE OF THE PKK in 1984 as a revolutionary organization in quest of Kurdish independence marks a major new phase in the evolution of the Kurdish national movement, entering a stage of sustained armed struggle now of over thirteen years' duration—the longest Kurdish rebellion in modern Turkish history.[1] The transformation of the Kurdish problem in Turkey into its present form is not only due to the PKK: Events in other parts of the Middle East, specifically the Iran-Iraq and the Gulf wars, provided the PKK with significant political and military room to maneuver. The organization's ability to profit from geopolitical changes and its resilience on the ground have clearly touched a nerve within Turkey. Whether the organization survives or not in the longer run, the fact remains that it has managed to change Turkey's foreign and domestic politics. This is why we start with an analysis of the organization. It is not the purpose of this section to detail the evolution of the PKK or recount its military successes and defeats.

The PKK is in fact an unusual phenomenon among Kurdish nationalist movements, particularly in its left-wing origins. Most other Kurdish parties—particularly in Iraq—have emerged from more traditional Kurdish circles with a specific regional and tribal orientation.[2] They represented the least assimilated of the Kurdish populations. The PKK, by contrast, grew out of the anarchy and turmoil during the 1970s when a number of radical

left-wing Turkish groups emerged, many of them violent. Emerging from
among the more assimilated elements, left-wing Kurdish students in Ankara began to talk of founding a movement as early as 1973, and in 1978
the PKK decided to hold its first congress and established itself in secret
under the leadership of Abdullah Öcalan. Its initial actions targeted Kurdish landlords, including an assassination attempt on a member of parliament from the Justice party of Süleyman Demirel. With such operations,
the PKK made a name for itself as a fighter for the disenfranchised.[3] It also
became the most effective Kurdish group in the southeast and caught the
attention of the security apparatus.[4] Early police pressures led Öcalan to
decide that he and most of the party leadership had to flee to Syria and
Lebanon, where he has remained ever since,[5] escaping the post-1980 coup
dragnet. Although Öcalan managed to escape, many others were incarcer-
ated by the military regime. However, the regime's indiscriminate repression in the southeast and east helped the PKK gain many adherents, a large
number of whom were in prison in Diyarbakir. Under Syrian tutelage in
Lebanon, where the PKK recruits got their first real training, Öcalan and
his small group established close links with some of the Palestinian groups
as well as Syrian intelligence.

The PKK launched its military operations against the state in earnest in
August 1984 after consolidating its position in the southeast following a
bitter internecine struggle with rival Kurdish organizations. From then on,
the PKK began to gather strength. Though amateurish at the beginning,
its recruits with time gained experience as the PKK reached its peak between 1991 and 1993. Ankara was caught unprepared for the kind of challenge the PKK offered. This was not to be one of the many small bands or
groups that had appeared and disappeared over the years, but rather one
that had a well-defined political agenda and could exercise unparalleled
discipline. The PKK, in line with its political agenda, has divided itself into
three elements. The party itself—that is, the PKK—is the foremost organ.
In 1985 it created the National Liberation Front of Kurdistan (ERNK) to
bolster its recruitment, provide intelligence, and engage in propaganda
activities in Turkey and abroad. Finally, the third leg in its structure is the
People's Liberation Army of Kurdistan (ARGK), formed in 1986.[6]

Ankara's initial reaction, which consisted primarily of military responses, included air raids across the border that invariably caused more
casualties among the Iraqi Kurds than the PKK. With time the Turkish
state too learned from its mistakes and began to target significant re-

sources, primarily military, on the region and to score important military successes against the PKK.[7]

The onset of first the Iran-Iraq War (1980–1988) and eventually the Gulf War in 1991 provided the PKK with strategic depth in its confrontation with the Ankara government. In the first instance the regime in Baghdad was forced to reduce its troop concentrations significantly in the north, creating a power vacuum. Similarly, during the much shorter Gulf conflict, Iraqi troops were thinned out of northern Iraq; more important, a de facto Kurdish autonomous zone emerged under the protection of the U.S., Britain, and France. The PKK has benefited from the absence of a military presence to impede its activities. On the other hand, the Turkish assumption that the Iraqi regime would be sympathetic to Ankara should it one day regain control of the area is not necessarily true. To impede the PKK's freedom of movement in Northern Iraq, Turkey has mounted numerous military operations—land or air, large or small—across the international border.

Goals

From the outset, the PKK has proclaimed its goal to be the creation of a unified, independent Kurdish state, and thus it has made no secret of its pan-Kurdish aspirations. The PKK sought not only independence, but also a political and social revolution among the Kurds in order to transform their society's feudal structure. It described itself early on as Marxist-Leninist and adopted the generally left-wing anti-imperialist rhetoric of the period to oppose "imperialism," including "Turkish imperialism" in Turkish Kurdistan. The PKK's program mirrored the slogans of the extreme Left: Kurdistan with all four of its segments, controlled by Turkey, Iraq, Iran, and Syria, represented the weakest link in "capitalism's chain," and the fight against imperialism was a fight to save Kurdistan's natural resources from exploitation. The PKK adopted a tight paramilitary structure and Leninist "democratic centralism" that essentially denied any internal debate or any transparency of organization and activity—features that largely have remained intact today, even if Marxism-Leninism has been abandoned in keeping with the new post–Cold War environment.

As an organization, the PKK takes itself very seriously. It has attempted to demonstrate that it is a "national liberation" organization that can institutionalize itself to survive the long haul. It periodically organizes national congresses, in which decisions are taken "democratically." It has laws regarding military conscription, promotions in its army, and so forth.[8] While these congresses and the publication of its decisions are intended to dispel the notion that the organization is totally controlled by one person, there is no doubt that these activities are designed to show that this is a movement with a structure, goals, and the political means to achieve them.

Claiming to have abandoned Marxism-Leninism, the PKK justifies its earlier radical stance as a reflection of the broad, extreme-leftist milieu that dominated Turkish politics at the time. In addition, PKK spokesmen claim that the Turkish state had then succeeded in winning over a large number of the wealthy Kurdish landlords, or aghas, as well as the mercantile class, leaving the PKK to seek adherents among the poorer classes of workers and peasants. Armed struggles worldwide, too, were nearly all from the left and propagated the appropriate leftist revolutionary rhetoric and ideology to justify their movements. The PKK thus very early on became committed to revolutionary violence against the Turkish state.

In fact, behind the left-wing rhetoric, the PKK had always been a nationalist movement. Its promise to save the exploited of Turkey and the rest of the Middle East notwithstanding, its very formation represented a break with the Turkish Left and abandonment of the "common struggle."[9] To be sure, this may have been directly and indirectly caused by a Turkish Left that sought recruits from the east and southeast as cannon fodder in its own particularistic struggle of the 1970s. Hence, its assumption of a nationalistic image is in fact not just in keeping with the times but also a return to its real self. Although a product of the doctrinaire Turkish left-wing movements, the PKK watched from close these groups' destruction by the military in 1980. The radical and violent Left failed to succeed anywhere in Europe or the Middle East. By contrast, nationalist groups proved to have much longer shelf life. Nationalism has proven to have no equal in mobilizing them.

Although the PKK is primarily a nationalist organization, it would be wrong to assume that it has completely abandoned the political Left. Its discourse is that of a national-liberation movement dedicated to the construction of a socialist state. Öcalan, in acknowledging the decision to do away with the hammer and sickle on the party flag, also stated that this did not represent a distancing from socialism.[10] If it has not completely abandoned its "left-wing roots," it is because of both tactical and strategic considerations. Tactically, it is easier to modify one's ideology than abandon it altogether. Also, a consistent ideological worldview is important in continuing to recruit and discipline adherents. In addition, the left-wing discourse is what they know best. Strategically and politically, the PKK still needs the support of the Turkish Left; although the PKK is disappointed with the Left's disregard of the Kurdish issue in the 1970s and its inability to survive the 1980 coup, the PKK knows that it cannot win on its own against a well-armed and determined Turkish state without the support of left-of-center forces in Turkish politics and society who themselves challenge some of the traditional ideological tenets of the old Kemalist state. The PKK is not the only one among Kurdish groups that adheres to left-wing dogma and terminology; as one Kurdish intellectual, Orhan Kotan, has pointed out, most Kurdish groups still use the terminology of the 1970s and are simply regurgitating the same old ideas, passing them off for new.[11]

Since the beginning of 1995, the PKK has been undergoing a significant shift in its political orientation. Although Marxist-Leninist thinking is no longer prominent in its rhetoric, one might argue that the party still contains some Leninist features of "democratic centralism." The PKK has moved away from an earlier condemnation of Islam as "exploiting the people" to an acceptance of Islam: Indeed, an Islamist movement (Parti Islami Kurdistan) is now in the process of being accepted within the pro-PKK parliament in Exile (see below). The PKK now speaks of a political settlement within the existing borders of Turkey.[12] In an interview with the London Arab daily *al-Hayat,* Öcalan stressed that his vision of the future for the Kurdish areas of the Middle East consisted of a series of federations: Turkish-Kurdish, Arab-Kurdish in Iraq, and Persian-Kurdish in Iran.[13] The PKK no longer claims to be the sole political representative of the Kurdish people. Öcalan has reportedly said that if and when negotiations take place, they need not necessarily be held with him personally. In this way the PKK is seemingly moving toward greater reality in its assessment of the current political environment. At the fifth PKK Congress, held at an undisclosed location in 1995, the party consolidated many of the changes in policy mentioned above.

How genuine is the claim that the PKK has abandoned the ultimate objective of an independent Kurdistan? At one level, this is a reflection of realism: The end of the Cold War and the loss of powerful potential patrons such as the Soviet Union, together with the growing realization of the power of the Turkish state and, most important, the lack of genuine support for outright separation among Turkey's Kurds, make it difficult to make a serious case for independence. On the other hand, PKK recruits appear not to have absorbed this change. While they recognize the impossibility of achieving a military victory, they expect that the cost of the PKK-led struggle will force the Turkish government to abandon the east and southeast and, thereby, lead to the creation of an independent state.[14] Clearly, the PKK must be able to engage in two different types of discourse: As it attempts to modify its international stand, it must also motivate its recruits, who do the fighting. It must be cognizant of the limited appeal that cultural autonomy and Kurdish language schools would have in comparison with the promise of independence when it comes to recruiting fighters and maintaining them in the field under very adverse conditions.

It would be incorrect to assume that the PKK is simply a military cum terrorist organization. No nationalist movement has ever achieved as much as the PKK has without recourse to political activism and preparation. The group's military prowess has only made it easier to organize politically. The PKK is first and foremost a political organization with distinct political objectives—even if they are modified when necessary—that employs violence, often extensively and even erroneously from its own standpoint. This violence is basically secondary to its fundamental character; while this does not imply that violence is unimportant for the PKK, it does mean that violence is used to define and pursue political objectives.

In late 1995 the PKK dedicated increasing attention to the role of outside forces in helping to strengthen its political clout for negotiations with the Turkish government. Two factors could be at work here. The first could be increasing concern about the military setbacks dealt to the PKK in the field in the period. In contrast to the early 1990s, when it controlled towns, villages, and even roads, especially after nightfall, it has now lost control of many of the major cities in the southeast; visitors note that the cities witness fewer incidents and are safer to walk in. It has had to curtail protest actions such as boycotts and shop closings. On the other hand, this relative quiet has been bought at high cost, as the military has had to saturate the region with troops and other security forces. The state can probably suppress PKK operations in the cities and in many parts of the countryside as long as it is willing to dedicate massive force to the task. It would seem likely that once the military begins to cut back on it presence,

PKK activities will spring back into place once again. It may be tempting for the state to argue that, when the PKK makes major new efforts for a dialogue with the government, it is dealing from weakness. But one need ask if this apparent weakness is transient or permanent. In our view, the government has not been able to repress the broader Kurdish nationalist movement—of which the PKK is the main leader and beneficiary—and probably is contributing to a continuing growth and deepening of the Kurdish nationalist movement on the political level despite military setbacks.

The second reason for the PKK's emphasis on negotiations with Turkey is that they represent the ultimate political goal of the PKK at this stage—to gain legitimacy in the eyes of the Turkish state as an interlocutor. The PKK can resist the government's military operations indefinitely—with greater or lesser strength—but in the end some kind of Kurdish-Turkish negotiations must occur if the armed struggle is to have meaning. The PKK cannot win the armed struggle in any military sense. "Winning" can only mean forcing the state into recognition of the PKK in some form. Here, the PKK may be growing more distraught about its ability to reach an accommodation with the Turkish state; indeed, the state seems paralyzed within its own toils and unable to break out into any new initiative, even if considerable groundwork already exists. Thus the PKK must place additional external pressures upon the state to accelerate the states's willingness to "negotiate" with a Kurdish identity.

The anomalous situation in northern Iraq provides the PKK with a temporary opening to Western news media and interest groups. The fact that the U.S., France, Britain, and Turkey protect the Kurds of northern Iraq against Saddam Hussein's wrath indirectly lends support to the broader "Kurdish cause," even if these governments are not individually well disposed toward the PKK.[15] The plight of the Kurds, while different in each country, nevertheless has been bleak; as long as Saddam's threat persists, foreign involvement will continue. The porousness of international borders and the demonstration effect of Iraqi Kurdish successes also nourish the Kurdish cause in Turkey; events in northern Iraq have always had an impact on Turkey's Kurds. Other secessionist or independence struggles—many held dear by Turkey's leaders and public, such as those of the Chechens, Abkhazians, and Bosnian Muslims—all add further psychological fodder to the cause of Turkey's Kurds.

Tactics

The PKK from its inception has employed classic insurgency tactics, blending violence and terror with political organization. The terror has systematically and primarily been directed first at potential rivals within the Kurdish camp, including other leftist organizations, and then at "collaborators"—in other words, other Kurds suspected of benefiting from interactions or cooperation with the state. It is only after the PKK made a name for itself that the violence began to be directed at the state and its representatives again in a structured way. The violence against other Kurds has been particularly gruesome: The PKK's most hated target are the village guards who, in its view, do the state's bidding for money. In order to discourage further recruitment, village guards and their families have fallen victim to revolutionary justice, often being attacked and killed en masse. Öcalan has in the past suggested that while terror may not be his preferred instrument, "the violence alternative may be difficult and painful, but it provides results."[16] As a result, violence is employed in crude and simplistic ways that damage the Kurdish cause. The PKK's effort to lessen Turkish state presence in the southeast by killing Turkish schoolteachers and civil servants, and by burning schools and other public institutions, has particularly enraged the Turkish public, which has seen innocent functionaries, who have no say in where they are assigned, made victim to the struggle.

By far, the PKK's primary focus has been the Turkish military presence in the southeast. Using standard insurgency tactics against a military at first unprepared and untrained to confront such a challenge, the PKK achieved impressive results, denying its enemy large sections of the southeast. It even engaged the Turkish military in large skirmishes, but suffered heavily for doing so. Fighting the Turkish military and surviving against the efforts to eradicate it are what have made the PKK popular among Kurdish masses.

On the other hand, the PKK's emergence and its mode of operation have ushered in a new era of hardship for the Kurdish population in the southeast. Guerrilla operations against the state introduced a massive new Turkish military and security presence into the southeast that has made the lives of ordinary Kurds far more difficult than before. The PKK sought to provoke the state into engaging in counterinsurgency tactics that were violent and indiscriminate. This had the goal of radicalizing Kurdish attitudes, forcing the Kurds to choose sides and banking on the fact that decades of ill treatment would make the PKK the natural repository of the local population's loyalties. In that respect, the PKK benefited from and exploited existing tribal divisions in the area. In the end, the combination of PKK operations and state violence in response have contributed to precisely such a radicalization.

At its zenith (1991–1993), the PKK tried to create a political vacuum in the southeast not just by denying the state access to towns and villages but also by limiting the access of mainstream Turkish institutions, including the press and political parties, to the region. It also encouraged civil disobedience campaigns, such as store closings and sit-down strikes. It set up secret tribunals to judge and arbitrate disputes among the residents of the region. All of these were designed to show that it could effectively challenge the rule of the central government. It subsequently attacked other state institutions, primarily schools and teachers, to deepen the cleavage between Kurds and Turks.

The violence against civilians and representatives of the state, and the military campaign against the security forces, were intermeshed with a political strategy designed to win both the respect and the support of the local population. The political component, which relied heavily on utilizing built-up Kurdish resentment, is a crucial component because so much of the livelihood of individual insurgents and units roaming the countryside depends on the willingness of the citizenry to donate food and shelter when necessary. In addition, the political education process is necessary if the organization is to continue to recruit to replace its manpower losses.[17]

By its own admission, the PKK was not very successful with its civil disobedience campaign. These campaigns were initiated too frequently, without clear political goals, and resulted in exposing the civilian population to retribution and in ultimate suppression by the security forces.[18] As a result, the PKK has clearly decided to refocus its energies on pursuing military operations and, in response to the increased effectiveness of the Turkish military, to expand its areas of operation as much as possible.

Financing

The success of the PKK in becoming the preeminent Kurdish organization in Turkey is due to many factors, some of which we have already discussed, such as its political savvy, the duration of the insurgency it has unleashed, and the perceived price in blood and sacrifice it has paid; this commitment has won it the respect of large numbers of Kurds, even if not their love. But it would be a mistake to attribute PKK success solely to the realm of heroism, brutality, or even ideals: Money is also a factor. The PKK is exceptionally well financed, which gives it important leverage in spreading its message, underwriting its operations, and creating a broad infrastructure that facilitates its recruitment campaign.

The sources of PKK financing is a highly controversial subject.[19] The PKK claims that most of its funds are from contributions, both from Kurds within Turkey and, especially, from those abroad. The Turkish government claims that the bulk of PKK funds come from burglaries and robberies (especially true in its early days), from extortion and protection money levied on Kurds and Turks wherever possible,[20] and especially from a massive narcotics trade between Turkey and Europe. Other analysts also add the factor of PKK small and medium business investments as a source of income.[21]

It is very difficult for the outside analyst to judge the extent of the accuracy of these two claims. In fact, it appears that there are some elements of truth to both accounts. Considerable numbers of Kurds speak of "taxation" levied by the PKK upon Kurds all over Turkey, and there is a great deal of circumstantial evidence that points to the PKK's effectiveness in extorting funds from all kinds of businesses, Kurdish—and Turkish, where possible. The PKK itself admits that it is able to gain funds by collecting customs taxes at the border from incoming trucks (including smugglers), an activity conducted also by the main Iraqi Kurdish groups. Income can also be seized from "collaborative landlords."[22] Another important source of revenue is the large Kurdish population living in Western Europe. Numbering as many as 500,000, Kurds in Europe have contributed generously to the PKK. These funds are used not only to support the organization's activities in Europe but also to purchase arms. Just as in Turkey, some of these funds are raised from willing contributors, who donate as much as 20 percent of their salaries, while other funds are raised forcibly. There is no doubt that many Kurds contribute quite willingly to the PKK cause, but most of them would probably prefer not to be taxed, even if they show some support for the cause. Reports of intimidation and demand for protection money are frequent.

In the conditions of guerrilla warfare in the southeast, it is extremely easy to imagine how intimidation is frequently employed. Some villages are pro-PKK for various reasons—conquest, tribal ties, commitment, desperation—others are anti-PKK for equally diverse reasons. Clearly the PKK can threaten "enemy" areas and extract protection money from many Kurds linked to the government who might otherwise be targets of guerrilla action. "Taxation" also extends to all kinds of economic activities within the southeast—especially narcotics.

The extent of PKK involvement in the narcotics trade is particularly controversial. The Turkish government claims that the PKK is responsible for the bulk of narcotics entering Europe from Turkey. The reality is that the region has traditionally been a major conduit for drug trafficking; under conditions of lawlessness and guerrilla warfare and the incredible temptation of the large profits to be made, many organizations and individuals, Turks and Kurds, are profiting from the trade. Those dealing in drugs even include members of the government and various security organizations, operating privately.[23] Narcotics-related corruption is widespread,[24] and, as in many Latin American states, it is growing in proportion to the size of the narcotics trade—against which few individuals can remain invulnerable. There can be no doubt that the PKK "taxes" the narcotics trade extensively. And certainly the Kurdish—and Turkish—population in Europe in general is deeply involved in the drug-running business. But the PKK, in the eyes of many Western analysts, is not the sole, or even the primary, source of European drugs from Turkey. Much of the information from official Turkish sources may be politically motivated. But while the PKK, along with other groups in the region, is involved in narcotics, its political success cannot be attributed primarily to this factor, nor can it be written off as a "narco-terrorist organization." Such labels are misleading and tend to conceal the more fundamental national, political, and social basis of the PKK movement, of which the narcotics trade is neither the raison d'être nor a permanent feature.

Finally, critical to the PKK's success is the clandestine support it receives from other states. To the extent that the Kurdish question is Turkey's most vulnerable point, for the countries threatened by Turkey or with which Ankara has severe disagreements and conflicts, the PKK is a valuable tool with which to punish Turkey. Thus, Iran and Iraq certainly have major reasons to help fund the PKK. The Syrian regime has been the foremost supporter of the PKK; it provides the PKK with training facilities in the Syrian-controlled Bekaa valley in Lebanon, and Öcalan shuttles between Damascus and the Bekaa. Syria, which has tense relations with Turkey over territorial and water disputes, made the most of Öcalan's forced exile in Damascus and Syrian-controlled areas of Lebanon and uses him as a card against Ankara. Beyond these, states hostile to Turkey such as Greece and Armenia, are known to have at least unofficial contact with the PKK; individuals within those states might well wish to pressure Turkey through support to the PKK. Finally, the Soviet Union had well-established contacts with the Turkish Left in the past; Russia today openly hosts PKK conferences in Moscow whenever Turkey pursues policies perceived by Moscow to be hostile to its interests. The Russian ability to support the PKK unquestionably places a damper on any Turkish government willingness to look too sympathetically at the Chechen resistance or pan-Turkist movements in Azerbaijan and Central Asia.[25]

`   In the end, the question of PKK financing remains extremely elusive for the outside observer. But there can be no doubt that the PKK is extremely well funded, enabling it to conduct a broad range of activities, from guerrilla warfare and bombings to political organization, the printing of Kurdish literature, and general support for the propagation of Kurdish culture and media—especially abroad—as well as the establishment of "diplomatic representation" via offices under one name or around Europe and in the United States.

The hub of the PKK's external activities is in Germany, where a majority of the Kurds, who arrived there primarily as guest workers, reside. These guest workers were joined in the 1980s by large numbers of politically active Kurds escaping the military regime installed on September 12, 1980. They provided the leadership and the organization for the guest workers. More important, they provided the link with the PKK and enabled it to mobilize and organize these Kurds. Though banned in Germany, the PKK routinely organizes large-scale demonstrations, sit-ins, hunger strikes, and the like. The efficacy of the organization and its later decision to attack Turkish targets, both those representing the Turkish state and Turkish nationalist organizations, ultimately led to its being banned. Yet it continues to operate actively under the guise of cultural and other forms of self-aid organizations. Even the anti-PKK Kurdish organizations in Germany readily concede that the PKK has managed to gain the support of an overwhelming segment, maybe 90 percent if not more, of the Kurdish population there.

In addition to financing, the PKK also recruits would-be guerrillas among the Kurds in Europe and uses its diaspora population as a political trump card of sorts. Clearly, the German government has been forced to coexist with the PKK on its soil, despite the ban on the organization. It has also engaged it in discussions at significant levels with the hope of curtailing its attacks on Turkish targets.[26]

The PKK has also put its financing to important use in the establishment of a PKK-dominated Kurdish-language TV station that operates by satellite transmission out of the U.K. The broadcasts are widely available to Kurds in Europe, Turkey, and even in northern Iraq by satellite. The station, called "Med-TV,"[27] provides daily news and commentary on the Kurdish world in both Kurdish and Turkish. Its reporting on the greater Kurdistan region employs traditional Kurdish names for places now renamed in Turkish, Arabic, or Persian—such as Dersim for Tunceli in the southeast. Live reports from PKK commanders in the field are regularly broadcast, as well as announcements and ceremonies held by the PKK. Öcalan often participates, by telephone, in the talk shows and uses the broadcasts to convey messages and make important announcements. Other programs are devoted to Kurdish arts and music. Med-TV is an important source of alternative news and information about the PKK and things Kurdish. But most important, it fills a large cultural vacuum: This is the first time Kurds in Turkey have ever had television programming dedicated to aspects of their own culture. As a result, the programming commands a wide viewership.[28] With the yearly rental cost of the transponder estimated at $6.5 million and a staff of two hundred,[29] the broadcasts represent an important financial outlay for the organization. (It seems amazing that the Turkish government would prefer that Kurds get their TV news and culture in Kurdish from PKK-TV rather than provide Turkish state or private TV in Kurdish inside Turkey from non-PKK sources.)

In view of Med-TV's large viewership, the government in Ankara has made combating it a major priority. Security forces in the southeast have tried to destroy satellite dishes and in some cases have even prosecuted people for watching the station.[30] Most of the government's efforts have been directed at convincing European countries not to lease transponder time on their satellites.[31] It finally succeeded in July 1996 in forcing the annulment of the contract the station had negotiated with a Portuguese firm; however, it appeared that by mid-August the station had found another outlet, this time a U.S.-based independent firm. Frustrated, Turkish officials have been considering electronic countermeasures and banning the use of satellite dishes in the southeast altogether.[32] This cat and mouse game is likely to continue for the foreseeable future because both sides clearly appreciate the importance of video images in the modern-day struggle for influence.

The Kurdish Parliament in Exile

One of the most important indicators of tactical change in the PKK, however, has been the creation of the Kurdish Parliament in Exile (Sürgündeki Kürt Parlamentosu, or KPE). The parliament sets itself the critical task of serving as the "authoritative representative of the Kurdish people" and the eventual interlocutor with the Turkish state in reaching an eventual settlement of the Kurdish problem in Turkey. It denies that it is an instrument of the PKK, although most of its members are at least sympathetic to the PKK, if not actual members. In fact, there are few identifiable elements within it that are clearly distinct from the PKK. The political wing of the PKK, the National Liberation Front of Kurdistan, ERNK, is a key element within KPE ranks,[33] although the leadership of the parliament states that the ERNK is expected to conform to political decisions taken by the parliament as a whole.

The KPE claims to represent Kurdish aspirations by being "elected" by all Kurds willing to participate in a vote while living outside of Turkey, Iraq, Iran, and Syria. Some of the KPE's members, especially the Turkish ones, do in fact offer the organization an element of credibility, having been elected to the Turkish Parliament in the 1991 elections from the People's Labor party, HEP. The evolution of legal Kurdish representation and political parties is analyzed later. Suffice it to say here that HEP was banned by the state as was its successor, the Democracy party. After the DEP was banned, a number of DEP parliamentarians fled Turkey and sought refuge in Europe. It is they who have provided some of the core of the KPE.[34]

Even though the PKK now speaks of a solution within the existing borders of Turkey, the Kurdish Parliament in Exile in its own program demonstrates considerable ambiguity in reflecting its own basically pan-Kurdish character. It ambitiously purports to be broadly representative of all Kurds in the world. Article two of the founding by-laws of the parliament states that the KPE "represents the will of people both inside and outside of Kurdistan." Article three states that "the KPE will constitute the first step of the Kurdistan National Congress. . . . It rejects all forms of foreign occupation of Kurdistan. . . . It respects peoples' right to self-determination. . . . It favors a diplomatic and political solution. . . . It represents the people of Kurdistan and their struggle in the international arena and undertakes diplomatic and political relations in that regard. . . . It represents the people of Kurdistan who have been forced to live in diaspora."[35] This language demonstrates at least ambiguity, if not a contradiction to arguments that the PKK now seeks a political solution within the borders of Turkey, while the PKK-dominated KPE still speaks for "all Kurds."

In order to legitimate itself to the maximum extent, the KPE has been careful to establish the trappings of democratic process and transparency of process in its founding. According to the parliament's own information bulletin, a Preparatory Commission was established in late 1994 to oversee the work of the parliament. The Preparatory Commission consisted of twenty-three individuals, of whom five were active members of the Turkish Parliament—in exile because of proceedings that were opened against them and six other deputies (then still in prison) on grounds of linkage with a subversive organization (the PKK). In early January 1995 "elections" were reportedly held among Kurdish communities in Russia, Kazakhstan, Azerbaijan, Armenia, Georgia, North America, and Australia to select delegates to the new parliament; elections inside Turkey were obviously impossible. Some sixty-five delegates were ultimately elected. The chairman of the parliament is Yasar Kaya, a long-time Kurdish activist, former chairman of the Democracy party (DEP), and publisher of *Özgür Gündem,* a pro-Kurdish newspaper eventually banned by the authorities in Turkey. The parliament reportedly represents many different political trends within Kurdish society, but in fact most of the non-PKK/ERNK members represent only relatively small splinter groups—a few communists, a few Islamists, women's groups, and Alevi, Yezidi, and Assyrian religious minorities.[36]

The KPE Executive Council includes in its own program the following goals:

- to establish a national congress and a national parliament of a free Kurdistan;
- to enter into voluntary agreements with the neighboring peoples, guided by the principle of self-determination for the Kurds;

- to support and strengthen the national liberation struggle to end the foreign occupation of Kurdistan;
- to undertake programs to safeguard the political, cultural, and social rights of the Kurds;
- to engage in lobbying for the purpose of convincing members of the international community to initiate military, economic, and political embargoes on the Turkish state;
- to undertake to improve the Kurdish language;
- to establish national institutions in cultural fields;
- to work with youth to put an end to its alienation;
- to ease the return of the Kurdish people to Kurdistan;
- to protect the natural riches in Kurdistan and see to it that these resources are used for the people's happiness and liberation;
- to establish close links with the democratic public in Turkey;
- to derive its authority for the memory of the martyrs;
- to prepare draft resolutions relating to a constitution, citizenship laws, conscription laws, civil laws, tax laws, penal laws, and an environmental protection act.[37]

This program presents yet further contradictions. Is the KPE dedicated to a political solution in Turkey, or to the broader issue of liberation for "all of Kurdistan?" What does it mean to "strengthen the national liberation struggle to end the foreign occupation of Kurdistan?" Is this the creation of an independent state, or is it simply hyperbole for removal of the heavy-duty Turkish military presence from the region? What of "protection of the natural resources of Kurdistan?" Does this imply that the mineral and water wealth of the southeast will be totally at the disposal of the Kurds—an economic declaration of independence—or will there be a single shared economy with Turkey at large? Draft resolutions relating to constitutions, citizenship laws, conscription, penal laws, tax laws, and so on suggest that the parliament will be arrogating to itself nearly all the attributes of sovereignty—leaving virtually no legal relationship with a Turkish state. What does "single-state solution within existing borders" then mean in this context? In February 1996, Yasar Kaya explicitly restated a one-state federal solution.[38] In brief, the KPE program is formulated in such a way as to shed reasonable doubt on the willingness of the Kurds to remain part of Turkey in any meaningful way. It raises, in fact, the problem of the "pan-Kurdish" dimension that cannot be readily isolated from existing Kurdish politics.

In fact, nearly all Kurdish groups, parties, and organizations demonstrate ambivalence on the question of "pan-Kurdism." It is necessary here to distinguish between "pan-Kurdism" as a political movement, which in principle would seek to found a single state comprising all Kurds, and a more modest cultural "pan-Kurdish" interest that would demonstrate a concern for the welfare of all Kurds and view their own political struggles for greater rights as having direct impact on the struggle of all other Kurds, therefore requiring regular contact and even some degree of political coordination.

In actuality, nearly all Kurdish political movements today, including the PKK, state that they seek solutions only within existing state borders of the Middle East. These claims may be largely accurate—on two grounds. First, it is simply not feasible for any Kurds to aim at complete independence from the states in which they currently reside; they lack the capability to achieve independence on their own by force. Furthermore, no international support exists for such an aspiration, which is perceived as highly destabilizing to the region. Thus separation is not the stated goal of any major Kurdish party anywhere at the present time.

On the other hand, this more limited political stance need not exclude the prospect of independence, or even the ultimate creation of a "pan-Kurdish" state, at some indeterminate time in the future. It is quite common to hear Kurds admit in private that their dream is of a future united Kurdish state, but they do not know whether it will ever be possible. In the interim, achievement of greater human and cultural rights, and perhaps some degree of local autonomy, represents a critical step toward alleviation of their major problems and grievances.

The parliament in exile thus faces a serious representational problem. It has sought, so far unsuccessfully, to enlist other, more serious, Kurdish movements into its ranks. The very important moderate and active (Turkish) Kurdish Socialist party, for example, headquartered in exile in Sweden under the leadership of Kemal Burkay, has declined to join the parliament. Burkay feels that the KPE cannot be taken seriously as a parliament since it is in many ways self-appointed; as a parliamentary body it is also premature in its establishment, as it controls no territory and has no international recognition. The two leading Iraqi Kurdish political parties, the Kurdistan Democratic party (KDP) led by Massoud Barzani and the Patriotic Union

of Kurdistan (PUK) led by Jalal Talabani, have also declined affiliation
with the KPE. The Iraqi Kurds' concerns reflect the same questions about
the KPE: If it is a pan-Kurdish organization, then these Iraqi parties—who
value their links with Ankara and Washington—do not necessarily wish to
link themselves to a pan-Kurdish agenda; if the KPE really speaks for Turkey's Kurds, then it is not appropriate for Iraqi Kurds to be involved. The
mainstream Iranian Kurdish organizations have also not joined. In a sense,
then, the KPE cannot be said to represent more than the PKK and a
broader group of sympathizers who see it as the major vehicle of organized, internationally oriented Kurdish power. The absence of other serious Kurdish organizations at this point weakens its representational
aspirations.

The KPE also suffers from its lack of recognition by any existing government in the world. Unlike the Palestine Liberation Organization (PLO),
which for years maintained "embassies" abroad and gained formal observer status in many international organizations, the KPE so far has not
attained this status.[39] It has, however, gained the sympathy of a number of
private international supporters from many European countries who are
willing to lend their names to the Kurdish cause. KPE leaders recognize
that they have a formidable task ahead of them in seeking diplomatic recognition; they may, over time, in fact come to gain greater recognition
than at the present early stage of the diplomatic offensive—depending on
how the Turkish government reacts. The Turkish government's strong and
inflexible denunciations of the PKK and the KPE may have somewhat
helped the parliament. Ankara severely criticized both Belgium and the
Netherlands for allowing the KPE to gather for meetings in their capitals;
in the case of the Netherlands, Ankara even temporarily retaliated by banning military purchases from The Hague. Ankara also reacted vehemently
to subsequent meetings of the parliament in exile in Austria and then in
Moscow. The great consternation with which these meetings are received
in Ankara has obliged Turkish leaders to initiate political démarches that
far exceed the political embarrassment these meetings of the parliament in
exile may cause Ankara.

Another goal of the KPE is to create a Kurdish National Congress (Ulusal Kongre), quite consciously modeled on the Jewish National Congress,
which for so long served to keep the idea of the Zionist state alive in public
opinion. The congress purportedly is to be a permanent body, higher than

the KPE itself, designed to attract Kurds of all political persuasions and from all countries who are dedicated to the national cause. Such a body would broaden the Kurds' public visibility, internationalize the movement, create further legitimacy for itself, and serve to deepen and spread a national identity among Kurds themselves.

In the end, then, the future of the KPE is uncertain. But it is important to recognize that it could become caught up in a new dynamic that will change its character. Most Kurdish thinkers and activists are not likely to remain indefinitely satisfied with either traditional PKK policies or its authoritarian, closed, modus operandi. Kurdish intellectuals are likely to want a more flexible approach to policies in order to deal with a changing world and a gradually changing Turkey. The establishment of the KPE in Europe opens up an entirely different world to Kurdish political activists. Instead of operating as does the PKK in secret in the Bekaa valley in Lebanon, or conducting guerrilla operations in the mountains of the southeast, Kurds living in Europe have the freedom and opportunity to openly seek political goals through political organization. Indeed, the PKK's struggle may now be gradually shifting toward the political and diplomatic phase, in an effort to increase pressure upon the Turkish state from abroad. Such a task will require a new cadre of Kurdish activists, more open, more educated, more European, and more flexible. This cadre is likely to grow in number as the nature of the political struggle evolves.

There are four possible future scenarios for the KPE, depending upon the policies of the Turkish government. First, it remains a strictly PKK vehicle and even the means through which the PKK tries to gain respectability abroad. Second, the KPE may expand as the Turkish government digs in its heels on the issue of reforms, thus making it easier for groups such as Burkay's to join the parliament to create a united front. Under this scenario, the influence of the PKK will be diluted, but the overall Kurdish movement strengthened.[40] A third outcome includes the possibility that the PKK may come to be entirely superseded or taken over by the KPE, creating quite a different organization—more open, transparent, democratic, even if not fully abandoning the armed struggle. Finally, the KPE itself may become irrelevant if the People's Democracy party (HADEP), the present successor to the banned Kurdish parties in Turkey, manages to become the legal focal point for Kurdish activities. The corollary is also true: The repression of HADEP may give greater visibility to the KPE.

The Öcalan Factor

How important is Öcalan to the PKK? By all accounts, the PKK is very much Öcalan's creation. Although based in Damascus and the Bekaa, Öcalan has succeeded in imposing himself on the Kurdish psyche by sheer force, ruthlessness, and single-minded determination. There is no question that he has a genuine following among rank-and-file Kurds, even those who do not belong to the PKK. Indeed, by all descriptions Öcalan is secretive, withdrawn, suspicious, and lacking in self-confidence. He does not like group discussion; his close associates reportedly seem uncomfortable around him. He does not treat others as equals and he often demeans his subordinates in front of others, demands self-confessions from his lieutenants, and keeps his distance from nearly everyone.[41] He has elevated the art of self-criticism to new heights. Arguing that the movement started with self-criticism, developed with self-criticism, and that victory will result from continued self-criticism,[42] he has used this notion effectively to maintain his hold on the organization and its membership. The lack of pluralism within the PKK ought not come as a surprise given its Marxist-Leninist roots. "Kurdish 'Marxism' in Turkey, like Turkish Marxism itself . . . offered little opportunity for political pluralism."[43] Not unlike other organizations of its kind, the PKK has been subjected to numerous purges by its leader. This type of structure is not appropriate for the overt political phase of PKK activity. He has very limited direct personal contact with European statesmen of the sort that Yasir Arafat consistently sought to encourage.[44] Constrained by the Syrians, he is limited in the contracts he can develop from his Damascus base.

Some Kurdish observers believe that Öcalan has begun to show considerably more maturity, realism, and balance since 1993. This version shows him moving away from ideology toward greater pragmatism, as evidenced in changing PKK positions on key issues ranging from separatism to Marxism-Leninism. He first demonstrated this pragmatism in 1993 when he declared a unilateral cease-fire that was well received by the Turkish public and media.[45] The positive Turkish response was encouraged by then-president Özal, who even asked the HEP parliamentarians to attend the announcement of the cease-fire's renewal. The death of Özal and the subsequent collapse of the cease-fire dashed any hopes of a cessation of hostilities. Öcalan has again tried, but this time without success, to seize the initiative by declaring a unilateral cease-fire to coincide with the December 24, 1995, Turkish parliamentary elections.

Öcalan's grip on the organization remains an important question. After all, the collapse of the 1993 cease-fire was the result of insubordination: In a deliberate attempt at undermining the cease-fire, a local PKK commander in Bingöl intercepted a bus carrying military conscripts and killed thirty-three of them.[46] Despite the potential for many more such would-be disloyal commanders and the natural handicaps arising from running an insurrection from a foreign capital, Öcalan has maintained a semblance of coherence and unity. In part, he has managed to do this by instilling a sense of blind dedication among his followers. He has used his aloofness and harshness to create a charismatic image for himself. Should he pass from the scene, the PKK will undoubtedly experience a period of internecine fighting until another leader emerges or the movement evolves into a new and unexpected—perhaps less, or even more, violent—form. Here again the future role of the KPE may have a major impact on the form a future PKK takes.

There has been speculation for some time about the absence of any PKK-related violence in the main cities of the country, where hundreds of thousands if not millions of Kurds reside, some of whom are fairly recent arrivals escaping the conflict. Among the reasons offered are the efficiency of the security services; the vulnerability of the daily lives of these Kurds, afraid to get involved in the violence from which they have yearned to escape; the lack of professional PKK cadres in the cities; and finally the control exercised by Öcalan, who correctly calculates that a major escalation of this sort would doom, at least in the medium term, any hope of Turkish-Kurdish reconciliation.[47] In fact, it might trigger the kind of inter-ethnic fighting that has not yet materialized in this conflict. That is not to say that soft targets in the cities have not been attacked directly by the PKK. Some attacks, such as the bombing of a railroad station that killed a number of military cadets, created a furor. Other attacks against tourists in Antalya, which shook the tourist industry in 1993, have not been resumed despite periodic threats by Öcalan. If the government's military campaign against the PKK genuinely succeeds in the southeast, this option in the cities may then appeal to Öcalan. More radical members of the PKK may not share this view, but, for the time being, the PKK is not about to disappear from the southeast.

On the other hand, the possibility exists that the recent expansion of the political and diplomatic arm of the PKK into the KPE will in fact impose change on the political leadership of the PKK—if not in removing Öcalan himself, at least in diluting his influence and pushing the organization in more moderate and open directions by those most prominent and active outside of the Bekaa valley and Damascus. The expansion of legal political activity in Turkey would similarly force Öcalan to respond to changes he cannot totally control or manipulate.

An important constraining factor in the life of Öcalan is his host, the Syrian government. As much as this situation shelters him from the Turkish military, it nevertheless makes him a client of the Assad regime. While it is impossible to discern the degree of control Syrian officials have over Öcalan, it is safe to argue that Syrian help does not come without strings attached. The situation makes him vulnerable in the unlikely event that Ankara and Damascus can cut a deal satisfactory to both sides. Although it is hard to see Öcalan's being delivered to Turkey by Assad, there was increasing speculation in Ankara that the government formed by Necmettin Erbakan would at least request from Damascus that Öcalan be sent somewhere not adjacent to Turkey's borders. Erbakan, it was thought, with his Islamic anti-Israeli credentials, stood a better chance of convincing Assad than a traditional Turkish government. Still, not only did his tenure in office not suffice to initiate discussions with Damascus, but as his dealings with the Iranians who clandestinely support the PKK demonstrated, it is unlikely that these countries would willingly give up a political cord.

The Syrian connection notwithstanding, the fact remains that for the time being Öcalan is the uncontested leader of the PKK. Irrespective of the terrorist label that has stuck to him, he has achieved, at least among a significant segment of Turkey's Kurdish population, a stature that no other Turkish Kurdish personality has reached, certainly not since Shaykh Said.

Kurdish Attitudes toward the PKK

The PKK today is the single most important political fact of life for Kurds in the southeast. The PKK decision in 1984 to begin its "armed struggle" pushed large parts of the region into violence and vastly increased the armed presence of the Turkish army, gendarmerie, special forces, police, and intelligence elements. Some Kurds argue that the emergence of the PKK actually worsened the situation for the Kurdish cause overall; it polarized the situation and reduced yet further the already limited organizational freedoms that the Kurds had gained as they sought to build national consciousness over the long term in nonconfrontational ways. The heavy military presence in the southeast has significantly diminished other forms of Kurdish political activities as well, including demonstrations, shop closings, strikes, and other forms of civil disobedience.

Beyond the difficulties of everyday life, the insurrection led by the PKK had deepened divisions within Kurdish society. Governmental attempts at recruiting village guards (see below) often pit village against village, hamlet against hamlet, and tribal organization against other tribal groupings as the PKK and the state compete for the support of individual villages. Even the feudal system that the PKK has vowed to dismantle may have received a boost, as the state and the PKK have both sought to recruit along tribal lines. If the Turkish-Kurdish struggle is one day resolved, the seeds for internecine Kurdish fighting may have been sown: There will surely be many accounts to settle.

Therefore, it is difficult to ascertain exactly the extent of the PKK's support among Kurds in Turkey.[47] Despite some of the deep divisions that the insurrection has generated, and whether or not Kurds approve of all the PKK's tactics or like its leadership, the PKK has imposed itself upon the Kurdish political scene as the single central reality and has dominated its dialogue for many years. As a result, few Kurds are in fact willing to oppose the PKK openly. While there are three reasons for this, they can be summarized as an absence of rivals or alternatives.

1. The PKK's Hostility to Rivals

In its early years of paramilitary operations, the PKK tended to act on the principle that "all those that are not with us are against us." The PKK struggled quite harshly against all other Kurdish groups and activists, and it railed against what it perceived as their minimalist goals or narrow ideological perspectives. In fact, it did not take on the Turkish state until it had virtually eliminated all other potential military rivals. In the eyes of the PKK's Kurdish opponents, the violent paramilitary character of PKK operations transformed the operating environment in very negative ways. Whereas the state had once tolerated a minimal number of publications, demonstrations, and even some political organization by Kurdish political parties, the violent assault against the state forced it to crack down harshly against almost all forms of Kurdish political activity. Thus, for those Kurds involved in daily political activities, there is a certain degree of nervousness about taking on the PKK publicly. It is not simply the PKK's past reputation for intolerance that deters people, but also pressure from rank-and-file supporters, who tend to view such criticisms as traitorous to the cause.

The PKK has in fact tolerated those political parties it thought it could influence, or at the very least use. The first was the HEP, the People's Labor party, which was subsequently banned by the state after having succeeded in entering parliament in a temporary alliance with the social democrats. With the closing down of HEP, the same members formed the DEP, the Democracy party, which was subsequently also banned. Many of its parliamentary members, including the most famous of them, Leyla Zana, were imprisoned on charges of sedition. While they may have had strong sympathies for the PKK, these parties were not monolithic, containing pro-PKK as well as non-PKK elements.

2. Turkish State Opposition

In tactical terms, it might seem wise for Turkey to allow a moderate Kurdish opposition to emerge that could then eclipse the PKK, attracting the support of the majority of the Kurdish population via more moderate goals and methods. Such an alternative movement, one might argue, would severely undercut the support of the PKK. Indeed, Öcalan himself, in a long interview in May of 1991, demonstrated some of his greatest resistance to the idea of any Kurdish political alternative to the PKK. He viewed any alternative Kurdish political organization or move to seek the support of the U.S. as a disguised attempt at liquidating the PKK and the Kurdish cause. Although he accepted that non-PKK political parties have a right to exist, he clearly viewed them as state-sponsored agents intended to divide the resistance.[49]

Yet despite Öcalan's clear sense of paranoia about potential rival movements emerging against him—especially those created by the government—there is no indication that the government has ever seriously tried to implement this idea. In fact, in the eyes of many Kurds, the PKK actually turned out to be a kind of blessing for Turkish hardliners. It was easy for the state to rally domestic and international support against an enemy like the PKK. Many Kurds have observed that the Turkish government prefers to have the PKK as its enemy: What more ideal enemy than one that has practiced massive violence, the killing of members of its own eth-nic group, has espoused for long periods a Marxist-Leninist and maximal-ist ideological position, has alienated most other Kurdish groups, and is headed by a leader broadly seen as a megalomaniac? A more moderate, cooperative, nonviolent, and attractive Kurdish leadership would make it much harder for the state to justify its own violent response and heavy-handed policies in terms of domestic and international opinion.

Although a more detailed analysis of the Turkish government's position is presented below, suffice it to say that its systematic suppression of mod-erate Kurdish groups has played into the hands of the PKK by exposing the "futility" of moderate behavior. Among such actions, the banning of HEP and DEP were the most radicalizing, as they did away with legally elected parties and members operating within the system. Unlike their pre-decessors, which were either illegal (as in the case of the Iraqi-affiliated Turkish Kurdistan Democratic party, founded in 1965) or had never suc-ceeded in developing past student-type organizations (such as the Eastern Revolutionary Cultural Hearths (DDKO)) HEP and DEP were bona fide parties that had a mass following, especially in the southeast.

The state has been equally harsh with small, nonradical Kurdish-based parties. Serafettin Elçi, a former minister in Bülent Ecevit's last cabinet in the late seventies, has tried to form a pro–free enterprise Kurdish party; initially called the Kurdish Democratic platform, it was finally constituted on January 7, 1997, as the Democratic Mass party (Demokratik Kitle Par-tisi).[50] Ibrahim Aksoy, a former DEP secretary general and close confidant of Kemal Burkay, the exiled Kurdistan Socialist party leader, has tried to come up with a left-leaning political organization, the Democracy and Change party, as an alternative to DEP and its most recent successor, HADEP (People's Democracy party). Such party leaders and members are continuously harassed by state security bodies, which initiate legal action against them. In fact, in recent years the state has found that the most effective way of silencing Kurdish groups in general is through the legal system, which can impose harsh prison sentences and monetary damages often far beyond the means of defendants. Such policies are not new: In fact, the state has been consistent in its pursuit of any kind of Kurdish activism, including the most peaceful, through the court system. Large trials occurred in the 1950s as well as in all the subsequent decades, and individuals have been sentenced to long terms in prison for evoking Kurd-ish nationalist themes.[51]

The Turkish policy has clearly benefited the PKK, which, unlike other groups, relies on its military capabilities to make its point. In effect, this gives a premium to violence and ensures that the PKK has a near monopoly on the political discourse as it relates to the Kurdish issue. The fate of HADEP, the latest transmutation of the HEP and DEP members, remains to be seen. Although allowed to participate in the 1995 parliamentary elections, HADEP may also follow in the footstep of its predecessors and find itself banned by the state. The decision taken in June 1996 to close down the Labor party (Emek Partisi), a small left-wing non-Kurdish party, on charges of sedition because it advocated a peaceful solution to the Kurdish problem in the southeast serves to underscore that, at least as far as the hardline elements within the state are concerned, political dialogue remains out of the question. Such actions invariably augment the PKK's ranks.

3. Political Support for the PKK among Kurds

The PKK has been relatively successful in perpetuating not only its own existence but also the armed struggle against the Turkish state. The resulting prestige it has derived has also led to defections from rival organizations deemed ineffective by their own militants.[52] Even Kurds who dislike its methods or its leadership style recognize that the reality of PKK operations, more than any other single activity, has raised the Kurdish issue at the international level, focused attention upon the problem, and created pressures—so far not yet decisive—upon the Turkish state to reconsider its policies.[53] In their thinking, it is the PKK that forced the then incoming prime minister Demirel in 1991 to state that he recognized "the Kurdish reality." Furthermore, Kurds distrust the state's rhetoric to the effect that reform is impossible while a "terrorist" campaign is being waged, and therefore reforms will occur only after the defeat of the PKK. Nearly all Kurds recognize that it is the PKK that has created the political space in which other Kurdish organizations and parties have been able to operate in recent years—even though they too have been subjected to prosecution, fines, and closure on a periodic basis.

Many potential alternative Kurdish political figures believe it is not feasible for them to form alternative political movements within Turkey—at least now. This is not to say that attempts have not been made, and a few were described above. Apart from the potential danger of reprisals against them from the PKK, there is a sense that alternative opposition figures offering themselves at this juncture would not sit well with the Kurdish public at large and may be viewed as fronts for the state. HEP, DEP, and HADEP are unlike other parties (as will be discussed in a later section) in that many of their rank and file are sympathetic to the PKK. Even the Welfare party's (Refah) Kurdish members who directly compete with HADEP and PKK will concede that they do not want the PKK eliminated totally, although they may seek to justify their position on humanitarian rather than political grounds. There is a widely held belief that fighters for the PKK—whatever one may think of the movement's leadership and tactics—have truly "paid their dues"—that is, demonstrated their sacrifice in blood for the Kurdish cause over a prolonged period.

Indeed, many Kurdish families have been directly affected by the PKK-led insurrection: By military estimates, over 11,000 PKK members have been killed in the years since the beginning of the "armed struggle." In addition, there are some 10,000 in jail for PKK-related or Kurdish-national-ist activities; tens of thousands have been arrested, served time, and have been released; there are perhaps as many as 5,000–10,000 guerrillas in the countryside and neighboring countries; and there is a militia estimated at 50,000.[54] Given the large but tightly knit nature of the average Kurdish family, and the impact of so many deaths, imprisonments, and the contin-ued battlefield activity, large numbers of extended Kurdish families have been directly affected by the fighting, and especially by PKK political activ-ities. In one of the few surveys conducted in the southeast, of the 35 per-cent of those surveyed who responded to a question on how well they knew members of the PKK, 42 percent claimed to have a family member in the organization.[55]

From the perspective of individual Kurds, the PKK has achieved a de-gree of success that has eluded them since the inception of the Turkish republic. The PKK has managed to marry political activism to armed resis-tance and internationalized an issue that had previously received little at-tention. While no one expects the PKK to defeat the Turkish military, its success in getting Ankara to commit vast amounts of manpower to the southeast and the ability of the organization to fight the army to a standstill are a source of pride. In comparison to its Iraqi or Iranian counterparts, the PKK has managed to achieve a great deal more with significantly less. Furthermore, having publicly anointed the PKK as its sole enemy and then addressed it with a purely military response, the state has created two distinct consequences for itself: At one level it has elevated the PKK's status in the eyes of the public, friend and foe alike. Second, by abandoning the political arena among the Kurdish public to the PKK, the state has de facto put itself at a terrible disadvantage in the race to win the hearts and minds of this most important constituency. In effect, it allows the PKK to set the agenda among Kurds. All of these factors also serve to create an atmosphere of intolerance within the Kurdish community in which criticism of the PKK is often equated with treason to the cause. Not surprisingly, this mirrors the developments within Turkish society, in which criticism of state policies is often interpreted as support for the PKK.

As it is with most diaspora communities, the Kurdish diaspora is more radical than the Kurds living in Turkey. This is the result of both the ease with which an organization can operate, recruit, and mobilize away from the control of security services, and the tendency of aggrieved groups to express their feelings and ideas without fear. In the Kurdish case, the fact that the diaspora communities tend to be of the working class and unintegrated in the European societies they predominantly live in further facilitates the PKK's task.

Support for the PKK today among politically active individual Kurds, including even those opposed to the PKK, undoubtedly contains a self-serving element. That is, they may expect to benefit in the long run from the PKK's bloody struggle if it opens the door to greater political participation and recognition of cultural rights. Clearly, past political activity—clandestine or legal—has brought them little gains in this regard. As a result, few on the Kurdish political spectrum would like to see the PKK defeated—including even those hostile to the PKK. Such a defeat would be perceived as removing the major leverage the Kurds currently have against the state. Not surprisingly, therefore, few are willing to criticize the PKK openly.

Turkish Kurds, Iraqi Kurds, and Operation Provide Comfort

Turkey has always feared the influence of events in Iraqi Kurdistan on the Kurds in its own midst. It has, therefore, not just opposed independence for Iraqi Kurds but has also been displeased by any discussion of federation or even autonomy for the Kurds of Iraq. Ankara's fears notwithstanding, the relationship between Turkish and Iraqi Kurds has not always been easily discernible. Separated by an international boundary and by regimes that have been anxious to limit the mobilizational potential of their respective Kurdish populations, the two Kurdish populations have been kept together by little else but family and tribal ties and cross-border trade. In the early 1920s, the new government in Ankara set its eyes on Mosul, the oil-rich province of Iraqi Kurdistan then occupied by the British. Ankara quickly abandoned any claims it had, once the Shaykh Said revolt erupted in 1925. The Kemalists always suspected the British of having encouraged the revolt to discourage them from advancing their claim.

The international boundary between Turkey and Iran is the oldest and most established of all of Turkey's frontiers. By contrast, the demarcation line with Syria and Iraq is a twentieth-century phenomenon. The creation of Iraq was particularly disruptive, as it divided the Kurmanji-speaking areas of Turkey from Kurmanji-speaking parts of northern Iraq, stranding families, clans, and tribes on different sides of the international divide. Over the years, trade between the Kurds residing in different states continued at a much reduced level and assumed a contraband character. But there were attempts at political cross-fertilization: Kurdish students from different countries began to mingle among themselves in Europe in the 1960s, and there was an abortive attempt by Iraqi Kurdish students studying in Turkey to set up branches of their European organizations.

The political connection between Iraqi and Turkish Kurds was rekindled with the successes of Molla Mustafa Barzani. As van Bruinessen argues, "Barzani in his lifetime became a legendary superhero, whose feats were sung and told in all corners of Kurdistan. . . . Admiration for, pride of, and consequently loyalty towards Barzani strengthened an awareness of Kurdish identity and loyalty towards the abstract idea of the Kurdish nation."[56] The fact that Barzani was a Kurmanji speaker from across the border, with close family connections, also helped his stature among Turkish Kurds. The Barzani movement, in victory and defeat, influenced Turkish Kurds and provided them with an impetus for their ethno-political activities. His military successes and his ability to force the Baghdad regime to accede to an autonomy agreement, such as the one reached on March 11, 1970 (the first one ever to be concluded by a sovereign state and the Kurds), reverberated throughout the Turkish Kurd population.

Turkish Kurds clandestinely formed the Turkish Kurdistan Democratic party (TKDP) as the Turkish counterpart of Barzani's Iraqi-based organization. The TKDP managed to gather an impressive following before it fell into disunity—mirroring events in Iraq—and disappeared altogether in Turkey. The struggles between the leftist elements among Iraqi Kurds and the more traditional Barzani were replayed in Turkey.[57] Similarly, the 1975 collapse of the Iraqi Kurdish revolt[58]—following the Algiers agreement between the shah of Iran and Saddam Hussein of Iraq that put an end to Iranian support for the Iraqi Kurds—confirmed the trend toward radicalization among Turkey's politically active Kurds. Disillusioned with the capitalist-Western camp, Kurds in both Iraq and Turkey were further pushed in the direction of the Soviet Union and other Third-World liberation struggles, especially the Palestinian one.

To this day divisions among Iraqi Kurds, between Molla Mustafa's son Massoud on the one hand and Jalal Talabani on the other continue to be reflected among Turkish Kurds. In 1975, Talabani left the Barzani's Kurdistan Democratic party to form the Patriotic Union of Kurdistan (PUK). Talabani, a Sorani speaker, represents the more urban middle- and lower-middle-class elements of Kurdish society, whereas Barzani's movement is more tribal and peasant based. The advent of the PKK has not changed the view of Turkish Kurds about Iraqi Kurdish politics. Turkish Kurds continue to be divided: Those who oppose the PKK remain attached to the Barzanis and regard Talabani as neither genuine nor trustworthy. They blame him for dividing the Iraqi Kurdish movement and betraying Molla Mustafa Barzani. By contrast, PKK supporters and leftist Kurds belonging to parties such as HADEP, while not automatically pro-Talabani, are more positively disposed toward him. Barzani, insofar as he resembles the traditional conservative Turkish Kurdish elements, represents everything Öcalan is ideologically opposed to. Talabani has also had more of an influence on Öcalan. He was quite instrumental in getting Öcalan to consider the 1993 ceasefire and was present when Öcalan publicly renewed it. Talabani, to some extent, can afford to have a more balanced relationship with the PKK, since his territory does not abut Turkey as does Barzani's, although in the past (as in 1992) he did participate in anti-PKK military operations with the Ankara government.

Ironically, it is Saddam Hussein and the PKK who have brought the Kurds in both countries closer together—at least physically. Saddam's repression in the 1980s and 1990s caused large population movements from Iraqi Kurdistan toward Turkey. Because the revolt against Saddam in the aftermath of the Gulf War was so comprehensive—it included not just the *peshmergas* but also civil servants, the middle classes, the professionals, and the peasantry—the refugee flow into Turkey was much larger and different than before. Their suffering, which prompted international food drops, also mobilized Turkish Kurds. Local officials, without relying on Ankara's help, organized large food convoys for the Iraqi Kurds. The refugee influx not only mobilized them but also further politicized them when they thought that Ankara was being less than generous.

On the other hand, the growth of the PKK and its use of northern Iraqi territory to base its fighters and supplies introduced a Turkish dimension into Iraqi Kurdish politics. During the Iran-Iraq War, Turkey signed a security agreement with Iraq that allowed Turkey to conduct operations against the PKK in Iraqi territory; the Turkish military has continued to intervene in the north almost at will and without Iraq's permission since the end of the Gulf War in 1991. These operations, especially air attacks, have not always ended up hitting PKK bases; sometimes they hit Iraqi Kurdish villages, causing casualties among their civilian populations. In effect, by traversing across the border into Iraq, the Turkish-Kurdish conflict is influencing developments there and forcing the two Iraqi Kurdish parties to deal with the PKK.

There is no question that Turkish Kurds now follow developments in northern Iraq more carefully than ever. The connection between the two areas is real, although this does not mean that one would necessarily emulate the other when it comes to political choices. Turkish Kurds are still very much interested in the fate of their brethren in northern Iraq, despite the failure of the two Kurdish factions to build upon their initial achievements after the conclusion of the Gulf War. The future of the de facto autonomous region, which had a promising beginning with the holding of free elections in 1992—a first in Iraqi territory—is in serious jeopardy, as the KDP and the PUK have initiated a furious internecine struggle against each other. Kurdish interest in the fate of the north is best seen during the debates over Turkey's renewal of the Operation Provide Comfort (OPC) mandate, the U.S.-led multinational force that has served since 1991 in northern Iraq to protect the Kurds from attacks by Saddam Hussein.

OPC, under attack from a variety of sources, including Islamists, nationalist elements among the center-left parties, and even indirectly from the military, which is anxious about the indefinite prolongation of such a force and its consequences for Turkish sovereignty, began to run into serious trouble in the Turkish parliament. The debates on its periodic six-month renewal assumed an increasingly vitriolic character, with OPC being accused of deliberately fomenting revolt by the PKK and other ills.[59] The resulting acrimony over the subject put parliamentarians of Kurdish origin, irrespective of their affiliation, in a quandary. While supporting the renewal of OPC's mandate, these parliamentarians have found themselves in difficult situations when their parties have required them to vote against any extension. Nowhere is this more visible than within Welfare. Welfare's Kurdish MPs have told their leaders that they would like to see OPC's mandate renewed, despite Erbakan's very determined and relentless opposition to it. Kurds in Turkey recognize that the operation in fact saved tens of thousands of Kurdish lives among the Iraqi Kurdish refugees who fled into the mountains in 1991 after the Gulf War to escape Saddam's revenge. They also acknowledge that this operation was among the catalysts that brought the whole Kurdish issue to greater Western attention and that resulted in the precedent-setting visits of Iraqi Kurdish leaders to Ankara during Özal's presidency. Hence, for Turkish Kurds, the operation helps focus attention on the Kurdish factor in Turkish politics and serves to strengthen their cause.

The advent of the Welfare-led government in June of 1996 ironically may have helped save the operation. Prime Minister Erbakan not only agreed to its extension but at the end of 1996 also gave his assent to a revamped—admittedly less extensive—OPC, renamed Operation Northern Watch. This allowed Erbakan to claim to have fulfilled one of his election promises. In the long run, the multinational force, which since January 1997 no longer includes France, is more threatened by developments in northern Iraq. Massoud Barzani's deal with Saddam Hussein in August/September 1996, which until he was pushed back allowed him to gain control of all of northern Iraq, underscored the limits of OPC and its successor force. While some Turkish Kurds welcomed the ascendancy of one faction over another, especially because their preferences were with Barzani in the first place, they were angered by the KDP's deal with Saddam, who is equally hated on both sides of the border. In the end, however, Turkish Kurds publicly supported an end to the conflict, and Welfare party's Kurdish members even initiated attempts at bridging the gap between the two Iraqi factions. Still, it remains to be seen how the August/September 1996 events will impact Turkish Kurds.

The PKK, however, has been much more wary of Operation Provide Comfort. It believes that the U.S. and other Western personnel participating in Provide Comfort are cooperating closely with the Turkish government, and particularly with Turkish intelligence. They also claim that the force, based at the Turkish-U.S. base in Incirlik, is providing intelligence to the Turkish army on the whereabouts of PKK forces in northern Iraq in order to facilitate the army's attack on the PKK there.[60]

The PKK as a whole continues to be suspicious of U.S. intentions toward it, based in particular on Washington's leading role among Western states in denouncing the PKK as a "terrorist organization." The PKK also sees the U.S. as Turkey's main source of arms used against the Kurds in the southeast, and the principal diplomatic support to Turkey in defending the government against European criticism that Turkey is violating human rights in the southeast.[61]

Finally, Özal, in his final years as president, decided to capitalize on the close connection between Iraqi and Turkish Kurds. By inviting the Kurdish leaders to Ankara, he sought an alternative way of defusing the conflict within Turkey. Working on the assumption that any move by Turkey designed to help the Kurdish enclave in northern Iraq would be well received among Turkish Kurds, Özal started to lay the groundwork for a strengthened relationship between Ankara and Iraqi Kurds. This would demonstrate to the Kurds in Turkey that the Turkish state was not necessarily hostile to Kurds, but just to the violence perpetrated by the PKK: It was largely a symbolic move. It did, however, turn traditional Turkish policy upside down. The nationalist center-left politician Mümtaz Soysal, by contrast, during his short tenure as foreign minister, acted in the opposite manner. He tightened the restrictions on journalists and nongovernmental organizations crossing into northern Iraq and sought to get rid of OPC.[62] Both political leaders had started with the same assumption regarding the influence of northern Iraq, but they devised opposite policies.

Notes and References

1. It is exceeded only in Iraq by the long armed struggle of the Kurdish Democratic party of Iraq—later joined by the Patriotic Union of Kurdistan in Iraq—both of which have also maintained an armed struggle for decades against the Iraqi state.

2. There are, however, exceptions to this. Following the 1975 debacle of the Kurdish movement in Iraq—abandoned by the shah of Iran after he concluded an agreement with Iraq—a disenchanted KDP became increasingly leftist in orientation as it tried to curry favor with the ascendant Third Worldist movements. The

KDP followed the lead of its rival, the Patriotic Union of Kurdistan (PUK), which has traditionally been more middle-class oriented, and in the 1970s it assumed an anti-imperialist discourse. The aim of both movements was to align the Kurdish cause more closely with the "national liberation struggles," and principally with that of the Palestinians—who never sympathized with them. Both these Iraqi movements, however, especially the KDP, maintain strong regional and tribal ties.

3. Ismet G. Imset, *PKK: Ayrilikçi Siddetin 20 Yili* (The PKK: 20 years of separatist violence in Turkey) (Ankara: Turkish Daily News Yayinlari, 1992), 59–71.

4. Rifat Balli, *Kürt Dosyasi* (The Kurdish file) (Istanbul: Cem Yayinevi, 1991), 204–5.

5. *Ibid.*, and also see Hidir Göktas, *Kürtler-II: Mehabad'dan 12 Eylül'e* (The Kurds: From Mahabad to 12 September) (Istanbul: Alan Yayincilik, 1991), 127–29.

6. For the composition of the PKK's central committee, see Michael M. Gunter, *The Kurds and the Future of Turkey* (New York: St. Martin's Press, 1997), 23–59.

7. For a more detailed account of the formation of the PKK, see Imset, *PKK: Ayrilikçi Siddetin 20 Yili* and McDowall, *A Modern History of the Kurds.*

8. See, for instance, *PKK 5. Kongre Kararlari* (Decisions of the 5th PKK Congress) (Germany: Wesanen Serxwebûn, 1995). In this particular congress it was decided not to recruit youth younger than sixteen to fight and to make military service for women voluntary.

9. In a fascinating insight into some of the racist or class aspects of Turkish society as perceived by the Kurdish Left, Öcalan had early on spoken of his desire also to liberate the "real Turks" or "Turkmen" of eastern Turkey, who had also been marginalized over a long period of Turkish history by the "white Turks"—the Istanbul-Ankara elite—who contained much Balkan blood as opposed to the purer Turkish blood of the Anatolian Turk with his closer blood ties to Central Asia, the cradle of the Turkish people. Whatever the truth of the observation about mixed blood, no Turks at least were moved by this kind of talk coming from a Kurdish organization.

10. See interview with Öcalan, *Yeni Politika,* July 18, 1995.

11. *Pazar Postasi,* February 2, 1995.

12. See David Korn's interview with Öcalan, reprinted in the PKK publication *Serxwebun,* April 1995, 12–14.

13. *al-Hayat,* reprinted in *Mideast Mirror,* November 20, 1995. Öcalan reiterated these views in an *al-Wasat* interview after Massoud Barzani's KDP swept northern Iraq, defeating its rival, the PUK, with Iraqi help in August–September 1996. Öcalan, in fact, stressed that Barzani ought to set up a federal democratic Kurdish government that would use the Arab world "as its strategic depth . . . [and that] Federalism in Iraq was a golden opportunity." Reprinted in *Mideast Mirror,* October 4, 1996.

14. Kadri Gürsel, *Dagdakiler: Bagok'tan Gabar'a 26 Gün* (The mountain dwellers: from Bagok to Gobar in 26 days) (Istanbul: Metis Yayinlari, 1996). This is an

account by a Turkish correspondent of Agence France Presse who was kidnapped by the PKK in 1995 and taken through large swaths of territory in the southeast, where he encountered some two hundred PKK fighters. He observed that as far as the guerrilla rank and file were concerned, this was not a fight for cultural autonomy or even regional autonomy but rather for complete independence. While some of the fighters envisaged a "socialist state," most simply seemed to care only about independence. They seemed to be realistic enough to understand that they could not militarily defeat the state, even though Vietnam was often proposed as an analogy.

15. The French pulled out from the protective force, Operation Provide Comfort, when it was renegotiated with the Turkish government in January 1997 and renamed Operation Northern Watch.

16. See Rifat Ballis's interview with Öcalan in *Kürt Dosyasi*, 252.

17. For a vivid account of the relationship between the PKK and the local population, see Miyase Ilknur and Çagri Kiliççi, "Cizre'yi Medya Vurdu" (Cizre was exposed by the media), *Nokta*, April 5, 1991. They describe how, on the eve of Nevruz, the Kurdish New Year, the townsfolk in Cizre demonstrated with PKK flags, pictures of Öcalan, and with gun-toting "guerrillas."

18. *PKK 5. Kongre Karalari*, 105–10.

19. In a briefing to Turkish journalists, the Turkish general staff claimed that the PKK's annual budget was of the order of $2 billion (*Hürriyet*, April 30, 1997). As well financed as PKK may appear to be, this figure is highly exaggerated.

20. According to one former PKK operative on trial in a state security court, numerous local businessmen contributed to the PKK. The organization charged each transportation company 1,000 DM a year per bus, and it obtained 25,000 DM from businessmen and 200,000 DM from factory owners in Diyarbakir (*Anadolu Ajansi*, August 6, 1996). Although these claims may be exaggerated because the operative may think that this is what the state authorities would like to hear, the fact remains that the implication of his testimony is that this is more than an extortion racket.

21. Imset, *PKK: Ayrilikçi Siddetin 20 Yili*, 207–10. Prime minister Çiller in 1993 accused some businessmen of contributing to the PKK; this assertion was responsible, many Kurds claim, for the assassination of a number of Kurdish businessmen, including two abducted from the Çinar Hotel near Istanbul.

22. Imset, *PKK: Ayrilikçi Siddetin 20 Yili*, 207.

23. In the summer of 1996, the security services uncovered two Mafialike organizations involved in protection rackets and drugs that extended into the security services. The first of these, the Söylemez gang, had in its midst not only former police officials but also active-duty soldiers and officers, including a first lieutenant serving in the southeast (*Yeni Yüzyil*, June 13 and 14, 1996; *Cumhuriyet*, June 13 and 14, 1996). In November 1996, a traffic accident near the town of Susurluk in western Turkey further revealed the relationship between some state security officials and Mafialike figures engaged in money laundering and drug trafficking. Although the investigation into these links has not been formally finished—it may

never be—a number of officials have been arrested and the minister of interior, Mehmet Agar, had to resign because of his perceived involvement with the protagonists.

24. In a dissenting minority report to the parliamentary investigation committee looking into the Susurluk accident, an opposition member, Fikri Saglar, argues that there is a perceptible increase in the wealth of security officials serving in the southeast, and that allegations of drug-related trafficking against some of these officials are common (see Mehmet Altan, "Güneydogu ve Susurluk 3" [The Southeast and Susurluk 3], *Sabah,* April 24, 1997). In fact, there have also been accusations in the past by state officials against one of the large Kurdish landowning families, the Bucaks of Siverek, known for their close relationship with first the Justice party and presently with its successor, the True Path party. In fact, it was in the villages controlled by Sedat Bucak, a True Path parliamentarian representing Sanliurfa, and from his village guards that large amounts of drugs were confiscated (*Cumhuriyet,* July 6, 1996). Sedat Bucak, ironically, was the only surviving passenger in the Susurluk crash that also claimed the lives of a high-ranking police official, a most-wanted right-wing assassin, and a former beauty queen. This has further implicated him in drug-related illicit activities.

25. The role and significance of the PKK and the Kurdish question as they relate to Turkey's foreign policy are discussed in a later chapter.

26. In the fall of 1995, a conservative member of the German Bundestag and a high-ranking security official of Chancellor Helmut Kohl visited Öcalan in Damascus. Because Öcalan hungers for international acceptance, these visits may have helped defuse some of the violence on German soil.

27. The name "Med" refers to the ancient Medes (of biblical "Medes and Persians"), who are believed by Kurds to have been the forerunners of the modern Kurds.

28. Even the Welfare (Refah) party's internal report on its performance following the June 2, 1996, local elections complained about the impact of Med-TV; it argued that "even in the smallest village people watched it with a small satellite dish" (*Cumhuriyet,* June 27, 1996). In interviews, the authors determined that viewership extends straight to official Ankara. The Welfare party mayor of Diyarbakir admitted that he has occasionally watched the station's cultural programming (see interview with Ahmet Bilgin, *Yeni Yüzyil,* August 12, 1996). Similarly, a DYP parliamentarian, Faris Özdemir, admits that people in the southeast watch Med-TV broadcasts (Sedat Ergin, "DYP'den Güneydogu'ya Yeni Bir Bakis" (A new perspective on the southeast from the True Path party) *Hürriyet,* April 4, 1996).

29. *Turkish Daily News,* June 26, 1996. While these figures supplied to the journalist by official sources may be somewhat inflated, they nevertheless give an indication of the resources the PKK has managed to marshal.

30. In a recent case, a village headman who in the past had complained to the European Human Rights Court for relief was charged with engaging in "separatist activity" because he watched MED-TV (*Cumhuriyet,* June 22, 1996).

31. France Telecom was threatened with exclusion from a proposed bid on a

third cellular network being built by Turkey to convince it not to renew Med-TV's lease on one of its transponders (*Sabah,* June 12, 1996).

32. Zaman, February 2, 1997.

33. In fact, of the parliament's sixty-five members, ERNK is the largest group, with twelve, followed by the banned DEP with six. See Gülistan Gürbey, "Options for the Hindrances to a Resolution of the Kurdish Issue in Turkey," in *The Kurdish Nationalist Movement in the 1990s,* ed. Robert Olson (Lexington: University of Kentucky Press, 1996).

34. Gürbey argues that, in an ironic way, by banning the DEP the state pushed the party into the hands of the PKK. *Ibid.*

35. See "Kurdistan Parliament in Exile," April 12–16 1995, 18–19 (an information bulletin published by the parliament's headquarters in Brussels).

36. "Kurdish Parliament in Exile," 7.

37. "Kurdish Parliament in Exile," 23–25.

38. At a news conference in Palermo Sicily, Kaya said, "We want a federal constitution. At the same time, we consider untouchable the territorial integrity of Turkey, which must be based on equality between Kurdish and Turkish people" (*Reuters,* February 9, 1996).

39. The KPE's dilemma is different from that of the Palestine Liberation Organization, which consistently placed primary emphasis on obtaining international recognition as part of its process of gaining legitimacy among all Palestinians. The PLO's search for international recognition was greatly facilitated by its near automatic acceptance by most Arab states, which accorded the PLO virtually the status of a government in exile. The PKK will not readily gain this kind of automatic international recognition.

40. Murat Belge argues that as long as the likelihood of any liberalization in Turkish positions remains limited, the possibility that the KPE may evolve into a more moderate movement, within which the PKK is just one component, is not insignificant. *Türkler ve Kürtler: Nereden Nereye?* (Turks and Kurds: From where to where?) (Istanbul: Birikim Yayinlari, 1995), 373.

41. For an insightful account of Öcalan and his dealings with visitors, see Mehmet Ali Birand, APO ve PKK (Istanbul: Milliyet Yayinlari, 1992).

42. In fact, Öcalan devotes a whole chapter to this topic in his long and laborious report to the 5th General Congress of the PKK. Abdullah Öcalan, *PKK 5. Kongresi'ne Sunulan Politik Rapor* (The political report presented to the PKK's fifth congress) (Wesanen Serxwebun, 1995), 263–322.

43. Hamit Bozarslan, "Political Aspects of the Kurdish Problem," in *The Kurds: A Contemporary Overview,* ed. P. G. Kreyenbroek and S. Sperl (New York and London: Routledge, 1992), 110.

44. In addition to the meetings with German representatives mentioned above, members of the Greek parliament have visited him.

45. Even though he scored some impressive political points with the 1993 cease-fire, Öcalan later admitted that it was in part motivated by the need for the organization to take a breather and reorganize. Öcalan, *PKK 5. Kongresi'ne Sunulan Politik Rapor,* 327–28.

46. Henri J. Barkey, "Turkey's Kurdish Dilemma," *Survival* (Winter 1993/94): 54. The cease-fire had been one-sided, with the army continuing its operations. With the death of Özal, an important voice in favor of a peaceful solution had been lost, which, in turn, may have contributed to the unhappiness within some of the PKK's rank and file. Interestingly, General Dogan Güres, the then–chief of staff of the Turkish armed forces, revealed in a 1996 interview that he too had thought that Öcalan had not ordered the killing of the conscripts. See Hasan Cemal, "Güneydogu'da Siville Asker" (Soldiers and civilians in the Southeast), *Sabah,* April 14, 1996.

47. In a 1992 interview, Öcalan suggested that the Kurds in the western part of Turkey ought to avoid violence and any activity that would harm them, and instead concentrate on political activities and joining unions. *2000'e Dogru,* March 15, 1992.

48. One member of parliament, Welfare party's Van representative, Fethullah Erbas, suggested in a 1994 parliamentary debate that as much as 15 percent of the population in the southeast then supported the PKK, but he also warned that a large section of the populace could in the future become supportive of the organization. Türkiye Büyük Millet Meclisi, *TBMM Tutanak Dergisi,* vol. 68, October 18, 1994, 390.

49. Q: "What concrete steps would you adopt against any pro-American tendencies among the Kurds in Turkey?" Öcalan: "We can take measures. We might not get too involved against them in Iraq or Iran . . . but we will struggle against them here. . . . We will declare war against any collaborationists in Turkey . . . [in what is] certainly an ideological struggle. . . . We might have recourse to violence. I am taking this opportunity to issue a warning on this.

"After all, we're not talking about mere political struggle. This idea [of an alternative movement to the PKK] represents a dangerous collaborationist movement that is linked with Turkish state terrorism. . . . I'm warning [then–Turkish president] Özal. If he tries to set up collaborators against us, he will suffer. He should not try to secretly set up some organization for these collaborators. He is trying to coopt [a number of Kurds who were recently released from prison] to reach certain political accommodations with them. If he does so, he will be delivering the greatest single blow to the dialog that we want to develop between Turkish and Kurdish society and peoples. These collaborationists have no ties with their own people; they treat them with about as much respect as a dog." Balli, *Kürt Dosyasi,* 246–49. Admittedly, this interview was conducted at a time when the PKK perceived the political and military momentum to be on its side, which explains Öcalan's self-confidence.

50. Elçi, while minister in the last Ecevit government (1978–79), shocked public opinion by openly declaring that there were Kurds in Turkey and that he was one of them.

51. One of the most important occurred in 1959, when forty-nine intellectuals were put on trial. It was dubbed the "Trial of the Forty-nine," and many of those charged would later emerge in different Kurdish activities, ranging from the leader-

ship of TKDP to DEP and the KPE. See Naci Kutlay, *49'lar Dosyasi* (The 49ers file) (Istanbul: Firat Yayinlari, 1994).

52. Murat Belge, *Türkler ve Kürtler: Nereden Nereye?*, 392.

53. The situation is now increasingly reminiscent of Palestinian views of the PLO in past decades: While many Palestinians quarreled with PLO methods, disliked Arafat, and opposed terrorism and internecine killings among Palestinians, the PLO over time came to be the symbol of Palestinian resistance and the main vehicle of nationalist expression, whatever its faults. Thus, nearly all Palestinians defended the PLO against nearly all outside challengers. The PKK among Kurds has not yet reached the stage of the PLO among Palestinians, but with time it is moving increasingly in that direction.

54. An estimate for the 1984–1994 period by the Diyarbakir Bar Association has the number of people taken into custody by the State Security Courts at only 60,000. M. Sezgin Tanrikulu, "Ulusal ve Ulusalüstü Hukuk Mevzuati Karsisinda Kürt Realitesi ve Mevcut Durum" (The Kurdish reality and the present situation in the face of national and national legal norms). *Diyarbakir Bölge Barosu Dergisi* (June 1994–June 1995): 7.

55. Türkiye Odalar Birligi, *Dogu Sorunu: Teshisler ve Tespitler* (The Eastern question: diagnosis and findings) (Ankara: TOBB, 1995), 20. This controversial report, funded by the Turkish Union of Chambers of Commerce and Industry and conducted by Dogu Ergil, has many weaknesses, but it remains one of the few attempts at analyzing attitudes in the southeast. With respect to this particular question, when asked to categorize the nature of the relationship to known members of the PKK, some 65 percent of the sample understandably refused to answer the question. For a fervent criticism of this report, see Mehmet Turgut, *"Dogu Sorunu Raporu" Üzerine* (On the "Eastern question report") (Istanbul: Bogaziçi Yayinlari, 1996). For a serious analytical criticism of the same work, see Sakallioglu, "Historicizing the Present and Problematizing the Future of the Kurdish Problem," op. cit.

56. van Bruinessen, *Agha, Shaikh and State*, 316.

57. In the early 1970s, one of these Turkish Kurdish groups, the Turkish Kurdish Socialist party, also known as Özgürlük Yolu, led by Kemal Burkay, overtly criticized the feudal-tribal-bourgeois direction of the Barzani movement. Chris Kutschera, *Le Défi Kurde: Ou le Rêve Fou de L'Indépendance* (Paris: Bayard Éditions, 1997), 243.

58. In this context, the immediate execution in plain view by Iraqi security forces of forty-seven Kurdish refugees handed back by the Turkish authorities at the Habur crossing point had a galvanizing effect on Turkish Kurds. M. Siraç Bilgin, *Barzani'nin Son Yillari ve Kürdistan'da Çok Partili Sistem* (The last years of Barzani and the multiparty system in Kurdistan) (Istanbul: Berfin Yayinlari, 1993), 16–17.

59. The Turkish general staff, while publicly supportive of the operation, nevertheless was reluctant to completely commit itself to its continuation, in part because it hoped to obtain better terms from the U.S. This is further discussed in a later chapter.

60. A PKK representative stated that in early 1995 German television ran a program that "proved" that the U.S. was providing intelligence information to Turkey on the location of PKK camps in Iraq. There is some evidence that the U.S. promised, during a visit by the U.S. undersecretary of state, Lynn Davis, to provide technical assistance to help the Turks monitor their Iraqi border. See "Turkey Monitors Its Mountainous Border with Iraq against Infiltration by Separatist Kurdish Rebels," *Reuters,* November 1, 1995.

61. See interview with Öcalan in *al-Hayat* reprinted in *Mideast Mirror,* November 20, 1995.

62. Baskin Oran, *"Kalkik Horoz:" Çekiç Güç ve Kürt Devleti* ("Poised hammer:" The hammer force and the Kurdish state) (Istanbul: Bilgi Yayinevi, 1996), 128–30.

3

The Building of Kurdish National Consciousness

I F WE ARE TO UNDERSTAND Kurdish politics in Turkey today, we need to examine the dynamics of a deepening sense of ethnic or national consciousness. It is not just the state's policies that have hampered the development of the Kurdish identity. Divisions among the Kurds along geographical, linguistic, religious, and political lines have also contributed their share to the situation. In this section we focus on these divisions and their interaction with the changing economic and political environment.

Demography, Geography, and Language

A key task of the Kurdish movement over the past several decades has been to build among Turkey's Kurds a sense of national consciousness. This is, after all, an ethnic group divided territorially (and to some extent linguistically) among four regional states, whose own local linguistic development has been severely repressed within Turkey, a repression that has included prohibitions against education, publishing, or dissemination of news in Kurdish. The emergence of a Kurdish consciousness has been harshly discouraged. The Turkish state, intent on preserving a unitary state with a homogeneous population, has strongly opposed such "consciousness-raising." In turn, these factors have helped blur the ethnic distinctions within society. Who is a Turk or a Kurd or a member of any other minority in Turkey is an often difficult question to answer. Here we adopt van Bruinessen's definition of a Kurd in Turkey: "All native speakers of Kurmanji or Zaza, as well as those Turkish-speaking persons who claim descent from Kurmanji or Zaza speakers who still (or again) consider themselves as Kurds."[1]

While even Kurds may find this definition limiting, Turks also maintain quite legitimate fears that enhanced awareness of differing ethnic identities within the state will inevitably lead to calls for special community interests and the possibility of political movements in search of community rights. That, under the worst scenario, could result in a separatist movement. These phenomena, after all, are hardly unknown in other societies in the world.

How many Kurds are there? There are no established numbers. The most often used number is 20 percent of the population; that ratio was popularized by the late president Özal. David McDowall has estimated the percentage of Kurds in Turkey to be around 19 percent.[2] The 1965 census represents one of the rare instances—and certainly the most recent—in which people were asked to identify their mother tongues. In that survey, some 2.2 million claimed Kurdish as their mother tongue and 1.2 million said it was their second language.[3] The 1965 census had also identified 150,000 Zaza speakers.[4] A recent study based on the 1965 census concludes that the Kurds represent 12.6 percent of the population (corresponding to just over 7 million in 1990).[5] Of course, the problem with such surveys is that they are more likely to underestimate the numbers because some respondents, fearing the state-employed questioner, do not always tell the truth. In addition, there are many Kurds who have lost the use of Kurdish but consider themselves to be Kurds, or who have, over time, regained Kurdish identity.[6] Moreover, centuries of coexistence between Kurds and Turks have given rise to a considerable amount of intermarriage, which may result in assimilation in either direction.[7] The population figures and fertility rates are the subject of intense controversy; a December 1996 NSC report warned about the burgeoning Kurdish population.[8]

While the southeast and east are considered the traditional Kurdish areas, and those regions have suffered the brunt of the insurgency and counterinsurgency campaigns, the fact remains that of the Kurds living in

Turkey only a minority inhabit these regions. Over the course of this century, many Kurds were forcibly resettled in western provinces or left to their own volition to pursue better economic opportunities in the faster-growing areas. Others, especially since the beginning of the PKK insurgency, have had their villages destroyed by security forces or to a lesser extent by the PKK, or have simply fled from military operations that have destroyed homes, crops, and livestock. Some 2 million Kurdish refugees have, as a result, been displaced in the last seven years.[9] The resulting refugee flow has found its way to some of the main cities of the region, such as Diyarbakir, or to Mediterranean cities such as Mersin and Adana, or to the main western cities of Istanbul and Izmir, where large Kurdish populations already existed. None of these cities are equipped to absorb the flow of refugees whose skills are not adaptable to city life. In Adana, for instance, 80 percent of the youth among the migrants are unemployed.[10] Seeking jobs as unskilled day laborers in the construction industry or as street peddlers, they end up competing among themselves for the few jobs or crowd each other out in the market.[11] The implications of this outflow has serious ramifications for the future of the Kurds. Does it create the conditions for a deepening of the assimilation process, or does it further radicalize them?

The development of Kurdish as a language has been inhibited by a number of factors, including the fact that it was not used as a written language during the Ottoman Empire for administrative, religious, or literary purposes, and the restrictions imposed on it by the modern Turkish state.[12] In addition, there is not a single Kurdish language to speak of. The existence of two main language groups, Kurmanji and Sorani, has also complicated matters. Kurmanji is spoken primarily in Turkey, northern Iraq, Syria, and a few parts of Iran, while Sorani is dominant in Iran and southern parts of Iraqi Kurdistan. The two languages can be mutually understood at an educated level with some practice. In Turkey itself, the overwhelmingly dominant dialect is Kurmanji in the east and southeast; a second dialect, Dilimi or Zaza, is spoken only by a very small group in central Turkey and is not mutually intelligible with Kurmanji. But the general suppression of written and spoken Kurdish in Turkey for any official or public purposes, including education, mass media, and broadcasting, has created problems in raising the linguistic level of the language to that attained, for example, in Iraq (especially the written language). The language has survived, but not flourished, in isolated villages and hamlets untouched either by the regional economy or by the state. At a time when urbanization increased, such as in and following the 1950s, the language of the villages and hamlets could not cope with the different lifestyles and environment, further depressing its use. If the language were "released" it could quickly adapt to modern conditions, much as modern Turkish has developed a highly rich vocabulary under the tutelage of the Turkish Language Institute.

Not surprisingly, reversing the trend toward cultural irrelevancy has been the goal of many Kurdish nationalist groups and parties as they undertook consciousness-raising activities as important elements of their agenda, including the sponsoring and dissemination of research—often illegally—on Kurdish history, literature, culture, language, and music. When unable to print in Turkey, these groups imported the material from abroad, mainly from Iraq, provoking the state to pass the 1967 law that officially banned the importation of publications and recordings in Kurdish. In 1983, in a further tightening of restrictions on language, the government passed a law declaring Turkish to be the native language of its citizens and banning the use of any other native languages, as well as participation in activities aimed at propagating their use.[13] This law, No. 2932, was revoked by Özal in April 1991, which has provided an opportunity for the reemergence of Kurdish-language publications that, under the ever-watchful eyes of the authorities, have to carefully regulate their content. Cultural organizations intent on teaching Kurdish and Kurdish history and culture, such as the Mesopotamia Cultural Center, have also emerged in recent years.[14] Only recently did the Turkish authorities allow for the registration of a cultural foundation, the Kurdish Foundation for Research and Culture, Kültür ve Arastirma Vakfi. Perhaps of more importance is the fact that it is the first such foundation to legally incorporate the word "Kurd" in its name. By and large, these publications and centers, operating under severe financial constraints in addition to the legal ones, have had an impact, although a limited one, on the resurgence of Kurdish.

If language is an important building block of national identity, is it possible to construct a nationalist movement without a common language? Unlike Iraq, where there is real competition between Sorani and Kurmanji, in Turkey the overwhelmingly dominant Kurmanji dialect has to compete only with Turkish as the primary language of the Kurds.[15] For practical purposes, then, the Kurds of Turkey do have a unified language. The linguistic problem becomes more severe only when speaking of a pan-Kurdish state. Examples from other countries, including Israel and India, demonstrate that language, while a critical ingredient, does not have to be shared by all. The revival of Hebrew, or rather the emergence of modern Hebrew, is purely the product of efforts in this century.

Societal Structure

Two characteristics of Kurdish society, its tribal nature and its religiosity, have played an important role in guiding it through the momentous socio-economic and political changes experienced in this century: from the disappearance of the Ottoman Empire to the formation of the modern Turkish republic under Kemal to, finally, the resurgence of ethno-nationalism among Kurds.

The Kurdish areas were not immune to the forces of change buffeting the area in the aftermath of the collapse of the Ottoman Empire. Serif Mardin has argued that "the provincial population of Anatolia was 'unhinged' by the transformation from a setting in which Islam had occupied a central place to a secular 'laic' society."[16] Although the new republican state officially abolished the *tariqats,* these Sufi orders continued to exist in the Kurdish areas because they provided the inhabitants, especially after the decision to do away with the caliphate, with an identity and a means of dealing with what was quickly becoming an alien ethnic environment. Similarly, the tribal structures played a dual role: While offering an identity to these villagers, who had previously thought of themselves as Muslim citizens of an Islamic state, they also played a mediating role between the economy and the average peasant and, more important, between the individual and the state. Tribal leadership, although based on kinship, is a far more complex institution than one in which loyalty is automatically offered to clan leaders. As Lâle Yalçin-Heckman demonstrated in her research on Hakkari, leadership was not always automatic, as the individual peasant expected his agha to produce results and offer patronage and protection. Hence, it is not surprising that an agha family will support different parties and clandestine nationalist groups simultaneously.[17] This ability to maneuver among competing external forces has, at one level, strengthened the tribal structure in the southeast since the outbreak of the PKK-led rebellion. The PKK itself has had a contradictory impact: It has in places strengthened the feudal structure by aligning itself with the local feudal structure, while, in other areas of the southeast it has come to represent the antithesis of the feudal representative, the agha, by bypassing the latter altogether and appealing to the population directly.

The strengthening of the tribal system comes at a price for the local inhabitants: Its tendency to try to resolve conflicts without recourse to local authorities increases the importance attached to blood feuds. These feuds tend to last for long periods of time before getting resolved and, therefore, result in much bloodshed. In the present-day southeast, the manipulation by both the state and the PKK of tribal differences not only accentuates the conflict but also increases the degree of bloodletting between rival Kurdish groups. We will return to this subject later on.

It is still too early to assess the long-term impact on tribal structures of the depopulation of the southeast. When villages are razed and the population is forced to move out, the inhabitants tend to leave en masse and therefore can carry their clan leaders with them; unfortunately, these aghas are woefully unprepared for the life that awaits them in the towns and cities. Already processes were at work undermining the loyalty of the peasants to their tribal leaders. Van Bruinessen identifies two such influences: first, the tendency of economic relations to become too exploitative, and, second, the ideological support system for tribal and religious leaders being continuously undermined by the process of education and the mass media.[18] The rise of the left-wing Kurdish nationalist movements in Ankara and Istanbul among students and workers is one such manifestation of this development.

In sum, two processes are at work simultaneously: While tribal structures are being dismantled by the movement of Kurdish populations, those Kurdish remaining are increasingly caught in a conflict that strengthens the hold of the clans on their daily lives. Still another observation is worth noting here. The controversial Chambers of Commerce and Industry report found that the areas with the strongest tribal and feudal links experienced the most significant rates of PKK recruitment.[19] Whether this was simply a reflection of the PKK's ability to manipulate these divisions or also of the fact that it represents a way out for youth increasingly disenchanted with the restrictions imposed by traditional authority remains to be seen. The weakening of the tribal structure has not escaped the notice of political authorities: In a report submitted to his party leader, Tansu Çiller, a minister of state, Salim Ensarioglu, defended the tribal system and lamented its weakening, which "allowed illegal organizations to fill in the vacuum."[20]

Religious Divisions among the Kurds: The Alevi Factor

The Kurdish identity question is further complicated by a profound religious split across the population, between Sunnis and Alevis. In fact, the Alevi issue represents one of the more obscure and least understood of important political and social phenomena in Turkey today. A major cultural and political struggle is under way for the souls of the Alevis of Turkey. Increasingly disenchanted with the status quo, Alevis have increasingly taken to the streets to protest and have sought alternative venues for representation, including the formation of their own parties. This is a process that will be a long time in unfolding, and one with potentially dramatic consequences for Turkey.

Figures about the Alevi population in Turkey are notoriously vague, but they range from approximately 10 percent to 30–40 percent of the entire population.[21] Even the Alevi faith is variously interpreted by different scholars. One interpretation is to see it as fundamentally a brand of Shi'-ism, which insists on religious leadership only through blood ties descending from the Prophet Mohammed. An alternative version sees the Alevis as descended from a much more ancient pre-Islamic tradition of fire-worship stemming from Iran, a tradition linked to Zoroastrian and Manichean beliefs.[22] Indeed, most Kurds in the twelfth century had largely resisted Islamization and were still adherents of older religions in the region, including Christianity, Judaism, and, most particularly, the "Cult of the Angels," derived in part from ancient Iranian religions including Zoroastrianism and its successors and offshoots. The "Cult of the Angels" describes a syncretistic faith that has broadly absorbed and integrated many other faiths around it, including strong elements of Shi'ism in the medieval period.[23]

The theological origins may be obscure, but the reality of the social distribution has unleashed much violence in Central Asia and Turkey for over a thousand years, and there are prospects for more of the same in the future. What is at stake is the struggle to redefine, in political and social terms, just what Alevism is today and what the considerable Alevi demographic strength will mean for political alignments. The process is hardly just an intellectual one, since approximately 10–30 percent (or even more) of Turkey's Alevis are Kurds; and nearly 30 percent of Turkey's Kurds are Alevi.[24] Another factor that has helped make the Alevi issue politically potent is the migration to the cities and the creation of shantytowns. Those

Alevis who tended to live in isolated localities became aware via urbanization not only of their minority status in religious terms but also of their lower economic status. In March 1995, riots in Istanbul's predominantly Alevi neighborhood of Gaziosmanpasa ended with at least seventeen people being killed by riot police. Understated at the time of the riots was the fact that most of these Alevis were Kurdish migrants from Tunceli.

Alevis perceive themselves as having suffered throughout history at the hands of their Sunni oppressors. Ottoman history is replete with chronicles of Alevi uprisings against the state, which in turn suspected them of loyalty to rival Iran. The depth of Sunni resentment against the Alevis is seen in the Sunni refusal even to acknowledge the Alevis as Muslims.[25] In Turkey's Republican period, the Alevis readily embraced the Atatürk revolution because its strong promise of secularism in principle would no longer leave Alevis as second-class citizens—as they had been in the officially orthodox Sunni Ottoman Empire. The Alevi-Sunni conflict produced widespread violence between 1975 and 1980, when the military took power. These bloody clashes were often publicly presented as right-left clashes, but more often than not they had deeper Sunni-Alevi characteristics. Some antileftist Sunni Kurds are even willing to vote for extreme Turkish nationalist Alparslan Türkes because of his antileftist platform.

Alevis have thus been staunch advocates of secularism in the Turkish Republic, out of concern for the traditionally repressive character of the official Sunni state, placing them on the left of the political spectrum. Alevis have been important elements of all major Turkish leftist parties including the Turkish Labor party, which was banned in 1971, and many others including the communists. In Tunceli, TIKKO (Turkish Workers' Peasant Communist Army), another local insurgent group, is primarily Alevi in origin and operates independently of the PKK. Today Alevis are dismayed at what they see as the betrayal of Kemalist secularism by the state-tolerated growth of Islamist movements and the role of Islam, now accepted in most mainstream political parties. Some Turkish Alevis believe it is they themselves who represent the heart and soul of traditional Turkish culture: In their view, it was only the Alevis who maintained the purity of language and the culture of the Turkish tribal period during the sweeping Arabization and Persianization of mainstream Turkish life during the Ottoman period. In a sense, they are thus staking a claim to being culturally "more Turkish" in a historical sense than their Sunni Turkish fellow citizens, who continue to treat them as second class.

To some Kurds, their religious community—either Alevi or Sunni—is more important than even ties to a common Kurdish ethnicity, especially where Sunni and Alevi Kurds live in towns with mixed Turkish-Kurdish population, such as Malatya, Erzincan, Elazig, and Maras. Here, Alevi-Sunni friction can be more important than Kurdish-Turkish friction, cutting right across ethnic lines. Historically, the Sunni and multiethnic character of the Ottoman Empire readily provided the Sunni Kurds a privileged place in society. Sunni Kurds assumed all the bigotry that their other Sunni compatriots held against the Alevis. To this day, there is less likely to be a family incident if a Sunni Kurd seeks to marry a Sunni Turk than for the same person to marry an Alevi Kurd. The political ramifications of the Sunni-Alevi divide among Kurds can be seen in the Shaykh Said rebellion of 1925, which was led by Zaza-speaking Sunni Kurds. Feeling betrayed by the new republic, which did away with the Islamic symbols of unity such as the caliphate, these Sunni Kurds were betrayed again by their Alevi brethren in Dersim (Tunceli) who cooperated with the state. In 1937–38 the favor was returned: In the Dersim revolt, which featured Alevi Kurdish rebels in what was one of the more bloody rebellions, the Sunni Kurds did not come to the rescue of their Alevi brethren.[26]

Many Turkish Alevis show some sympathy to Kurdish Alevis—in a way that Sunni Turks could never show to Sunni Kurds. Because many Alevis have increasingly come to believe that theirs is a fight for identity and recognition, they have come to identify with the plight of the Kurds,[27] and they think that at some level they deserve to have their democratic and national rights respected. However, these same Turkish Alevis, who have no territorial claim, are very opposed to any change in Turkey's borders. Still, Alevis are uneasy about the fact that most Sunni Kurds belong to the Shafa'i sect, which is viewed as one of the most conservative and regressive of the Sunni sects.[28] The Alevi factor thus casts considerable complications into the Kurdish question.

On the other hand, ethnic solidarity among Kurds has now begun to outweigh the religious tie nearly everywhere, but the intensity of these ties to some degree depends on the level of education, sophistication, and the degree of homogeneity in the communities in which they live. In Alevi Kurdish strongholds such as Tunceli—one of the most volatile and rebellious of all the Kurdish areas—opposition to Turks is far deeper than to Sunni Kurds. Heightened Alevi-Sunni rivalry has worked well for the PKK as demonstrated most recently in Sivas, where the PKK, by targeting Sunni villages, managed to unleash a counterreaction by state forces against Alevi villages, some of which are Kurdish. In the ensuing conflict, the state evacuated some sixty-three Alevi villages,[29] unleashing a storm of protest among the Alevi community, including their Germany-based mass organizations.

In fact, the PKK has had to bow to reality and adjust its policies and ideologies to such facts: It has now dropped its former hostility to Islam and has been actively fostering Islamic tendencies within the PKK. It has supported the building of mosques in Europe and the creation of a pro-PKK Islamist Kurdish movement, the Islamic Party of Kurdistan (PIK). The PKK leadership, while not Alevi in character, has increasingly had to accommodate itself to the Alevi community in recent years in order to attract this extremely important segment of the Kurdish community. The PKK has also fostered the creation of a confederation of thirty organizations called Kürt Alevi Birligi (Kurdish Alevi Union, KAB), while also catering to orthodox Sunni dislike of Sufi sects.[30] One of the more visible leaders of the KAB, Ali Haydar Celasun, is not only a member of the KPE but is also an avowed follower of Öcalan.

The full implications of the Alevi-Sunni divisions within Turkish and Kurdish communities have yet to unfold. Alevi Kurds have played a prominent role in the recent evolution of the Kurdish nationalist movement: Among some of the best known are Kemal Burkay and Ibrahim Aksoy. What is missing from the discussion above is the role of political parties in accentuating these divisions. Every political party has tried to manipulate this complex picture for its own narrow electoral gains. The Republican People's party (CHP) has over the years been the main repository of Alevi votes. Even before the September 12, 1980, coup, and especially since then, provinces with large Alevi minorities—Turkish and Kurdish—have witnessed a great deal of unrest. In part this is due to the increased urbanization of Alevis; once tending to live in secluded villages, they have now moved into the regional provincial capitals, thereby falling prey to the ideological hostility of organizations close to either the Welfare or Nationalist Action parties. These groups in targeting the Alevis and Kurds are motivated either by simple religious hatred or by political considerations, such as their wish to dislodge the Republicans. The province of Sivas has been particularly affected by such intercommunal tension.[31] Yet the Islamists, as represented by the Welfare party, today advocate a much less confrontational policy on the Kurdish question. The role of parties will be discussed in a later section.

Political Divisions among the Kurds

The de facto dominance of the PKK in the political field today should not conceal the fact of splits among the Kurds and varying degrees of opposition to the PKK among them. There is hardly a Kurd in Turkey who is not well aware of, and probably shares, the special grievances Kurds have—underdevelopment and neglect of the southeast, harsh security measures employed there, and the lack of cultural rights. Yet not all Kurds, even nationalist ones, have chosen to pursue the nationalist cause as their first or exclusive goal, either via the PKK or membership in radical parties. Many Kurds, even including nationalists, have joined mainstream Turkish parties and have become members of Parliament. What are some of these differences among the Kurdish population in Turkey as it affects the ethnic or nationalist struggle?

Viewed from a Turkish-Kurdish perspective, the options available to them in recent years have ranged from violence to political activity to assimilation. In this section we look at these options in a more systematic way. The PKK represents one facet of the violence option; the other is the opposition to violence engaged in by Kurds who oppose the PKK. Political activities can in turn be separated into three divisions: mainstream politics, legal and illegal Kurdish political parties, and Islamic politics.

Violence and Counterviolence

Since the PKK has been discussed in great detail in earlier sections of this work, here we take up only the question of counterviolence. The most important violent counterreaction to the PKK among Kurds has been the institutionalization of the village guard *(köy koruculari)* system. These are Kurds in the pay of the state who have been co-opted by it to provide security for selected villages and to act as a front line of defense against PKK incursions. The village guard system is a direct outgrowth of the societal structure in the region. Aghas, who not only owned large tracts of land but also commanded the loyalties of the peasants residing in their "villages," were willing participants in the village guard system. To them the PKK represented a genuine threat to their power and influence, especially if they have also enjoyed the patronage of the state. Indeed, given the PKK's radical leftist origins, it was not surprising that it vehemently opposed the tribal system on ideological grounds.

Recruitment of village guards is not based solely on these primordial ties but also can contain a considerable element of coercion: The state will force villages and villagers to choose sides. Violence in the village often springs from class or personality differences within the village, and the "struggle against the PKK" has been used by both sides in part as a means of settling old scores.[32] The village guard system also has an important economic motive; in the bleakness of the southeast, state salaries often represent the only source of income for many of these poorly educated and trained guards themselves. In addition, many of the aghas pocket as much as half of the salaries their guards receive. With the money they earn and the arms they carry, the guards exercise a degree of power in their areas. It is not surprising, therefore, that the guards have acquired a vested interest in conflict with the PKK; there are numerous anecdotal accounts of manufactured incidents designed to keep their profile high.

Nor should it be assumed that all tribal elements are more "traditional" and hence pro-state. Indeed, there are tribal and clan groupings who for a variety of historical, regional, and even accidental factors are either pro-state or pro-PKK. The competitive and often conflictual nature of intertribal relationships and the long-standing feuds between them that have nothing to do with the state or the PKK explain their preferences.[33] The PKK itself was forced by practical considerations to abandon its anti-agha attitude and make alliances with "patriotic" ones against collaborators; in the process, by going after the village guards and their families, the PKK has actually transformed this aspect of their "struggle" into an extension of tribal warfare.[34] It has been particularly difficult for those residents of villages who have refused to join either the PKK or the state-sponsored village guard systems. Often, they have had no choice but to leave their villages for the towns, where they are not welcome.

The village guard system poses a serious long-term danger: State policies to divide the Kurds politically on the PKK issue are sowing the seeds of long-term inter-Kurdish rivalries and hatreds, with many bitter political scores to be settled. Even if this conflict is resolved peacefully, the wounds created today will fester for long periods of time.

Another violent reaction against the PKK emerged among Kurdish right-wing religious nationalists who are strongly opposed to the leftist and Marxist origins of the PKK. Most notable among them is the Hizbollah, operating in key cities (Nusaybin, Batman, Diyarbakir, Van) in the southeast, which is responsible for a large number of assassinations of PKK members and sympathizers; they have killed dozens of people since 1991, especially intellectuals and journalists. The name Hizbollah suggests the basically Islamist origin of the organization, probably reflecting its formation from a nucleus of Islamist police and security officials purged from government in 1991. Hizbollah itself split into two groups, those with a purely Islamist orientation opposed on principle to political ethnicity within Islam, and those who combined Islam and nationalism in seeking to found an independent Islamist Kurdish state.[35] The group is sympathetic with Sunni Islam and opposed to Kurds who are not Sunni but Alevi in their religious beliefs. The Hizbollah soon began to emulate the tactics of the PKK and to extract "contributions" from businessmen and truck traffic.[36]

The state has often been held directly responsible for setting up or utilizing these "hit squads"—sometimes called "Hizbollah-contras"—for extrajudicial handling of pro-PKK activism; there is no evidence available one way or another to prove or disprove this, and the general atmosphere of lawlessness today in the southeast facilitates all kinds of terror and vigilantism, including irregular activities by the state. One can only say that the Hizbollah represents a group of Kurds, probably small, with their own religious rightist nationalist Kurdish agenda. Given the nature of the conflict, it is inconceivable that the Turkish state would not at least privately welcome Hizbollah activities, which have been so damaging to the PKK cause; indeed, until recently there have been almost no arrests or prosecutions stemming from the actions of the Hizbollah, further suggesting state disregard of, if not complicity in, the work of the hit squads. The situation may have changed with the reported accommodation reached by the PKK with the Hizbollah to cease assassination operations in 1993.[37] Despite the fact that Hizbollah in the past seemed to be pursuing the same agenda as the state, since 1995 confrontations between Hizbollah and security forces have begun, indicating that the state may have lost its control over the group. Nevertheless, the conflict between right- and left-wing Kurds is far from over. A spread of Hizbollah violence or Kurdish civil war to other parts of Turkey could be quite destabilizing.

Mainstream Politics

Not all Kurds have chosen to pursue their ethnic grievances through radical movements and parties. In the absence of any legal Kurdish parties in Turkey, in the past Kurds have joined existing Turkish parties on the right or left. This section discusses their motivations for joining such parties. The actual views of these parties is discussed in the next section.

Despite the difficulties Kurds have had in expressing nationalist views, they have had a remarkable success in getting themselves elected or represented in mainstream Turkish parties. Over the years, it has been estimated that as many as one-third of the members of any parliament may have been of Kurdish origin. Why have so many sought to become parliamentarians? Two general explanations can be advanced.

The first has to do with the conditions in the southeast: In economically deprived regions, politics offers individual Kurds a means of advancement. In a centralized state such as Turkey, Ankara is the locus of all power and of all decision-making, whether vital or trivial. Hence having a representative in Ankara is of utmost importance. With mainstream parties being the only game in town, access to power could be achieved only through them. Kurdish politicians have not run just for parliamentary seats but also at the local level for positions of municipal councilor or mayor. Some of the prominent tribal families in the east and southeast are expected to run for elected office; this not only validates their preeminent position in their communities but also helps them to perform the crucial intermediary function they have been accustomed to doing for so long. As a result, some of these families in every election will field two or more candidates, often from different parties, in order to spread the risk. Prominent families will also divide the elected offices among them: While one becomes a parliamentarian, another gets elected mayor of the town, and a third gets appointed—presumably with the help of the parliamentarian—to run one of the major state-owned installations, such as the district offices of the waterworks or the railroad. Tribal families and aghas have been eagerly sought by all political parties because they can deliver large blocks of votes at election time. This also explains why members of one family will appear on the ballots of more than one party. Irrespective of their position on the Kurdish question, these parliamentarians will seek to bring projects home, to help constituents with their problems, to get them jobs, and so forth.

Second, there are a myriad of individual motivations that explain involvement in politics: For some individual office holders, constituency services and easing the pain of their citizens back home are genuine ways of addressing the problems created by the Kurdish question. Clearly, for others, elected office represents a conduit to a share in the spoils generated by a political system in which patron-client relationships are highly prized. A number of Kurds, especially nationalist ones, have sought to join parties and get elected to protect themselves. They either hope that the party will provide them and their families with some protection from the security officials who may be investigating them, or, if they succeed in getting elected to parliament, that parliamentary immunity will protect them from being charged.[38] For Kurds who have traditionally maintained ties with the state and benefitted from state largesse, continued association with mainstream parties offers them protection from the PKK, which they fear.[39] Similarly, the same motivations also lie at the heart of the frequent changes in party affiliation.

Some of the MPs of Kurdish origin may elect not to be concerned with Kurdish issues, or to closely align themselves with the central government. Such is the case for the Bucak family or the Cevheris. While for some belonging to the larger Turkish melting pot is perfectly acceptable, for other Kurdish politicians the Kurdish agenda may not always have been the first public goal—even if the Kurdish cause may have been uppermost in their minds. To most Kurdish parliamentarians, it has simply been imprudent, given existing conditions in Turkey, to openly champion the Kurdish cause—and potentially costly on a personal basis as well.[40] As regionally elected representatives from Kurdish areas, Kurdish representatives, like all politicians, have sought to encourage legislation that economically benefits their regions and their constituents—without any mention of the Kurdish cause per se. Instead, they seek to get their non-Kurdish colleagues to bring up these issues. In general, despite the sometimes acrimonious nature of Turkish politics, Kurdish MPs from the region tend to have excellent relations with other members and tend to cooperate among themselves irrespective of party affiliations. This also explains why they have been viewed with suspicion by other parliamentarians and other institutional bodies.[41] Still, as Hamit Bozarslan points out, "Kurdish actors who were traditionally well integrated into the system could not remain indifferent" to the radicalization of Kurdish politics and were "forced to accept the minimum nationalist demands—the end to the state of emergency, to stop the destruction of the Kurdish countryside, to respect human rights and to recognize cultural rights."[42]

Which of the mainstream parties to join is a decision that is very much influenced by local conditions, such as historical alliances between individual parties and certain families, internal religious differences and the influence of Sufi religious orders, recruitment drives by parties, and the ability of the parties to deliver benefits or even to ensure success in the elections. Many have been uncomfortable with the violence (and attendant risks of association) that has marked PKK policies for so long, and the political radicalism of Kurdish parties as well. By and large, political ideology has not played much of a role in recent years, as it is not uncommon to see members of parliament switching parties when circumstances make it convenient to do so. Some of the more radical Kurds were at some point members of left-of-center and even conservative parties. While Ahmet Türk (a Kurdish MP) could boast membership in both the Justice party (the precursor of the present True Path party) and SHP (the Republican People's party's precursor in the 1990s) before becoming one of the leaders of DEP, Abdülmelik Firat, the grandson of Shaykh Said, got elected to parliament from Erzurum on the True Path ticket. He subsequently resigned from the party and became an independent deputy.[43]

The Republican People's party (CHP), which until recently was the sole center-left party, has long been detested by Kurds as Atatürk's creation, and also because of its role during the single-party era, when the state promulgated the key policies that denied the existence of Kurds as a separate ethnic group. On the other hand, as a left-of-center party, the CHP has also been more active in recent decades on the human rights front and more liberal in viewing Kurdish grievances and opposing state-conducted violence. In its previous incarnation, as the Social Democratic People's party (SHP), the party at first welcomed many members from the southeast, many of whom were to eventually form the Kurdish-based parties. But SHP/CHP ultimately suffered from its decision to join, as the minor partner, the government coalition with the True Path party. Paradoxically, as the party in charge of the human rights portfolio in the 1991–1995 coalition government, it alienated both Turkish and Kurdish nationalists. By defending Kurdish human rights it incurred the wrath of the security forces and all those who viewed the Kurds as a threat to Turkish unity. By contrast, as far as the Kurds were concerned, the party became associated with Prime Minister Çiller's uncompromising hard-line policies in the southeast. Suffice it to say that despite harboring some of the more liberal members of the parliament on the Kurdish issue, the party succeeded in alienating the bulk of the Kurdish population in the southeast. This became evident in the election debacle of 1995. In recent years, the center-left has been divided between the liberal, but inept, CHP and a nationalist wing led by Bülent Ecevit and his Democratic Left party (DSP), which few Kurds support.

In the case of the center-right political parties, the True Path party (DYP), despite its more uncompromising stand on the Kurdish issue, has regularly managed to elect a number of Kurdish representatives to Parliament. In addition to the deals constructed between party leaders and local aghas,[44] the DYP is the direct heir of the Democrat party, which in 1950 unseated the long-time oppressors of the Kurds, the RPP. Hence, some of the alliances constructed between certain tribal leaders and these parties have withstood the test of time. Other factors have also helped these center-right parties: The tendency of CHP to capture the bulk of the Alevi votes has made the conservative Sunni Kurds uncomfortable with the Left.

The other center-right party, the Motherland party (ANAP), created by Turgut Özal following the 1980 coup, has attracted and recruited its share of Kurdish politicians. Although responsible for many of the harsher measures initiated in the southeast, Özal eventually earned the admiration of Kurds for his willingness to discuss the issue in public and seek alternative solutions to the military campaign. What is not obvious is whether Özal had long coattails, especially after his death in 1993. Kurds vote or join ANAP for many of the same reasons they join any political parties. As a result, in many of the parties Kurdish nationalists coexist with their Turkish counterparts and uncommitted Kurds.

In the final analysis, mainstream parties' use of Kurdish representatives as "bulk vote generators" has not served Turkish democracy well. It has transformed part of the traditional leadership into a conservative societal force that seeks to prevent the local social order from being disrupted; at the same time, it has failed to articulate the critical needs of the local population beyond the accepted terms of the state-sponsored discourse. These traditional leaders were willing to limit their requests to safe needs, such as more schools or more services, only partially fulfilling real political and social needs. "Local traditional voters who gained new importance by delivering votes to the governments in the multi-party period, became supporters of the regime. In this sense, wider representation has come to mean a narrower representation for the Kurdish population."[45]

The Islamists

The Welfare party (Refah Partisi, RP) is treated here separately, although it aspires to be and in some senses is a mainstream political party. The reason for the differentiation is occasioned not by Welfare's discourse but rather by the way Kurds relate to this party. Of course, Welfare's discourse is one of the reasons that it has done well among Kurds.

There are two different Kurdish approaches to Welfare. One results from the relationship Kurds traditionally have had with Islam. The other is due to Kurdish perceptions that Welfare is an antiestablishment party intent on, if not destabilizing the Turkish political scene, then testing the limits of Turkish democracy and expanding them further.

The relationship between Kurds and Islam has already been discussed. In the years since the inception of the republic, Islam provided an alternative identity for Kurds, if not one approved of by the state. It also represented the social glue that had kept Kurds and Turks together in the Ottoman Empire. Not surprisingly, in describing the conditions in Hakkari, Yalçin-Heckman finds that "Islam is intimately linked with local culture. Islamic practices and beliefs, and the teachings of Islam, form a fundamental, if not the most important, part of the local cultural discourse."[46] Therefore, Welfare's message of Islamic solidarity, which deliberately underplays ethnic differences, has had much appeal to Kurds, though not to all. Clearly, from the Kurdish standpoint, it is the political party with the least hostile attitude toward them, the fewest ideological problems with the concept of Kurdishness, and the least historical baggage. Welfare has also succeeded in recruiting bona fide Kurdish nationalists who, ironically, do not share the Islamic message—at least to the same extent—that emanates from the party's hierarchy. Some have joined Welfare for many of the same reasons discussed above in relation to mainstream parties—that is, to get elected into parliament or the mayoralty, access to Ankara, and so on. For some of these MPs, the Islamic identity that Welfare has used as a means to paper over the Turkish-Kurdish divisions is secondary to their Kurdish identity. These Kurdish nationalists are different from those HADEP has courted; they are politically, economically, and socially more conservative and tend to view HADEP itself as being too close to the PKK. Many do not share the PKK's goals or methods, especially the killing of fellow Kurds, and are also alienated by the radical leftist discourse that Kurdish parties of the likes of DEP and

HADEP have used.[47] For them, the Kurdish question is fundamentally about identity and the recognition of this identity by the Turkish state and society. Their antipathy for the Turkish state and its policies is no less than that of other Kurdish nationalists, but it is reinforced by the treatment that religion has received at the hands of Kemalist "secularists."

Some of the Kurdish MPs of Welfare also believe that the party, while not necessarily the best vehicle for a resolution of the conflict, appears to have the best chance to democratize the system. Precisely because it is an antisystem party and rejected by the establishment, especially the military, its success in the polls and assumption of power, even in coalition, will force the Turkish political system to open up and include new groups. This would represent a first step in making the system more inclusive of the Kurds.

In the recent past, as for example in the 1994 municipal elections, Kurds voted for Welfare en masse because it represented a protest vote: In the absence of any Kurdish parties, this was the party that the establishment dislikes and fears—and therefore it deserved their vote. However, Welfare's status as a recipient of protest votes may change now because of the combination of the two factors stated above: Islam and the democratic opening produced by the 1995 elections, when Welfare increased its size from 38 to 158 members of parliament. With 34 Kurdish MPs, the party has a chance of becoming a serious contender for Kurdish votes. In other words, with the mainstream parties failing the Kurds, Welfare or Kurdish parties remain the only significant avenues for legal Kurdish political activity. But Welfare disappointed its own Kurdish activists during its time in office. To the consternation of Kurdish activists, it has adopted much of the state's discourse on the insurgency. This was primarily out of concern not to further antagonize the military establishment, which viewed the party with suspicion and disdain. The party's general attitudes toward the Kurds will be explored in a subsequent chapter.

Independents

The Kurdish political scene is not restricted solely to the political parties already discussed—mainstream, Kurdish, or Islamist. There are also cultural organizations and professional organizations of lawyers and others who participate daily in articulating different visions of the Kurdish question.

Among the more important independent political forces is a former minister of public works, Serafettin Elçi. Representing a liberal economic viewpoint, Elçi, like many other Kurdish politicians, has flirted with or joined different parties.[48] While rejecting the violent methods employed by the PKK, he has since 1994 been trying to form a political party of his own, called the Kurdish Democratic Platform. Its demands include the recognition of the Kurdish identity and calls for the reorganization of the state, but within the territorial integrity of Turkey. He has not had much success in the past, as other Kurdish groups view him as being too moderate. His new party, the Democratic Mass party (DKP), while differentiating itself from the likes of HADEP and DEP, which Elçi calls Marxist in tradition, considers suggestions such as a possible federal arrangement as potential solutions to the conflict.[49] Elçi epitomizes the difficulty independent Kurdish groups have in negotiating the small political space left to them by the PKK and the state: While in favor of the PKK's abandoning the armed struggle, he sees no reason why that organization should give up its arms unconditionally.[50] Still, despite its anti-PKK position, in June of 1997 the prosecutor for the Supreme Court initiated a court case to have the DKP banned.[51]

Kemal Burkay, who formed his Kurdistan Socialist party (PSK) in 1974, has lived in exile in Sweden. In 1978, Mehdi Zana, considered a close associate of Burkay's, won the election for mayor in Diyarbakir, the most important Kurdish city in Turkey. In fact, the PSK thinks it was on the verge of a major breakthrough in the southeast in terms of organization and influence until the 1980 coup and pressure from the PKK eventually succeeded in dismantling the PSK's organization. Known for his aversion to violence, Burkay did not make his peace with Öcalan until the latter extended his 1993 cease-fire offer, and then the two signed a protocol on cooperation—an agreement largely devoid of content. While his party is organized abroad, one of his confidants in Turkey, Ibrahim Aksoy, formed the Democracy and Change party. The PSK was one of the main casualties in the rise of the PKK. The PSK, though banned in Turkey and unlike the Democracy and Change party, is committed to a federal solution within Turkey. The latter, despite its more moderate stance, was sued by the state for advocating the division of Turkey. Ironically, the party's appeal in Turkey had remained small, and Aksoy, who has changed parties many times and served as leader of HEP, ended up being imprisoned.

Assimilation

In stark contrast to the nationalists, there are those Kurds who are considered as having "assimilated." What constitutes assimilation is a difficult question to answer in the Turkish context: Some Kurds are turkified (Türklesmis)—in other words, they may have lost all trace of their ethnicity generations ago.[52] They may also be considered—not always accurately—"assimilated," for quite disparate reasons:

- They may have elected to become Turkish, either as a result of the socialization process in schools and elsewhere, or, even if aware of their Kurdish origins, they may prefer to consider themselves Turkish as a result of a deliberate choice to belong to the larger, more powerful, and more prestigious Turkish mainstream.
- They may be deliberately concealing their Kurdishness and pretending to be Turkish.
- They may think that the politics of ethnicity is irrelevant or may be by and large apolitical.
- They may live in western and central Turkey and live and work in a purely Turkish environment, rendering Kurdish identity irrelevant if not forgotten.
- They may have lost any working knowledge of the Kurdish language.
- They may be the offspring of mixed marriages.
- It may be professionally more prudent for them not to state their Kurdish origins.
- To conceal any Kurdish origin may have certain opportunistic benefits, at the least to avoid possible problems, especially at a time of confrontation and rising Turkish national chauvinism in some circles.
- A handful may genuinely feel that Turkish culture is more advanced, may see the Turkish language as a greater vehicle for access to the world in general: to literature and the means of being part of an intellectual, business, and power establishment that is more attractive than a (deliberately) underdeveloped Kurdish culture.

It is impossible to state how many Kurds fall into these categories. For assimilated Kurds, the doors of opportunity have been wide open. In fact, until recently there have been few if any barriers to their advancement in the state bureaucracy, in politics, and in business. Former chiefs of staff, big city majors, and numerous parliamentarians have been of Kurdish stock.

There are a few prominent Kurds, such as the former mayor of Istanbul, Bedrettin Dalan, who simply say that Kurdish culture is ultimately a poor man's version of Turkish culture, that "both go back to the same roots." However anthropologically dubious this statement is, Dalan has chosen to drop his Kurdish heritage entirely as a dead-end street.[53] Kurds who assume such an openly anti-Kurdish pro-Turkish position are in a minority. Another prominent Kurd, the foreign minister of Turkey in 1995 and one-time leader of the CHP, Hikmet Çetin, does not at all deny his Kurdish heritage and has a good command of Kurdish. Çetin, however, sees himself as culturally a Turk within a Turkish establishment, from which a solution to the Kurdish question will come through working within the system; at this stage, he is unwilling to seek any special rights for Kurds, any more than for any other group in Turkey.[54] This is a slightly more widespread phenomenon among establishment Kurds, but it may likely be subject to evolution and change.

But in seeking a solution to the Kurdish problem, the difficulty is not with those who have no recollection of their past Kurdishness or who have deliberately elected to give up their original ethnicity. These are not the ones who have become politicized or who can potentially mobilize against the state. These are not among the nationalist elite. The key question is whether the strong process of growth of Kurdish national consciousness over the past decade has begun to reverse the slow process of assimilation. Is the conflict in the southeast, by giving rise to anger and large population movements, directly stimulating the rise of Kurdish self-awareness? The answer to this question has powerful policy consequences for the government of Turkey. Yet it is impossible to draw linear results from complex social processes. The propositions that assimilation has increased or has been reversed are not mutually exclusive. Given the large size of the Kurdish population in Turkey, both of these processes may be occurring simultaneously as the conflict spreads and affects the middle ground of the Kurdish community, which has hitherto sat on the sidelines.

The motivations behind the attitudes of "assimilated" Kurds thus vary considerably. President Özal believed in the proposition that, as Kurds move west, they tend to assimilate. To some extent, if the 1995 election results for HADEP were to be repeated, the fact that the party was unable to muster much support in Istanbul and Izmir would certainly support Özal's contention. On the other hand, the military was clearly unhappy at this prospect and did not have confidence in the idea that assimilation would increase with the outflow of Kurds from the southeast: quite the contrary, according to the former chief of staff, Dogan Güres. He claimed to have disagreed with Özal's wish to see more westward migration, fearing that the process of migration would "damage the psychology" of the migrant.[55]

Another key question is, might the views of assimilated Kurds change under changed circumstances in the future? If penalties no longer attach to proclaiming oneself a Kurd, or if the Kurds should gain widespread political representation in political parties, might not many of those "assimilated" decide to revert back to their original Kurdish identity? Indeed, under less strained circumstances, declaration of a clear-cut Kurdish identity within the framework of the Turkish state is not necessarily an unworkable formula in the future. Those who have been fearful of acknowledging their Kurdish identity in the past may feel less concern about doing so in the future. Exposed to reinvigorated Kurdish political and cultural activities, some "quiet" Kurds will inevitably feel a long-repressed sense of pride awakening within themselves and start taking a more active role in official Kurdish life. This phenomenon of a reactivated sense of identity and nationalism is well known throughout the developing world, and most recently is strongly asserting itself among the Turkic peoples (and others) in the former Soviet Union. There is every reason to expect that rising Kurdish national sentiments in Turkey will heighten the willingness of people to consider themselves Kurds and to take pride in that fact, especially as the penalties for doing so diminish. Few people anywhere in the world are comfortable in denying their own roots and identity.

More negatively, if the situation between Kurds and Turks should sharply deteriorate in the years ahead, perhaps nearly all Kurds will be forced to take sides in an uglier confrontation in a way that they had always hoped in the past not to have to do. History offers many such cases of evolving senses of identity in which conflict, for better or for worse, polarizes identity, denying individuals the right to remain neutral or disengaged. Chaim Kaufmann argues that "even those who put little value on their ethnic identity are pressed towards ethnic mobilization," primarily because of the behavior of extremists on either side of the conflict.[56] In short, identity can be a shifting characteristic—but under stress the search for identity is usually more a one-way street in the direction of one's most basic identity. Brutal repression can cause people to conceal their identities and even publicly proclaim other ones, but the phenomenon is not likely to last under peaceful conditions.

Legal Kurdish Political Parties

At the moment, the only legal Kurdish political party—although its leaders would cautiously argue that it is not solely a Kurdish party—is HADEP, the socialist-oriented People's Democracy party (Halkin Demokrasi Partisi). It is the direct descendant of HEP (the People's Labor party) and later DEP (the Democracy party). Its status today is in limbo in the aftermath of a tumultuous party congress in June of 1996 in which the Turkish flag was lowered and replaced with a banner depicting a likeness of Öcalan. Subsequently, the entire leadership of the party was arrested, charged with sedition, and jailed. As a result, the party runs the risk of being closed down.

HEP, formed in June of 1990, is the first legal and explicitly Kurdish party ever to exist and have a parliamentary representation in modern-day Turkey. It was an unprecedented event and a harbinger of a trend not readily reversible. At the outset, the party went through the motions of appearing to be a Turkish party; its first president was actually a Turk, Fehmi Isiklar, and its general secretary a Kurd, Ibrahim Aksoy. Yet given the fact that the initial impetus to form it originated with SHP's expulsion of seven Kurdish MPs who had attended a conference on the Kurds in Paris and its overwhelmingly Kurdish composition, there was little doubt as to what HEP's main purpose was. HEP made a remarkable entry into Turkish politics when it concluded an electoral pact with SHP, the center-left Social Democratic People's party,[57] in the 1991 parliamentary election. The pact allowed HEP to field candidates in the southeast and east and to overcome the prohibition on its participating in the elections because of a technicality in the election law.[58] It won twenty-two seats and caused a furor when its deputies wore the banned Kurdish colors to the swearing-in ceremony, some of them even using Kurdish for the oath of office—a highly provocative act.[59] Not surprisingly, these and other events undermined HEP's relations with SHP and caused the undoing of the pact. Soon thereafter, HEP was banned because of its alleged links to the PKK and activities endangering the state; it was ultimately replaced by DEP, the Democracy party.[60]

The formation of DEP coincided with the 1993 PKK ceasefire announcement. The ceasefire, which had the backing of then-president Özal, had created a favorable atmosphere all around Turkey until it was dispelled by the death of Özal and the subsequent killing of thirty-three Turkish soldiers. In this expectant atmosphere, DEP members perceived themselves not simply as a political party but moreover as party to future negotiations on the resolution of the Kurdish conflict.[61] In that vein, many of the intra-Kurdish divisions that had plagued their previous attempts had been pushed aside. DEP also represented an unambiguous choice: It was a Kurdish party determined to advance the Kurdish agenda. The party initiated a "Campaign for Peace" that essentially articulated the need for the state to recognize the "Kurdish identity," for negotiations with elected members of the population, for freedom to publish, educate, and broadcast in Kurdish, for abolition of the emergency rule in the southeast, for removal of the special security forces and village guards, and for introduction of economic measures and judicial reforms. DEP's creation had coincided with a hardening of the position of the government, especially after the ascendancy of Süleyman Demirel to the presidency and his replacement at the prime ministry by a novice politician, Tansu Çiller. With the increasing level of tension, DEP could not go much further with its agenda and found itself on the defensive: Soon after its formation, one of its MPs, Mehmet Sincar, was murdered, and the state prosecutors initiated proceedings to close down the party.[62]

In 1994, on the eve of the March municipal elections, Prime Minister Çiller, claiming that DEP was simply an extension of the PKK, engineered, in conjunction with the banning of DEP, the imprisonment of some of its parliamentary representation by having the Parliament vote to remove their immunity. While other DEP members managed to flee to Europe and eventually form the KPE, in a much-publicized trial the arrested members of DEP were sentenced to long periods of incarceration. The banning of DEP and the arrest of its MPs profoundly shocked the Kurdish population.

Unlike previous occasions, when a soon-to-be-banned party could create a new political shell to host its parliamentary delegation, the 1994 attack on DEP was designed to cleanse the Parliament of nationalistic Kurdish members. The banning of DEP and the harassment campaign conducted by the state and state-affiliated groups, which caused the deaths of many activists, dealt a significant blow to the ability of the Kurds to organize politically.[63]

A new party, HADEP, was formed to pull together what was left of DEP. Devoid of many of the better known Kurdish politicians, ranging from Leyla Zana to Ahmet Türk, HADEP did not, until recently, have the name recognition, visibility, political experience, or depth that its predecessors enjoyed. Despite its claims to the contrary, HADEP is primarily a Kurdish party. It includes a number of Turks attracted by the party's left-wing message and the concerns it expresses for economic and workers' issues. Arabs and Circassians are also represented in the party, especially because of their concentrations in the southeast. But fundamentally, for HADEP the Kurdish problem is its most urgent concern. HADEP did not participate in the 1994 municipal elections, claiming that the state's intimidating tactics made it very difficult for it to engage in a fair and honest campaign. The main beneficiary of HADEP's boycott was the Islamist Welfare party, which swept the municipalities in the Kurdish regions.

The 1995 elections were its first real test, and the results were mixed. HADEP received 4.17 percent of all the votes cast nationally. While it did well in the southeast, winning in many districts, it fared poorly elsewhere in the country. It did not manage to elect any representatives to Parliament because of the 10 percent nationwide minimum, or barrier, it needed to pass in order to obtain a seat in parliament. Without such a barrier, it would have elected approximately twenty-two members from the southeastern region. Welfare was once again one of the primary beneficiaries: In Diyarbakir, HADEP, with 46.3 percent of the vote, could not elect a single representative, whereas Welfare, with 18.8 percent, received five of the ten parliamentarians elected from this electoral district. Nor did HADEP fare well in the Kurdish districts of the big cities such as Istanbul, Izmir, and Adana. This was particularly disappointing given the party's expectations and the assumed level of politicization of the Kurds living there. In Adana and Mersin, large-scale emigration from the southeast has transformed these cities demographically. Yet despite the enthusiastic crowds that greeted HADEP president Murat Bozlak—far greater than those welcoming other party leaders—the final tallies did not reflect that enthusiasm.

A number of factors explain HADEP's disappointing performance: First, Kurdish masses in the cities are not as politicized as HADEP had expected. Second, in the cities, where incumbency and patronage matter a great deal, Welfare controlled many of the municipalities in which Kurds tend to live and, therefore, could fully exploit its advantages. Welfare collects the garbage, HADEP does not. Third, HADEP ran a poorly organized campaign. Fourth, its electoral alliance with two insignificant left-wing parties not only confused some of its electorate but also alienated some of the more conservatively inclined. And fifth, these elections, called on very short notice, were conducted with voter rolls that had not been updated since 1991.[64] In the southeast, HADEP did exceedingly well despite evidence of intimidation and vote rigging by the security forces in the more rural parts of the southeast.[65]

Ironically, with its less than stellar showing in these elections, HADEP succeeded in legitimizing itself. There are two reasons for this: First, it proved that it was the preferred choice for many in the southeast, despite the long years of war and violence. Second, its poor showing in the main cities was received with a collective sigh of relief by Turks who had feared that the party would score significant victories there as well. This result allowed Turks—perhaps erroneously—to talk about a Kurdish problem that is regional in nature rather than nationwide in character. A regionally contained problem would be easier to resolve. This combination of a regionally successful showing with a poor performance in the cities enabled politicians and pundits alike to argue for the elimination of the 10 percent minimum requirement, so that HADEP can be represented in Parliament in the future. This was an important turnabout in attitudes.

In early 1996, HADEP therefore seemed poised to grow and about to recapture the luster lost with the dismemberment of the DEP, and to become part of the Turkish political scene. It also appeared that it was unlikely that any future Turkish government would attempt to ban it.[66] The 1995 elections also demonstrated, as argued earlier, that HADEP and Welfare are in competition for Kurdish votes. This is why even HADEP officials concede that they are unlikely to get more than 10 percent of the national vote, even under the best of circumstances. There is, of course, an irony in this, because it effectively means that the Turkish establishment has to choose between alternatives it dislikes. HADEP may perhaps be closer to this establishment than is Welfare.[67] It is a modern, secular, and Western-oriented movement, except that its focus is on the Kurds. Ironically, pro-Welfare Islamist Kurds perceive HADEP as a Kemalist institution.

HADEP's focus, just like that of its predecessors, is on the immediate concerns of the southeast. Its demands are identical to those of the DEP and HEP: peace and security, the elimination of the state of emergency, and the protection of human rights. It also has longer-term goals that are broader in scope and that were shared but not always advocated by HEP and DEP. These include changing the internal political structure of the state, cultural reforms, end to the emergency rule in the southeast as well as to the conflict with the PKK, decentralization, and a new constitution that reflects the Kurdish reality. Whether or not these represent a consensus of Kurdish opinion or even one within HADEP's own members is difficult to tell, but it is extremely important to note that its political goals go beyond the cosmetic and cultural ones that some in the Turkish body politic are willing to provide, such as regional Kurdish-language television and private Kurdish-language instruction. Still, the party's thinking is somewhat muddled because its cadres have been thinned out as a result of the continuous state of confrontation all Kurdish organizations find themselves in.

Not unlike its predecessors, HADEP claims to be separate from the PKK. Although there are no organic links between the party and the PKK, its rank and file are sympathetic to the PKK. And the PKK has a significant sway over the party membership. Like all other Kurdish parties and organizations, it is not willing to see the PKK defeated, nor could it do so, given the preferences not just of its rank and file but of other Kurds as well. The PKK, in their view, has provided the bulk of the sacrifices for the Kurdish cause, and it is part and parcel of a larger Kurdish cause. To some extent, HADEP has been pushed into being a Kurdish nationalist party, and not just by the state. The state and the news media, by equating the search for identity with a Kurdish nationalist struggle, have succeeded in marrying HADEP to the Kurdish cause more than HADEP itself would have dared attempt.[68] There is, however, a danger in the state's constant suggestion that HADEP is a surrogate for the PKK. Such statements, in the wake of the 1995 elections, are tantamount to saying that there are at least 1.2 million people who voted for the PKK. Still, the inability to disassociate itself clearly and unequivocally from the PKK is an issue that continues to bedevil HADEP, just as it did its predecessors. It remains a dilemma for HADEP precisely because it cannot afford—at least in its own mind—to alienate the large numbers sympathetic to the PKK while cognizant of the fact that distancing itself from the PKK may win it some credibility with Turks in general but not necessarily a "legal status" from the state.

The volatility of the Kurdish issue in Turkey was once again demonstrated when, in the summer of 1996, six months after its quite respectable showing at the polls, HADEP faced the same fate that befell its predecessors: Its leadership was jailed and the State Security Court sought its outright ban. This followed the HADEP Congress in June 1996, which witnessed the removal of the Turkish flag and its replacement by an Öcalan banner. As this event unfolded, some of the audience applauded, while others booed the perpetrators. Stunned, the HADEP leadership failed to react immediately, and, with television cameras rolling, the damage had been done. The reaction within the Turkish public was swift, encouraged by the media, and people flew the Turkish flag in protest. The State Security Court jailed party leaders and fifteen days later charged them with sedition. The court ordered the HADEP headquarters raided and party membership lists confiscated. It ordered a nationwide "security investigation" of all the members and their relatives.[69] Clearly intended as intimidation, these investigations were also designed to find enough evidence, as the prosecutor admitted, to close down the party.[70]

The events surrounding the HADEP convention were widely interpreted at the time as a provocation.[71] But a provocation by whom? The two parties most likely to benefit from such an eventuality are the state and the PKK; the first because it gets to close down a party it despises and second because it demonstrates to the Kurdish public that there is no alternative but the armed struggle and complete adherence to the PKK.[72] Whether HADEP as a party survives the incident or whether another party is formed in its stead remains to be seen, but a sense of fatigue is settling on Kurdish activists: Not only do they have to incur the financial and other costs of setting up parties along with all their attendant local party organizations and so forth, but the personal risks are quite high. The night after the flag incident, three HADEP members returning home to the southeast from the convention were ambushed and killed near Kayseri. This brought the total number of HEP/DEP/HADEP leaders and members killed under mysterious circumstances in which the perpetrators were never caught to ninety-two since 1990.

Chapter Three

Notes and References

1. Martin van Bruinessen,"Ethnic Identity of the Kurds," in *Ethnic Groups in the Republic of Turkey,* ed. Peter Alford Andrews (Weisbaden: Ludwig Reichert Verlag, 1989), 613. According to this definition, Kurds who have willingly assimilated are considered to be Turkish, and Christians who have embraced Islam (such as the many Armenians who have assumed Kurdish Alevi identity over the centuries) are counted as Kurds.

2. McDowall, "The Kurdish Question," 32.

3. Andrews, *Ethnic Groups in the Republic of Turkey,* 100.

4. *Ibid.,* 121.

5. Servet Mutlu, "Ethnic Kurds in Turkey: A Demographic Study," *International Journal of Middle East Studies* 28, no. 4 (November 1996): 517–41.

6. In fact, Öcalan himself does not speak Kurdish and in a 1993 interview conceded that he could not even make time to study the language properly. Oral Çalislar, *Öcalan ve Burkay'la Kürt Sorunu* (A discussion of the Kurdish question with Ocalan and Burkay) (Istanbul: Pencere Yayinlari, 1993), 29.

7. In an article entitled "Istimlâl" written in 1923, Ziya Gökalp, one of the founders of modern Turkish nationalism, depicts how in the countryside of the southeast Turcoman and Turkish tribes became Kurdish over time, and how Kurds who migrated into cities assumed a Turkish identity. Reprinted in Ziya Gökalp, *Kürt Asiretleri Hakkinda Sosyolojik Tetkikler* (Sociological investigations on Kurdish tribes) (Istanbul: Sosyal Yayinlar, 1992), 125–30.

8. *Milliyet,* December 18, 1996.

9. The 2 million figure is an estimate made by the U.S. State Department. See *Turkey: Human Rights Report, 1996* (Washington, D.C.: U.S. State Department, 1996): "According to the Interior Minister, as of March, 2,297 villages had been evacuated or burnt down. In July the emergency region governor stated that 987 villages and 1,676 hamlets (settlement units of 3 or 4 houses) had been depopulated 'for various reasons,' including residents evacuated by security forces for security reasons; residents who left of their own accord for security or economic reasons; and residents who left because of PKK pressure." HADEP, in a report it prepared for the 1996 HABITAT II Conference, claimed that over the last four years some 3 million people had been made homeless as 3,000 villages and hamlets had been burnt down or evacuated *Cumhuriyet,* June 20, 1996). The government claimed that by the end of 1994, 988 villages and 1,676 hamlets had been destroyed, resulting in an outflow of 311,000 residents (*Milliyet,* July 28, 1995).

10. A. Rezzak Oral, "Kalmak mi Dönmek mi Zor?" (What's more difficult: To return or to stay?) Part 2, *Milliyet,* July 26, 1996. One district headman described how the number of his constituents increased from 6,000 to 63,000 in a matter of a few years.

11. Kadri Gürsel, in his account of the days he spent with PKK fighters, recounts how some of them have ended up in the large cities after the villages were razed. They worked at construction sites or as peddlers before joining the organization (*Dagdakiler,* 59–62).

12. Philip Kreyenbroek, "On the Kurdish Language," in *The Kurds: A Contemporary Overview*, ed. Kreyenbroek and Sperl, 69. This is not to say that there are no significant literary achievements in Kurdish. The seventeenth-century epic poem *Mem-û Zîn* by Ahmed Khani is the most widely known. By contrast, there as been a significant effort on the part of the state and others to claim, absurdly, that the Kurdish language does not exist. For such an account, which claims that the total number of Kurdish words in existence is no more than 300, see Tekin Erer, *Kürtçülük Meselesi* (Kurdishness question) (Istanbul: Bogaziçi Yayinlari, 1994), 17–18.

13. Kreyenbroek and Sperl, eds. *The Kurds: A Contemporary Overview*, 75. The Kurdish Socialist party of Kemal Burkay, with others, had long pursued an agenda aimed at expanding the use of Kurdish well before the PKK came into being, and it continues to do so today from its headquarters in Sweden. Kurdish exiles, especially in Sweden, Germany, France, and Austria, are busy publishing materials (often with the help of the government, as in Sweden and Germany) and facilitating education in Kurdish, especially at the primary level. With the lifting of the official restrictions on the use of Kurdish in 1991, this has become easier, although harassment by representatives of the state continues.

14. Interestingly, the Mesopotamia Cultural Center has had to incorporate itself as a private enterprise because authorities would not grant it nonprofit status.

15. For the PKK at least, the different Kurdish dialects are a sensitive issue, since one of the decisions of the 5th Congress was to unite all the dialects into one language (*PKK 5. Kongre Kararlari*, 136–37).

16. Serif Mardin, *Religion and Social Change in Modern Turkey* (Albany: State University of New York, 1989), 155.

17. Lâle Yalçin-Heckman, "Kurdish Tribal Organisation and Local Political Processes," in *Turkish State, Turkish Society*, ed. Andrew Finkel and Nükhet Sirman (London: Routledge, 1990), 308–10.

18. van Bruinessen, *Agha, Shaikh and State*, 310–11.

19. Türkiye Odalar Birligi, *Dogu Sorunu: Teshisler ve Tespitler*, 69.

20. *Yeni Yüzyil*, December 7, 1996. Ensarioglu is himself a Kurd.

21. Andrews, *Ethnic Groups in the Republic of Turkey*, 57.

22. Etymologically, the word can have dual origins. As a heterodox form of Shi'ism, the word *Alevi* is related to the Arabic word *'Alawi*, deriving from 'Ali, the son-in-law of the Prophet from whom the blood line descends. Alternatively, the word can be derived from the Persian (and Turkish) word *alev*, meaning flame, as related to "fire-worship" in Zoroastrianism.

23. See Mehrdad R. Izady, *The Kurds: A Concise Handbook* (Washington, D.C.: Crane Russak, 1992), 135–45.

24. These numbers have to be viewed with caution, as it is difficult to attest to their veracity. Alevi Kurds tend to live in the provinces of Bingöl, Tunceli, Malatya, Erzincan, Sivas, and Elazig. Andrews, *Ethnic Groups in the Republic of Turkey*, 116–17.

25. Although the Alevis consider themselves to be Twelver Shi'ites (followers of the Twelfth Iman of Shi'ism), Alevis, unlike Iranian Twelvers, do not follow the

basic tenets of Islam, such as the five daily prayers, the hajj, and they see no need for mosques, preferring instead ordinary houses for worship.

26. Peter J. Bumpke, "The Kurdish Alevis—Boundaries and Perceptions," in Andrews, *Ethnic Groups in the Republic of Turkey*, 514.

27. In an interview, the muhktar (headman) of the Gazi district argued that in the absence of concrete steps taken by the state to recognize their existence, the Alevis found themselves with a problem that very much mirrored the Kurdish one. See Ali Bayramoglu and Yavuz Baydar, "Aleviler Ne Istiyor?" ("What do the Alevis want?") Part 1, *Yeni Yüzyil*, July 28, 1996.

28. Most Turks belong to the Hanafi school. Riza Zelyut, *Aleviler ne Yapmali?* (What should the Alevis do?) (Istanbul: Yön Yayincilik, 1993), 219–20. Some Alevis believe that they are an even more aggrieved minority than the Kurds, since Kurds—at least assimilated ones—have been allowed to reach the highest echelons of the state, whereas Alevis have always had to keep secret their Alevi identity if they were to assume positions of power.

29. *Yeni Yüzyil*, January 1, 1996. In an unusual move, the state has had to retreat and pull back and redeploy its special teams responsible for the repression.

30. Rusen Çakir, "Degisim Sürecinde Alevi Hareketi: Apo, Bektasilige Cihad Açti," (The Alevi movement in transition: Apo calls for a jihad against Bektashis) *Milliyet*, July 8, 1995, 23.

31. The single worst incident occurred in July 1993 when 37 artists died at an Alevi celebration—burned to death when their hotel was torched by Islamic radicals. Noteworthy was the fact that the Welfare party was in command of the Sivas municipality at the time of this event. For a historical analysis of Sivas's travails, see Zeki Coskun, *Aleviler, Sünniler ve Öteki Sivas* (Alevis, Sunnis and the other Sivas) (Istanbul: Iletisim Yayinlari, 1995).

32. Former interior minister Abdulkadir Aksu in an interview admitted that people often falsely denounced their neighbors or competitors to the security forces as being members of the PKK (*Zaman*, August 6, 1995).

33. The weekly *2000'e Dogru* published a government report that purported to analyze tribal groupings in 23 provinces according to their origins, numbers, and loyalties to the state, December 13–19, 1987. It suggested that the security forces intervened in intertribal disputes to shore up pro-government groupings.

34. van Bruinessen, *Agha, Shaikh and State*, 317.

35. See Imset, *PKK: Ayrilikçi Siddetin 20 Yili*, 329–31. Other information on the Hizbollah is drawn from interviews in Turkey.

36. Türkiye Odalar Birligi, *Dogu Sorunu: Teshisler ve Tespitler*, 82.

37. See interview with Öcalan, Çalislar, *Öcalan ve Burkay'la Kürt Sorunu*, 45.

38. On the other hand, losing an election can be costly: In January 1996, Abdülmelik Firat, an independent MP from Erzurum, was charged with belonging to a terrorist organization and helping the PKK. He was detained immediately after his parliamentary immunity had expired. Similarly, Mahmut Alinak, another Kurdish former member, was sentenced to a prison term when he failed to win reelection in December 1995. Alinak has since had his prison term extended by three years

for inability to pay the approximately $1,000 fine (*Anadolu Ajansi,* January 16, 1997).

39. For instance, True Path party Hakkari parliamentarian and tribal chief Mustafa Zeydan vehemently objected to any suggestion of negotiations with Öcalan, whose primary aim, he claimed, "was not to obtain Kurdish-language television, but rather . . . the creation of a greater Armenian state" (*Hürriyet,* August 6, 1996).

40. The expulsion of Ahmet Türk and six other members of SHP, the Social Democratic People's party, in 1991 for having attended a conference in Paris on the Kurds best exemplifies the dilemma faced by the Kurdish MPs in mainstream parties, especially since the social democrats have been the most liberal on this issue.

41. For instance, a military sponsored study repeats unsubstantiated accusations against Kurdish members of parliament of "having welcomed the 500,000 armed [sic] peshmergas [in 1991 from Iraq] by telling them 'you are not refugees . . . these lands here are yours' " Mehmet Kocaoglu, *Uluslararasi Iliskiler Isiginda Ortadogu* (The Middle East in the context of international relations) (Ankara: Genelkurmay Basimevi, 1995), 262.

42. Bozarslan, "Political Crisis and the Kurdish Issue in Turkey," in *The Kurdish Nationalist Movement in the 1990s,* ed. Olson, 142.

43. A cousin of Abdülmelik Firat, Fuat Firat is presently a Welfare party MP from Istanbul.

44. For instance, in 1995, Tansu Çiller in a deal with one such party stalwarth and loyal Kurdish leader, Sanliurfa representative Necmettin Cevheri, made sure that his son would be elected from the True Path party from the province of Adana.

45. Sakallioglu, "Historicizing the Present and Problematizing the Future of the Kurdish Problem," 10.

46. Lâle Yalçin-Heckman, "Ethnic Islam and Nationalism among the Kurds in Turkey," in *Islam in Modern Turkey: Religion, Politics and Literature in a Secular State,* ed. Richard Tapper (London: I. B. Tauris, 1991), 110.

47. Still, Refah and HADEP do share constituencies. Where it has been difficult for HADEP to organize, Kurds have joined Refah only to return to HADEP when convenient, as was the case, for instance, in Sarayköy (a town in the western province of Denizli) when 58 of the Refah party leaders and members switched to HADEP, (*Hürriyet,* May 5, 1996).

48. He considered joining DEP but changed his mind when it became apparent that his candidacy for party leadership would be denied. He also considered joining Refah, and in 1995 he was the Republican People's party's unsuccessful candidate for parliament from Sirnak.

49. See interview with Elçi in the *Turkish Daily News,* March 17, 1997.

50. "PKK Silah Birakmali" (The PKK should abandon arms) *Pazar Postasi,* February 4, 1995.

51. *Yeni Yüzyil,* June 25, 1997.

52. On the complexities of the assimilation process, see Martin van Bruinessen, "Race, Culture, Nation and Identity Politics in Turkey: Some Comments." Paper

presented at Continuity and Change: Shifting State Ideologies from Late Ottoman to Early Republican Turkey, 1890–1930, Princeton University, April 23–26, 1997.

53. Based on the authors' interview with Dalan in Istanbul in August 1995.

54. Of course, other Kurds may not find him acceptable. Burkay, for instance, finds him to be more chauvinistic than most Turks because of his participation in government policy. In fact, for Burkay, such people cannot be considered Kurds (Çalislar, *Öcalan ve Burkay'la Kürt Sorunu,* 105–6).

55. Interview with Dogan Güres, *Milliyet,* November 19, 1995.

56. Chaim Kaufmann, "Possible and Impossible Solutions to Ethnic Civil Wars," *International Security* 20, no. 4. (Spring 1996): 143–44.

57. SHP, which was formed by members of the banned CHP, eventually merged with a reconstituted CHP in 1995 under the latter's banner and symbols.

58. The law stated that a party had to have been organized in more than half of the country's constituencies and also ought to have had its party congress at least six months before an election. HEP being a relatively recent party and given the fact that the 1991 elections were snap elections, HEP could not physically have fulfilled all the requirements in time.

59. Leyla Zana uttered a sentence in Kurdish that said she was taking the oath of office for the friendship of the Kurdish and Turkish peoples. Hatip Dicle said that he was taking the oath of office because the constitution required him to do so. The problem for HEP originated in the wording of the oath, which they believed excluded Kurds altogether. The ceremony was a controversial issue for Turks, but there was celebration in parts of the southeast. For an account of the events from HEP's perspective, see A. Osman Ölmez, *DEP Depremi* (The DEP earthquake) (Ankara: Doruk Yayinlari, 1995), 160–67,

60. In between HEP and DEP, another political party was created with the explicit purpose of safeguarding the parliamentary seats won by HEP. The Constitutional Court banned this party, Özgürlük ve Demokrasi Partisi (ÖZDEP), within a year of its formation.

61. Ölmez, *DEP Depremi,* 273.

62. Sincar was not given a state funeral despite his being entitled to one, and DEP supporters were not allowed into Ankara for funeral services.

63. There were disagreements among the DEP members. Some suggested that the party be disbanded and a new one formed so as to save the representatives' seats, while others were intent on continuing the struggle to the bitter end as DEP members. Mahmut Alinak, *HEP, DEP, ve Devlet: Parlamento'dan 9. Kogusa* (HEP, DEP and the State: From Parliament to the Ninth Cell), Vol. 2 (Istanbul: Kaynak Yayinlari, 1996), 132–34.

64. This was an especially important obstacle for HADEP, a significant proportion of whose electorate had moved because of the conflict. In the nine days allowed for reregistering, voters had to obtain proper documentation from their place of origin, which, for many Kurds, no longer existed. The alternative means required special appeals to the district and the security services. As a result, most of those who had migrated to cities like Adana and Mersin could not vote.

65. There have been many reports charging that army officers had threatened villagers if they voted for HADEP. Similarly, voting results show that while HADEP did very well in city centers in the southeast, its votes declined dramatically in the villages that were attached to the same cities. Mardin is one such example. As one columnist also detailed, in places the results bordered on the absurd. In one village the local HADEP candidate did not receive a single vote in his own village; not even his own wife, children, or relatives voted for him. See Fatih Altayli, "Köyler HADEP'i Istemiyor mu?" (Don't the villages want HADEP?) *Hürriyet,* December 30, 1995.

66. There were other indications of HADEP's growing respectability: President Demirel invited HADEP leader Bozlak to the presidential palace for discussions with other party leaders, and Mesut Yilmaz, the ANAP leader, consulted with Bozlak during his efforts at forming a coalition government in February 1996.

67. In the 1995 elections, Welfare was convinced that the only reason HADEP was allowed to run was to limit the Islamists' influence. See chapter 4, note 24.

68. For an incisive analysis of HADEP's performance and reactions, see Ali Bayramoglu, "Kürt Sorunu ne Olacak?" (What will become of the Kurdish problem?) *Yeni Yüzyil* December 28, 1995, 5. By contrast, an influential columnist, Ilnur Çevik, clearly equates HADEP with the PKK. See "Güneydogu'da Seçim PKK için bir Test," (The election in the Southeast is a test for the PKK) *Yeni Yüzyil,* December 21, 1995, 7.

69. *Cumhuriyet,* July 6, 1996.

70. Almost all of the case brought to court by the State Security Court prosecutor on August 23, 1996, consists of circumstantial arguments that purport to link the party to the PKK. For details, see Ankara Devlet Güvenlik Mahkemesi Cumhuriyet Bassavciligi, *PKK'nin Legal Alandaki Uzantisi HADEP ve 23.06.1996 Tarihli Kurultayda Türk Bayraginin Indirilmesi Olayina Ait Iddianame* (The accusation against HADEP as the legal extension of the PKK and the lowering of the Turkish flag at the June 23, 1996 convention) (Ankara: Devlet Güvenlik Mahkemesi, 1996). Most party leaders, including the president, Murat Bozlak, were released from custody on April 15, 1997, pending the conclusion of the case.

71. As one columnist wrote, "Viewed by any point of view this is an unbelievable act of provocation. It is obvious it was well planned to the most minute detail." Mehmet Ali Birand, "Amaç HADEP'i Kapattirmak," (The aim is to have HADEP closed down) *Sabah,* June 27, 1996.

72. Just as the state was developing its long case against the party and its relationship with the PKK, Kurdish news media, such as *Özgür Politika,* a newspaper published in Europe, claimed on April 11, 1997, that an alleged police agent provocateur, Murat Ipek, who confessed to working for the Anti-Terrorist Section of the Ankara police, had entered the hall, equipped by the police with PKK documentation, and had helped stir up a small group of radicals to bring down the Turkish flag.

4

The Kurdish Issue in Turkish Public Opinion

O NE OF THE MAJOR GROUNDS for hope for a peaceful solution to Turkey's Kurdish problem is its relatively advanced stage of political development. At least three critically important qualities already exist in Turkish political culture: democratic process and governance, the existence of a large and vibrant civil society, and an open press. In each of these areas there is something left to be desired, but these characteristics nonetheless function quite impressively by any regional standards, including those of most of Eastern Europe and the Balkans. Unfortunately, these institutions have not functioned well in terms of handling the Kurdish problem. The Kurdish problem seems to fall well outside most of the normal processes of Turkish government and society. To put it another way, Turkey's democratic features are largely nonfunctional when it comes to the Kurdish issue.

Parliament and the Political Parties

Turkey has a functioning democratic order, in the sense that governments now regularly come to and leave power in accordance with an electoral process derived from the constitution. Turks actually believe that their lives can be changed by elections—an important sign of democratic principles at work at the grass roots. While the democratic order is far from perfect, it is increasingly solidly established; public opinion now exerts major impact on how Turkey conducts its policies.[1] In parliamentary terms, Kurds happen to occupy nearly one-third of the seats in the Turkish parliament. Yet only a handful of Kurdish deputies in the parliament have been willing to speak out at all on the Kurdish problem. Why so?

We noted earlier the extreme difficulties that have existed for anyone even talking about the existence of a Kurdish problem. To speak about Kurds was to run the risk of violating the constitution on the grounds of encouraging separatism. Hence Kurdish deputies, elected from primarily Kurdish regions, avoided directly addressing the problem, preferring at best to work behind the scenes or simply to focus upon the economic betterment of their regions. Even today, despite the emergence of a series of explicitly Kurdish parties, the parliament has yet to undertake a debate of the Kurdish issue per se. Kurdish-oriented parties such as the People's Labor party (HEP) and its successor, the Democracy party (DEP), were banned in quick succession over the last three years. Their successor, the People's Democracy party (HADEP), has had a tenuous hold on life. These parties have all walked on extremely thin ice and are vulnerable to accusations of constituting a separatist, or a PKK-affiliated, party.

Still, there have been occasions on which the Parliament has attempted to investigate developments in the southeast. Such efforts have not amounted to much, as they have tended to become political footballs among the various parties. One such effort was a parliamentary commission that submitted its findings in October of 1994. While timid in its criticisms of governmental policy and putting the blame for the ills of the region almost entirely on the PKK, the commission's report, nonetheless intimated the difficulties ordinary citizens experience at the hands of the security forces and the lack of interest on the part of both the public and private sectors. It even suggested that the operations of the security forces could resolve only 25 percent of the problems, while the remaining 75 percent had to be addressed within the state structure and its representatives operating in the region.[2] The two dissenting members' comments, by contrast, took the report and the commission to task. One of them even suggested that the report did not conform with the style of a parliamentary investigation, but rather with that of "a state-issued one." He went on to criticize the report for failing to mention, incredibly, that the southeastern problem was caused by the different ethnic origins of the region's inhabitants.[3]

Turkey's major parties have acted with a great deal of caution with respect to this issue. They have by and large differentiated between their own specific policy prescriptions and what they have termed as "state policy." By state policy, politicians mean the combination of the preferences of the civilian and military bureaucratic elite and the ideological precepts of Kemalism: Turkish nationalism and the maintenance of a centralized unitary state. Few if any among the mainstream parties engage in any revisionist thinking about the nature of the Turkish state. While substantial differences exist among them on issues such as taxation, privatization, worker's welfare, and so on, there are no deep philosophical divides; what is being argued is a matter of degree—and of course, personalities.

The two major exceptions on the Turkish political scene today are represented by the Islamist Welfare (Refah) party and the New Democracy Movement (Yeni Demokrasi Hareketi, YDH), both of which approach their understanding of Turkey from quite new and independent positions. The two parties ended at the opposite ends of the election results in December 1995: Welfare emerged as the single largest party, while YDH withered away.

The 1995 Elections

At the outset, the post-1995 election period augured well for the Kurdish question. HADEP's results, as discussed earlier, while not satisfactory by any means, nonetheless did give a boost to HADEP itself and did indirectly help legitimize the party in the eyes of the public. Despite the poor showing of Cem Boyner's YDH and the relative disappointment for HADEP, the elections provided an opportunity to discuss the Kurdish question. The social democrats, the Republican People's party (CHP), had for years engaged in a battle, fought mostly from within the government, that produced scarce little. This was due to the fact that they opted to become the minority party in a coalition with Tansu Çiller's, the one party that has embraced the "state policy" wholeheartedly. Both the CHP and ANAP went out of their way to emphasize the fact that they would seek a peaceful solution to this problem. While these can be interpreted as cynical efforts at minimizing Welfare's pull in the southeast, ANAP's statements were significant in that the party used them to differentiate itself from the ruling DYP. Even the DYP, which hitherto had been the architect of an uncompromising policy, can be said to have discovered the problem of the southeast.

The absence of a clear winner (see Table 4.1) in these elections meant that Turkey was immersed into a period of coalition formation. Welfare's first-place finish, while not a shock, posed a strange dilemma: Divisions within the center-right and center-left made it very difficult for a coherent government to emerge from the mainstream parties. Consequently, either one of the two center-right parties had to initiate a timid dance with the Islamists. ANAP chose to go first, drawing the ire of the secular forces around the country and the military. Such pressure convinced the center-right to form a minority coalition supported by the larger of the two center-left formations, the Democratic Left party of Bülent Ecevit.

The ANAP-DYP coalition did not survive long, as allegations of financial improprieties and parliamentary investigations fielded by Welfare against Çiller brought the government down. In a surprising turnaround, it was Welfare and DYP that in June of 1996 put together a rotational coalition agreement that envisaged that Erbakan would be prime minister for the first two years, to be followed by Çiller. By June 1997, this coalition government had succumbed to pressure from the military and other establishment forces and resigned.

TABLE 4.1
Distribution of Seats in the Turkish Parliament

Party Name	% of votes	seats 12/95	seats 7/96	seats 4/97
Welfare	21.3	158	159	160
Motherland	19.7	125	130	127
True Path	19.2	135	120	120
Democratic Left	14.6	76	75	68
Republican People's	10.7	49	49	49
Great Unity*		7	7	7
Great Turkey			1	7
Independents			8	10
Vacant				2

*Elected as part of an alliance with the Motherland party

The Islamist View: The Welfare Party and Others

The position of the Welfare party on the Kurdish question, as on many other questions, is of immense interest not just for Turkish politics but also for the region, since it represents the first Islamist party to come to power by the ballot box in the Middle East. On the surface, the Welfare party's vision of the Kurdish question has always been at odds with that of the mainstream parties—which was not necessarily very meaningful while Welfare had been in the opposition. But now Welfare had come to power. The Welfare party and Islamists in general view the Kurdish issue as a problem created by the state, based on the decision to use Turkish nationalism as the sole foundation of the new state, a policy that deliberately excluded and alienated the Kurds from the Turkish republic. To them, ethnic divisions are artificial; the Welfare party naturally contends that if Islam had formed the foundation of the state, the Kurds would not have felt excluded. Accordingly, a return to the Islamic identity in Turkey will comfortably accommodate both Kurdish and Turkish peoples. Welfare party members argue that the Kemalist state, by discriminating against both Kurds and Muslims, created a bond between the two groups.[4] With these criticisms of the state's founder. Atatürk, the party has tried to distance itself from the mainstream parties and appeal to Kurds. In fact, one observer suggests that Erbakan and his people deliberately avoid direct references to the Turkish people and insist on using substitutes, such as "our dear people" or "our dear people's valuable children."[5] Because of the belief in an overarching Islamic umbrella, the Welfare party and Islamists appear not to be threatened by non-Turkey identities and, therefore, have not had to deny the existence of Kurds, as have mainstream parties.

Still, the Welfare party's discourse is tame in comparison with that of Islamist intellectuals and activists. The reemergence of the Kurdish question in the 1980s has enabled Islamists to sharpen their critique of the Kemalist state they abhor. For them, the ideal arrangement was the previous one: The Ottoman Empire, in which all Muslims were equal irrespective of their ethnic background. In fact, the problems started with the intrusion of the West, specifically with the Tanzimat reforms in 1839 and the idea of the unitary state.[6] The theme that today's imperialist powers, just as they did in the past, use the Kurds to sow dissension among Muslims is a theme that permeates the writings and thinking of the Islamist camp, including the Welfare party.

Beyond this, Islamist thinkers have repudiated the concept of the nation state. Ali Bulaç argues for instance that, just as with the Kurds, he does not believe in Palestinians, the Polisario, and Kashmiris creating their own states.[7] This is because an independent Kurdish state in Iraq, for instance, would distance the Kurds from the logic of integration with Islamic societies. On the other hand, Kurds must be protected from the assimilationist policies of Turks and Arabs,[8] because he does believe that Kurds are a separate people endowed by God with a different culture and language.[9] Another such thinker, Abdurrahman Dilipak, goes even further in arguing that the Kemalist concept of nationalism has been vanquished and that the time has come to return to the Ottoman-style "millet" system.[10] Islamist publications have been more aggressive on this issue, and they have also not shied away from criticizing the Welfare party. In a series of articles on this question, for instance, Selami Camci has pointed out that while some of Welfare's theses regarding foreign intervention and the like are undoubtedly correct, the party fails to realize the complexity of the problem and specifically the fact that Kurdish nationalism is a natural outcome and is not about to disappear any time soon.[11] As sympathetic as they may appear to the Kurds, Islamists themselves are nonetheless wary of the international connections that Kurds, specifically Iraqi Kurds, have formed over time. Most worrisome to them are the politics of both Kurdish leaders in northern Iraq, who have had extensive dealings not only with Western powers but also with Israel.[12]

The Welfare party has incorporated into its discourse many of the ideas discussed above to attract the support of Kurds nationwide: It has consistently advocated the elimination of the Emergency Rule in the southeast, expressed its desire to resolve matters peacefully, emphasized the unity of all under Islam, worked for the liberalization of restrictions on language, and sent teams periodically to the southeast to investigate matters and produce reports. In the process, unlike other parties, it did not declare itself an enemy of a Kurdish identity; even Erbakan has occasionally mentioned Kurdish identity.[13] Although the party has been careful not to overly criticize the military's conduct of the conflict in its reports, it has, nonetheless, suggested that the people of the region have suffered unnecessarily. In its 1994 report, it argued that a large segment of the populace in the region are treated as potential suspects, and that residents were being forced out of their villages.[14] A 1996 report similarly argued that state officials were mistreating the inhabitants of the southeast.[15] In another far-reaching report, in addition to the steps outlined above, the party called for the election of provincial governors, the transformation of provincial assemblies into "state" assemblies, implying a federal structure of sorts, and the elimination of State Security Courts.[16]

As a party that has already attracted the ire of the state establishment in other respects, Welfare is careful of the limits it can reach on the Kurdish question.[17] Most of the reports mentioned above are produced by delegations sent by Erbakan to the southeast and are submitted to him and the party leadership, who are under no obligation to accept the recommendations; but they do make good press copy and show that the party is attempting to grapple with the issue.[18] On the other hand, writers who are sympathetic to the party have no qualms about arguing what they think is the obvious: The Welfare party perceives the issue as composed of three dimensions: the southeastern problem, the Kurdish question, and terrorism. While the southeast has been economically ignored over the years, the Kurdish issue is one of identity, and Welfare's aim is to attack all three problems simultaneously since they are intimately linked.[19]

As a result, Welfare has achieved a modicum of success: Hamit Bozarslan suggests that the party has managed to create an organic link with the Kurdish national movement through the religious orders that are so prevalent among the Kurds. It has succeeded in incorporating among its ranks not just Kurds, as other parties have, but even bona fide Kurdish nationalists.[20] As argued earlier, it has also benefited from the Islamic and socially conservative nature of the southeast—after all, the first Kurdish revolt of the republican era, the Shaykh Said rebellion, contained both religious and nationalist characteristics. The party had already made important headway among the Kurds in the 1970s. In the 1973 elections, the National Salvation party, Welfare's precursor, won 11.8 percent of the national vote and, with forty-eight members in Parliament, emerged as the fourth largest party. By 1977, it had lost half of its parliamentary delegation, receiving 8.6 percent of the vote, although the total, absolute number of votes remained constant. Between 1973 and 1977, however, it appears that the party consolidated its position in the southeast. Whereas in 1973 only one Kurdish province, Bingöl, figured among the top ten provinces, by the 1977 elections eight of the top ten and nine of the top eleven were unambiguously Kurdish provinces.[21] In recent years, the travails of DEP and HADEP have served the Islamists well: In the 1994 municipal elections, their absence allowed Welfare to sweep the southeast's municipalities. In 1995, HADEP's performance notwithstanding, it elected a number of representatives from the southeast to Parliament.

Success, however, comes at a price. With its not-so-subtle anti-Kemalist discourse, the party has anointed itself as a "countersystem" (*düzen karsiti*) political formation and, therefore, it is well poised to receive Kurdish votes and activists in search of such an alternative to the "statist" and "PKK-oriented" parties. And it has. Many of its supporters and activists in the southeast are fierce Kurdish nationalists, who (as argued in the section on Islam and the Kurds, above) see in the Welfare party an opportunity to push the political system further and democratize it, or even upset it. This creates a dilemma for Erbakan and the party leadership: While the party is now home to a large Kurdish contingent at both the national and local levels, there are also other and more dominant currents within it. Not everyone in the party shares the concerns of those in the southeast. In fact, quite naturally, many of the Islamists have criticized government policies in the southeast just because they were in the opposition. With Welfare having come to power as the senior member of a coalition, these tensions are bound to become more pronounced as the party tries to accommodate these factions to the necessities of governance.

Another interpretation of Welfare's ideology suggests that it is inherently "statist" in its own right. In other words, despite its call for the strengthening of local administrations, it does not look to the dismantling of state authority, but rather its reformulation along Islamist principles. While Welfare may have fewer problems than other parties on the question of a Kurdish identity within the state, it is equally unlikely that Welfare would tolerate any weakening of the central state in the name of accommodating any kind of nationalism. To all Islamists, nationalism is not a positive force, since in most cases it works to divide the Muslim community, the *ummah*. Welfare would therefore probably yield much on questions of expression of Kurdish identity, but very little by way of decentralization of state power, and it would move aggressively against actual separatism. Its economic approach to the southeast is reminiscent of its rhetoric of the 1970s, when it argued for state-sponsored investment almost everywhere. In other words, the Islamist focus would remain on the coherence of state power, and not on the nationalist Turkish basis of state power.

One cannot minimize the importance Islam plays in the shaping of Welfare's worldview. It has to this day articulated a consistently anti-Western discourse when it comes to Western policies and intervention in the Muslim world; it has sided, almost automatically, with countries that the West has for one reason or another imposed sanctions on or criticized, especially if they are Islamic. On Iraq, for instance, despite Saddam Hussein's violent suppression of the Kurds, whose rights Welfare supposedly champions, Erbakan has been a vociferous advocate of lifting U.N. sanctions, opening border posts, and removing Operation Provide Comfort, the U.S.-led Turkey-based military force that monitors and safeguards the Kurds of northern Iraq. In the 1995 election campaign, he argued for the creation of an Islamic NATO, Islamic Common Market, Islamic U.N., and so forth.

Yet, despite Islamist rhetoric, the Welfare party, even its previous incarnations in the 1970s, has exhibited strong nationalist tendencies. Erbakan is first and foremost a Turkish nationalist: His Islamic orientation reflects his preference that Turkey ought not play a secondary role in a Western-run world order. His approach to the Islamic world also betrays a desire for Turkey to lead and even dominate it. In fact, his and his party's approach to both foreign and domestic policy strongly suggest that they are Ottomanist in inclination. Erbakan envisages a strong Islamic Turkey leading the way for all Islamic countries.

In this configuration or vision of Turkey, it is unlikely that the Welfare party would be willing to agree to reforms on the Kurdish question that extend beyond the "cultural" realm while simultaneously acknowledging a separate Kurdish identity.[22] A Welfare parliamentarian, involved in many of the party's ventures in the Kurdish question, in defending why Kurds should have all the cultural rights they seek while remaining part of the Turkish republic, argued, "The creation of an Islamic union requires the leadership of Turkey. The Turkey that engages itself in this duty cannot be a smaller or a divided country, quite on the contrary. . . . To divide Turkey is the greatest injustice that can be done not just to the 60 million people living in Turkey but to all of the Muslims and peoples of the world."[23] Resolving the Kurdish problem à la Welfare, therefore, may be nothing more than a gateway to greater glories.

There is, however, one potential bottleneck, and that is the Kurds themselves. Given the competition for these votes between Welfare and HADEP, Welfare's strategy of capturing and holding onto Kurdish votes depends on one of the following scenarios being realized. In the first scenario, HADEP, or for that matter any other Kurdish-based mass political party, is prevented from participating in elections. Then, Welfare is quite likely to sweep the southeast and all other localities where Kurds live in

large numbers.[24] Had there been no national 10 percent threshold block-
ing HADEP's entry into parliament, Welfare's representation in the southeast would have been seriously reduced, perhaps by as much as fifteen
seats. In the 1995 elections, with HADEP running, Welfare lost votes in
all Kurdish provinces except Bingöl, where it actually increased its share.[25]

Alternatively, stiff competition from the likes of HADEP means that
while in power, Erbakan and his colleagues had to demonstrate that they
can change the lives of ordinary citizens in the southeast. It is not just
future Kurdish votes that are at stake here but also the cohesion of the
party. While there are thirty-four Kurdish members of the party, a group
of ten to fifteen are active supporters of the Kurdish cause, both in Turkey
and Iraq.[26] These Kurds do not necessarily share Welfare's vision of an
Ottomanist Turkey but tend to judge Erbakan on how well he performs in
the southeast.[27] They were also at odds with the rest of the party on issues
such as the extension of Operation Provide Comfort. While the party in
general saw it as an extension of Western influence, many of these Kurdish
parliamentarians wanted it to be extended.[28] Just as there are nationalists
among these Kurdish parliamentarians, there also are Islamists who tend
to attach more or equal importance to the idea of Islamic unity when compared with ethnic considerations. As a result, the Kurds in Welfare have
been unable to organize a common front against the party's leadership or
its policies.

The Kurdish vote is vital to Welfare if this party is ever going to become
a majority party, or at least one with a sizable plurality. As the decision to
align himself with Turkish nationalists in 1991 and HADEP's relative success in 1995 demonstrated, Erbakan cannot take the Kurdish vote for
granted. Therefore, by becoming prime minister, he also got a chance to
extend this base further. Irrespective of the sensitivities of establishment
forces in society, such as the military, he still needed to strike a delicate
balance within his own party: Despite the Islamicist rhetoric among Welfare parliamentarians who are not of Kurdish descent, Turkish nationalist
currents are quite strong.[29]

In addition to the constraints emanating from the military and his coalition partner, discussed below, Erbakan, therefore, has had to pursue a
timid policy with respect to the southeast since becoming prime minister.
He launched a number of trial balloons to test the reaction of his own
partisans and the other parties in parliament. Among the most important
was the aborted August 1996 attempt to send an intermediary to Öcalan

to explore the possibility that the PKK would abandon the "armed strug-gle."[30] The project, which was not kept secret, was immediately vetoed by president Demirel. It is possible that Erbakan, who had no intention of seeking a dialogue with the PKK, deliberately sought a public venue for a set of talks that, given their nature, ought to have been kept secret. He thereby ensured that their failure become public and thus also demon-strated to Kurds in Turkey that he had done his outmost on this issue. Packaged with that effort was an attempt to get the PKK to free Turkish soldiers kept captive by one of his parliamentarians, Fethullah Erbas. The initial attempt to get the soldiers released failed, but Erbas, who is not a Kurd and who hails from Van, succeeded in his second attempt in Decem-ber of 1996. On the other hand, despite the many hints that the party and the government were about to allow the diffusion of Kurdish-language television[31] little has been done on that score either.

In addition to party unity and consolidation, the Kurdish question poses two serious problems for Erbakan. The first concerns his relationship with the military and the second his foreign policy objectives—especially his desire to improve relations with Iran and Syria. The potential for discord with the military high command (already unsettled by Welfare's ascension) over this issue has been high from the moment Erbakan took over the reigns of power. To placate them, Erbakan increasingly mirrored the mili-tary's discourse with respect to the conflict, arguing in public that the issue was primarily one of terrorism. He praised and defended the military's conduct in the southeast.[32] Upon the formation of his government, Erba-kan acceded to the National Security Council's demand that Emergency Rule be extended for another four months in the southeast, something he and his party had strenuously objected to in the past and had always voted against. Eventually, he managed to extract one concession from them when, in November 1996, Mardin Province was left out of the scope of the Emergency Rule. The military has continued operations in the south-east and across the border without any interference from the government, or Erbakan in particular. It is unlikely that there would be any change in this aspect of the policy. After all, neither Erbakan nor the bulk of Welfare have any sympathy for the PKK, which stands in their way to claiming the Kurdish vote and indirectly provides support for the likes of DEP and HADEP.

Continued Syrian and Iranian support for the PKK has embarrassed Erbakan. During his visit to Iran and Iranian president Rafsanjani's return visit to Ankara, Erbakan strenuously tried to convince his eastern neighbor to stop harboring the PKK. He has sent signals to the Syrian leadership. He had hoped that his rise to power would convince these two countries to abandon policies they had deemed to be in their national interest in the name of Islamic solidarity. Their lack of cooperation, therefore, has had repercussions on other parts of his agenda and further undermined the little credibility he had with the military.

The New Democracy Movement

The New Democracy Movement (Yeni Demokrasi Hareketi) was created by Cem Boyner, a young and charismatic businessman and former head of TÜSIAD, the Turkish Businessmen's Association. Despite its relatively small size, it has had a major impact on the Turkish political scene, even though it fared poorly in the December 1995 elections.[33] As the other nonstatist party, it equally condemns the Turkish state elite for many of the problems created within the country and for its adherence to a narrow basis of Turkish nationalism as the foundation of the state and source of the Kurdish problem. From the beginning, Boyner sought to devolve state power, which in economic and political terms would empower the regions, including the Kurds, to develop their own local policies along their own terms. More important, Boyner had been the single major exception to the public political silence on the Kurdish issue—which in his view cruelly pits all citizens of Turkey against each other at great cost to all. Boyner pushed for the recognition of the Kurdish problem for what it is: a problem of identity. While intolerant of attempts to forcibly alter boundaries or any kind of separatism, he would have done away with the most restrictive of state policies, on issues ranging from cultural rights to local empowerment.

At the beginning of 1995, when it was a movement and not a political party, the New Democracy Movement was greatly feared by center-right parties. Boyner's perceived immunity from prosecution and harassment from the security forces allowed him to explicitly take the state to task for the conflict in the southeast. The character of his discourse, which would have landed anyone else in jail, provided an opening, a political space, in which some of the issues relating to the Kurdish question could and were aired. Boyner, who also took the powerful military establishment head on for the latter's interference in the political process, ultimately got too closely identified with the Kurdish issue in the public's mind. The New Democracy Movement fell quite short of its most pessimistic expectations in the December 1995 national elections, polling an insignificant 0.5 percent. To be sure, the party was new and had not consolidated itself, and it had unexpectedly to compete with HADEP for Kurdish votes in the southeast, where it had expected to do well.[34] In addition, because of the 10 percent national minimum a party had to obtain to win parliamentary seats, many would-be New Democracy voters chose to cast their votes in a more strategic fashion and not waste them. Still, Boyner's contribution has been of major significance: More than any other politician since former president Özal, he has succeeded in forcing open the Kurdish question quite bluntly, generating some kind of debate and preparing the groundwork for future dialogue.

The Turkish Left

The Turkish Left in the 1970s was the major force in spawning the PKK; violence was the vocabulary of a great portion of the Left and much of the Right. Today a few fringe leftover movements on the extreme Left still pursue violence in Turkey; while violence has escalated in the last few years, it is still far from the scale of the 1970s. The Left today is divided into roughly three groups, whose views differ somewhat on the Kurdish problem. The extreme radical left, which seeks the overthrow of the Turkish state, views the PKK with sympathy as a force willing to practice violence against the state. In fact, this radical Left admires the PKK because it has succeeded in doing what the Turkish Left has not been able to do: for over a decade, to conduct a successful guerrilla campaign against the Turkish military. As a result, some Turkish radical leftists have, over the years, joined the PKK. The Turkish radical Left, with the exception of one group in Tunceli, is primarily an urban phenomenon. As much as it admires the PKK, the urban violent Left has both benefited from the PKK and suffered as well. While the PKK created an atmosphere of chaos that has encouraged this violent Left, it has also been the primary cause for the massive expansion in the nation's security services, which, in turn, have the capability of focusing on all kinds of groups. This radical Left has managed to build a small following and it gained notoriety with the prison hunger strikes of 1996, which resulted in the deaths of twelve inmates before the incoming government of Erbakan negotiated a compromise. The most important of the radical leftist groups is the DHKP, the Revolutionary People's Liberation Army, which has an active presence among Turks living in Europe. On December 22, 1996, the PKK and the DHKP signed a joint statement calling for "a common revolutionary front." By and large, the DHKP and other similar urban-based organizations that conduct violent operations against members of the security services remain marginal.[35]

Turkey's internationalist Left identifies itself with other leftist movements in Europe, essentially of a social-democratic nature. Today this group is represented by the Republican People's party (CHP) (which, in turn, is the product of a 1995 union between the CHP and SHP). It is drawn toward protection of human rights and civil liberties, hence to a lessening of the power of the state, especially its security organs. The internationalist Left is the primary segment of Turkish society likely to respond more positively to Kurdish calls for national and/or cultural rights. These left-of-center parties regularly speak out for human rights and the amendment of the more repressive articles of the Turkish constitution and penal code. These parties' close ties to European socialists have rendered them sensitive to European criticisms of Turkish human rights policies and the treatment of the Kurds. Social democrats have spearheaded efforts, spurred on by the 1995 negotiations on Turkey's accession to the European customs union, to bring Turkey more into accord with European standards.

The CHP has advocated the recognition of cultural rights and has displayed increased sensitivity to human rights concerns. Some of its members have been in the forefront of struggles to get the security services to be more respectful of citizens', and especially of prisoners', rights. Some also challenged the behavior of the security services in the east and southeast, attracting the ire of the security chiefs. On the Kurdish question, the party, nonetheless, suffers from the fact that, in addition to being Atatürk's original party (and hence the originator of the policy of assimilation), it has vacillated a great deal on its approach. While still a separate party, the SHP at first dismissed some of its Kurdish MPs in 1989 for having publicly discussed the Kurdish issue abroad and having participated at a Paris conference on the same topic. Later, under pressure from the remaining MPs of Kurdish extraction, it issued a report on the southeast in July of 1991 that was quite conciliatory to their concerns. As discussed in an earlier section, it also constructed an electoral alliance with HEP at the onset of the 1991 elections.

This inconsistency became even more pronounced when the party served as the True Path party's junior coalition partner from 1991 onward, until the end of 1995. This period coincided with the worst of the repression in the southeast; not only were HEP and DEP closed down, but human rights violations in the east and southeast also reached their peak, as the army and security forces stepped up the campaign against the PKK. Party leaders concede that they were incapable of moderating the hardline policies of their partner, and especially of prime minister Tansu Çiller, who had replaced Demirel. Still, the SHP/CHP earned the wrath of the security services. Special team personnel even threatened the minister of state for human rights, the CHP member Algan Hacaloglu, during one of his visits to the southeast.[36] The Istanbul security chief, Necdet Menzir, went so far as to publicly accuse incumbent CHP ministers of aiding and abetting the violent groups battling the state.

Of all the mainstream parties, the SHP/CHP promised the most to the Kurds, but it was unable to deliver much. It is because of this gap between promises and deeds that, despite its more flexible philosophy, the party forfeited all credibility with the Kurdish populations.[37] Unable even to formulate a cohesive social democratic platform acceptable to the population at large, CHP experienced one of its worst defeats in the 1995 elections, as constituency after constituency abandoned it. It barely made it past the 10 percent national barrier. Perhaps as a consequence of this, the party decided to revisit the Kurdish issue by publicizing another Kurdish report in July of 1996. Prepared by the former minister for human rights, Hacaloglu, the report is a reconfirmation that CHP believes in the primacy of political solutions that recognize the existence of a Kurdish identity.[38]

There is also a nationalist Left in Turkey, whose roots draw upon longstanding Atatürkist and statist traditions. These groups, represented today by former prime minister Bülent Ecevit's Democratic Left party (DSP, Demokratik Sol Partisi), see patriotism in terms of loyalty to the idea of the Turkish state and the Atatürkist nation-building project. The DSP and Ecevit in particular are strongly wedded to a centralized unitary Turkish state. Any Kurdish entreaty—political or cultural—is perceived as a direct challenge to their formulation of the state. Intellectuals from these groups are unapologetic about the use of state power to preserve ideological conformity within the state, and they view both the Kurds and the Islamist movement as equal threats to the traditional vision of the Turkish state and its future.

Thus Ecevit has taken a strong nationalist position explicitly on the

Kurdish issue and is not likely to show sympathy to the notion of according the Kurds greater rights. For Ecevit, the issue is simply the result of economic underdevelopment and the feudal structure of the southeast and east, where the aghas wield an inordinate amount of power and influence. Therefore, with land reform and state investments in a variety of economic enterprises, the southeast and east would not suffer from terrorism—assuming of course that the external sources of support for the PKK are also dealt with. Unlike most of his colleagues on the international Left, Ecevit does not acknowledge the separate ethnic identity of the Kurds. In fact, he tries to avoid the use of the word *Kurd* as much as possible, arguing that "one cannot be a leftist and point to the racial components of an economic and social problem."[39]

As is the case with Erbakan, Ecevit views the Iraqi Kurdish problem and its impact on Turkey as an attempt by the forces of imperialism (read the U.S.) to divide up first Iraq and then Turkey. He has been as implacable as Erbakan in demanding the elimination of OPC and the lifting of sanctions on Saddam Hussein. In parliamentary debates on the extension of OPC, Ecevit has been able to play an increasingly influential role, given the distribution of seats among the different parties. In April 1996 he proposed a "Regional Security Plan," which included the creation of a security belt in Iraqi territory, to replace the U.S.-led OPC.[40] It is not surprising, therefore, that Mümtaz Soysal, another leading figure of the Turkish parliamentary Left, known for his nationalist ideas and who briefly served as foreign minister in 1994, defected from the internationalist RPP to Ecevit's DSP on the eve of the 1995 national elections.

In the 1995 elections, Ecevit and his party, with 14.7 percent of the vote, emerged as the single largest formation on the Left, eclipsing the Republican People's party. The party's gains reflect not only the CHP's difficulties—its coalition with DYP and corruption scandals—but also Ecevit's reputation as a "clean" politician. His party has lacked an organizational base, which has raised question marks regarding its long-term future. Should the party gain further strength, especially at the expense of CHP, it will considerably strengthen the hardline elements on the Kurdish question.[41]

The Right

The Right is divided, on the one hand, between the mainstream parties, the True Path party (Dogru Yol Partisi, DYP) and the Motherland party

(Anavatan Partisi, ANAP), and the extreme nationalist Nationalist Action party (Milliyetçi Hareket Partisi, MHP) of former colonel Alparslan Türkes. While both mainstream parties have espoused similar ideas on the issue, it is the DYP, as the ruling coalition member in the 1991–1995 period which has had the more responsible role for articulating and implementing the policy on the Kurdish question.

In the years she was prime minister (1993–1995), Çiller chose to make "antiterrorism" the primary basis of her policy on the Kurds. On the eve of the 1994 municipal elections, she also engineered the eviction of members of the pro-Kurdish DEP from Parliament. The party, as the heir of both the Democrat and Justice parties of earlier decades, has always represented conservative rural and urban interests, especially those of western Turkey. It is particularly strong in regions where agriculture is commercialized and among western Anatolian commercial and industrial establishments. In the Kurdish areas it has made deals with some of the tribal leaders that have allowed it to win seats. The Kurdish insurrection and revival of the identity issue has caught the DYP unprepared. The party has steadfastly maintained that "there is no ethnic problem in Turkey, but a terror problem."[42] It was not until 1996 that anyone in the party had attempted to develop alternative strategies to the problem. Both Demirel, the party founder, and his successor, Çiller, have toyed with reformist propositions, only to abandon them quickly in the face of the slightest sign of resistance. It is Çiller who, in the process of establishing her control over the party apparatus and expelling Demirel loyalists, brought some of the hardliners in the civil and military bureaucracy into DYP.[43] In this respect, among the mainstream parties, it is the one most committed to seeking a military solution to the Kurdish question. However, from June 1996 to June 1977, the DYP found itself in the awkward situation of being a minority party in coalition with the Welfare party, whose approach to the Kurdish question is radically different. When Welfare sought to find intermediaries to engage the PKK, the DYP initially equivocated, with some of Çiller's lieutenants responding positively.[44] But pressure from party hardliners and the military eventually brought the party back into line.[45]

A traditional DYP ally unhappy with the conduct of the counterinsurgency is the business community, especially the larger industrialists. They have increasingly come to regard the insurgency not only in financial terms—and hence its impact on the rate of inflation—but also in the dam-

aged relations with Europe and the United States. They have not, however, prevailed in influencing the party's positions in this regard.

The Motherland party (ANAP), by contrast, has in recent years pursued
a line typical of opposition parties—that is, it has sought to oppose government policy when convenient without articulating a coherent viewpoint of
its own. It is only with the onset of the 1995 national elections that ANAP
decided to formulate an explicit policy on the Kurds; it sought to differentiate itself from the DYP by emphasizing the need to recognize the cultural
distinctiveness of the southeast and the need to find a nonmilitary solution
to the problem. One of its leading figures, Korkut Özal, the brother of the
former president, even stated that he would be willing to talk to Öcalan
himself if it would guarantee a peaceful resolution. On the other hand, in
the fall of 1995, ANAP also played the role of spoiler by seeking to block
measures designed to "democratize" the constitution and the penal code—
indispensable to a solution to the Kurdish problem—at the time when
Turkey was trying to improve its chances for accession to the customs
union with the European Community, which it subsequently gained.

In the brief spring 1996 interlude when he was prime minister in the
short-lived ANAP-DYP coalition government, party leader Mesut Yilmaz
put forward proposals outlining some of the reforms he was planning to
undertake. Just like the Welfare party, ANAP also made use of its ethnic-
Kurdish parliamentarians to conduct studies in the southeast. One three-
member delegation visited the region in early 1996 and recommended the
liberalization of cultural and educational restrictions, along with the easing
of the military presence.[46] Yilmaz himself declared that prohibitions on the
Kurdish language would be removed.[47] This issue, however, took a back-
seat to intercoalition squabbling between ANAP and DYP, with which
Yilmaz shared power. In the end, his promises of more democracy and a
peaceful solution came to naught.

ANAP, in effect, enjoys a degree of freedom of action that other parties
do not have, and it can always wrap itself in the mantle of Özal, who
created and led the party. Even though during Özal's last years Yilmaz
emerged as one of his opponents, the Özal legacy is a powerful instrument.
Özal's legacy does not always play to ANAP's strength in this matter:
Özal's interest in attracting as many different political tendencies as possible when creating the party has meant that ANAP contains liberals as well

as extreme nationalists close to the Nationalist Action party. These nationalists have restricted party leader Yilmaz's room to maneuver.[48]

The late Alparslan Türkes's Nationalist Action party (MHP) is a classical neo-fascist party with an uncompromising stand on the Kurdish issue. In the past, at the forefront of the battle against the Left, it set its sights on the Kurds. As in the past, it has sought to infiltrate the state apparatus—and it has succeeded in doing so, especially in the security services. During Tansu Çiller's 1991–1995 tenure as prime minister, the MHP acted as her silent partner and, in exchange, was allowed unprecedented access to state institutions. Its fervently nationalist Turkish rhetoric has meant that it has been a primary beneficiary of the violence instigated by the PKK. The MHP's ranks are reportedly strengthened with each body bag that returns to the village of Turkish inductees from the war with the PKK. Having managed to place its militants in the quasi-military "Special Teams" (*özel timler*), which operate in the east and southeast with impunity, the MHP has also been, even if indirectly, one of the principal participants in the violence. In the 1995 elections, believing that it would do well on its own, the MHP declined an offer of alliance with Prime Minister Çiller. Although it garnered a respectable 8.3 percent of the vote, displaying its growing strength, it did not manage to overcome the 10 percent barrier needed to obtain parliamentary representation. Nonetheless the impact of its rhetoric on national policy is quite considerable.[49]

The MHP and Türkes have repeatedly stressed the "scientific fact" that Kurds are "descendants of Turkish tribes" and resisted the notion that Turkey is composed of a mosaic of peoples. While the party leadership must be cautious about its public statements, at the private level MHP members often exhibit an extreme chauvinism and one that is absolutely determined to deny any Kurdish identity within Turkey. Still, in public Türkes has berated all those who have suggested that a political solution ought to be sought, and he has even threatened to spill blood to prevent it.[50]

Another right-wing nationalist formation is the Greater Unity party (BBP), an off-shoot of the MHP. Ideologically, they occupy the space between the MHP and the Welfare party: They are both Islamists and extreme nationalists. Led by Muhsin Yazicioglu, the party has also taken a strong stand against any political solution to the Kurdish question. Interestingly, because the party was formed by right-wing elements interned by the military hierarchy during the 1980–1983 interregnum, unlike the MHP it does not exude the same kind of confidence in the officer class.

Turkish Civil Society

Turkish civil society is the most developed among all Muslim states of the Middle East. Private groups and organizations are widespread, and their numbers are growing, but their indirect role vis-à-vis the political system is still evolving. The main problem is that they are still too timid to take on the state on an issue as controversial as the Kurdish question. Although major strides have been made by the Turkish government toward accepting the explicit existence of Kurds by the growing use of the word in public discussion in recent years, the magnitude of military operations against the PKK has created a quasi-war situation in which questions about the goals of the war can possibly call into question one's patriotism—a situation not unknown in other countries. Successive Turkish governments over the past years have encouraged nationalist elements to frame the issue precisely as one of patriotism—witness the widespread campaign undertaken by many newspapers, collecting donations for Turkish troops in the southeast and northern Iraq in March and April of 1995 under the slogan "let's back our boys" (*Mehmetçikle el ele*). The campaign had an intimidating effect on anyone inclined to raise questions about the nature, wisdom, or efficacy of the military operation.

General Public Opinion

Understandably, Turkish public opinion has grown less tolerant and more anti-Kurdish over the past decade, as the magnitude of the military struggle has grown. Many families have now lost sons in the army to the conflict, and many parents speak with great anxiety about their sons' early due dates for military service and the risks they entail. Bodies have been coming back from the southeast on a regular basis; at the height of the insurrection, the number of coffins brought to the main Kocatepe Mosque in Ankara for funeral ceremonies before being sent back home would sometimes reach ten a day. While over time the impact of casualties could in principle lead to a popular desire for policy change on the Kurdish issue, so far it seems only to have strengthened right-wing opinion, which is convinced that Turks are more willing to suffer casualties than the softer

Americans. As noted earlier, the extremely nationalist Nationalist Action party (MHP) can only be bolstered by the phenomenon of dead Turkish boys coming home from the front.

Reaction has not been limited to the nationalist Right. There has also been a resurgence in Kemalist secular nationalism in reaction both to Kurdish nationalism and to the rise of Islamic forces and parties. There is an irony, as one author has suggested—with some hyperbole—in the fact that the emergence of the PKK and its terror tactics in the 1980s have done more to define the Turkish identity than seventy years of republican policies aimed at the homogenization the population.[51]

The PKK has itself considered the pros and cons of adopting a policy of total polarization of the population in Turkey. In the past it has sought to publicize its cause and carry it to the mainstream Turkish population via terrorism—especially bomb attacks in the big western cities of Istanbul and Izmir and in major tourist locations such as Antalya. The PKK has reportedly taken credit for these operations, which do indeed polarize the population and create visceral hatred between Turks and Kurds. In one sense, from a harsh PKK point of view, this might be an arguable strategy, if the goal were total separation of the two communities. But it is extremely ill-considered, since the Kurds themselves will be ultimately the biggest losers if urban Turkish workers decide to carry out acts of vengeance against the Kurdish population in western cities and towns. Extreme radical Kurds and extreme Turkish nationalists might share a common goal here, but fortunately both have been restrained from the most violent acts. The PKK mainstream says that it has no quarrel with the Turkish people, only with the state, but even a few urban terrorist acts like this give the lie to that contention.

The ease with which public opinion can be aroused was evidenced in the reaction to the manufactured flag incident at the HADEP convention in June of 1996. Still, in view of the length of this conflict, intercommunal incidents have been kept to a minimum. While many such events have taken place,[52] at times instigated by the news media or local authorities, there is genuine confusion about Kurds within mainstream Turkish public opinion. To begin with, this is a relatively new issue as far as the public is concerned. After all, the very concept of any separate Kurdish identity had been ridiculed for many years as a deliberate feature of state policy; the government has propagated over the years the ideas that Kurds are really just "mountain Turks," that Kurdish is a dialect of Turkish (whereas structurally they are totally unrelated), and that even if Kurds speak a different language, it is debased and not a serious vehicle for communication—hence it is foolish to demand special linguistic rights. By contrast, those Kurds who attempt to raise the issue peacefully or seek state recognition of their identity are portrayed as traitors, separatists, or terrorists. When all Kurdish political activism is automatically identified with the PKK, terrorism, and separatism, dialogue within society becomes impossible.

At this point, the state has created for itself one of the single biggest obstacles to future dialogue: the formation of public opinion that finds the concept of "Kurdish identity" absurd, unnecessary, and subversive, and that all who talk about Kurdish rights are terrorists and enemies of the nation. But because the issue is relatively new to the public, it is also malleable. While the Kurds may be a notable exception, given the size of their population, Turkey has other minorities who have not necessarily articulated any demands but who have always been conscious of their hyphenated nature. The saliency of the Kurds has raised their consciousness. Because of the hard-nosed attitude of state officials, the role of other civil society institutions becomes even more crucial in delimiting the parameters of the Kurdish problem and its resolution.

Intellectuals and the Private Sector

So much of the debate on the Kurdish question has been framed by the perception that it represents an existential threat to Turkey's well-being. Therefore, it is not surprising that the debate in general has been rather muted. The combination of laws that tend to punish speech and the strong sense of patriotic duty imbedded in the Turkish public inhibits a great deal of criticism. This is not to say that there are not pockets of opposition.[53] By and large, intellectuals as a class, especially academic circles, play almost no useful political function, because of their failure to examine and question Kurdish policies. University students do not usually argue over Kurdish issues in class, and faculty do not discuss it among themselves. The issue is functionally nonexistent in academic circles—meaning that a critically important segment of society that is equipped to examine this Turkish social problem is a nonparticipant in stimulating a national conversation.

To be sure there are some notable and brave exceptions to this generalization, but they have been insufficient to sustain a meaningful national dialogue. This situation is not apparently the result of any specific formal government policy; it simply stems from a feeling that it is prudent not to question too openly. Among the more prominent intellectuals, novelists Yasar Kemal and Orhan Pamuk have often expressed their opposition to the military approach to the problem. Yasar Kemal, a Kurd by birth who only recently began to identify himself publicly with the Kurdish struggle, and his younger colleague Pamuk have relied on their international fame to protect them from judicial action. This has not stopped the State Security Courts from charging Kemal with sedition for articles he has published, resulting in the self-exile of this international figure. But such actions are counterproductive internationally because they tend to draw more attention than the Turkish government is willing to tolerate. Some artists, on the other hand, have taken risks on their own, by challenging conventional attitudes and sanctions.[54]

This is not to say that there is no debate in Turkey. There are internationally linked organizations, such as the Helsinki Citizens' Assembly, that have offered Turkish intellectuals a modicum of protection.[55] Another nongovernmental organization created for the explicit purpose of searching for common ground between Turks and Kurds living in Turkey is TOSAV, Toplum Sorunlarini, Araştirma Vakfi or Foundation for the Research of Societal Problems. It too gets its funding from the European Union and the United States. Individuals in academia have spoken out on this question in newspaper articles, and journals such as *Birikim* and *Türkiye Günlüğü* have discussed the problems associated with both Turkish and Kurdish identity formation. The Kurdish question has also given rise to other debates in which the Kurds may not figure directly in prominent fashion. One such debate, influenced by the difficulties the state has had recently with the Kurds, has been on a presumptive "Second Republic," a discussion on recasting the state. As the Islamist thinker Abdurrahman Dilipak has suggested, there are three social forces behind the push for a renewal of state institutions: the Islamists, the Kurds, and the business community.[56]

Islamist intellectuals have received the greatest boost from the reemergence of the Kurdish question. They, unlike their secular counterparts, have an alternative to offer which, in the short term, appears to be nonthreatening to state interests. On the other hand, the Islamist agenda as a whole clearly represents a fundamental challenge to the Kemalist establishment. Because they stress the unity of the two peoples (and of other Muslims as well) within the confines of an Islamic society and abhor the notion of ethnic differences, they possess a natural advantage over their secular counterparts, who can construct a resolution only through compromises along ethnic lines. But are the modern-day Islamist intellectuals and their movements a mirror image of the left wing of the 1970s, for whom the Kurds were nothing but cannon fodder in their struggle against the capitalist system? The Kurdish question has opened another front for the Islamists in their struggle with secularism. As one Islamist thinker openly confesses, as a Muslim, he takes delight in the fact that the Kurdish issue has created the possibility for society to rid itself of this "despotic" Kemalist regime, even though he grieves for all the lives that are being lost in the process.[57] Secular intellectuals challenging the state's official policy have written columns in daily newspapers, but, as will be discussed later, they have had remarkably little impact on policymaking.

Until recently, other segments of society, such as lawyers or businessmen, had not formally stimulated public discussion of these issues either, although many as individuals have spoken out occasionally in the press. Local bar associations in the southeast and Kurdish lawyers in the main cities have been quite active, although they are focused primarily on human rights cases. Human rights foundations have also taken up the cause of individuals imprisoned or tortured by the system. These lawyers have gone about their business in the face of considerable personal risk, as many have disappeared.

More recently, however, Turkish business has begun to openly criticize the rationale behind a military campaign that has burdened the treasury. As such, businessmen have become one of the most liberal elements in Turkey in seeking a political (nonmilitary) solution. Their motivation is purely pragmatic: They are aware of the significant financial drain on the budget and the inflationary impact that the military campaign in the southeast causes. They are also well aware that the conflict has had negative consequences on Turkey's international standing, and that it may have even come close to endangering the accession to the European Customs Union.

The first attempt at an institutional study of the southeast came from the Istanbul-based Economic Development Foundation (Iktisadi Kalkinma Vakfi, IKV). In a far-reaching report, IKV's then head, Sedat Aloglu, discussed a series of economic, social, and cultural reforms, including the creation of institutes for the study of Kurdish and TV and radio broadcasts in Kurdish.[58]

The IKV report was followed by one commissioned by the Turkish

Union of Chambers of Commerce and Industry and Commodity Exchanges (TOBB), the main quasi-official business organization, to which almost all businesses belong. Unlike the IKV report, the TOBB study, because of its methodology and the importance of the institution issuing it, achieved an unprecedented amount of notoriety. IKV was a small foundation that occupied itself mainly with European Union–related concerns, while the TOBB was intimately linked with the state and leading personalities in the center-right parties. Similarly, Sakip Sabanci, one of the two most influential business leaders, also issued a report on the southeast, in which he argued that money alone would not solve the problems of the area and that Turkey had to look at other countries, namely Spain, Britain, and Italy, to learn how to deal with these kinds of ethnic problems.[59] Halis Komili, then leader of TÜSIAD, proclaimed in 1995 the Kurdish question to be Turkey's most severe quandary, saying that without a solution to it, other problems would not be resolved.[60] In January of 1997, TÜSIAD issued a wide-ranging report on the need to deepen the process of democratization in Turkey in which it advocated a number of measures designed to alleviate the cultural and other inequities Kurds face.[61] These concerns of the business circles and interest in a pragmatic approach were best reflected in the genesis of the New Democracy Movement of Cem Boyner, mentioned above, the single most outspoken politician of prominence in the country on this issue. Boyner's efforts also gave an impetus to other young businessmen who have joined the fray: The Young Turkish Businessmen's Council (TÜGIAD) organized missions to the southeast and issued reports advocating a change in the approaches to that region.[61]

All these reports and efforts by individuals have resulted in greater political space in which to discuss these issues, even though they have not yet succeeded in changing policy. Nonetheless, intellectuals and business classes remain the most potent source of opposition to and influence on government policy.

The Media

The Turkish press is one of the most open in the Middle East today, embracing a wide spectrum of views from far left to fundamentalist Islamist and proto-fascist nationalist. Yet this relatively free press has not been so open when it comes to the Kurdish issue, or indeed any issue that directly touches on the national security. It appeared as if most of the press took its guidance on national security issues from the official bulletins of the government, the military, and the National Security Council. Most coverage of fighting was contained in relatively brief stories about the number of PKK terrorists who were captured or killed the day before, or about terrorist incidents carried out by the PKK. Since there was no formal national debate in Parliament or elsewhere about the Kurds, there was no serious debate in the press either, even though this is not, strictly speaking, a government-controlled press. With the exception of columnists, the press finds it safer to avoid probing discussions of the problem; most journalists describe it as "self-censorship," which can often be more stifling on a specific issue than review by a state censorship board.

All is not in solid conformity, however, even in the mainstream press. An important distinction has to be made between the reporting end of the news and columnists. Nearly every day in one paper or another—most often in the more liberal or intellectual papers, or even in the Islamist press—there are analyses or pieces by columnists who take a more critical and thoughtful approach to the Kurdish problem, not directly critical of government policy but reflective on the broader nature of the problem. There is almost an indirect relationship between the level of PKK activities and the ability of columnists, as well as others, to discuss nonmilitary solutions to the Kurdish question. The best such example came about during the cease-fire of 1993, when newspapers were full of stories on the PKK, which—while mostly negative—did not exhibit the hard edge they usually do. The level of discourse in the news media seems also improved when the security apparatus has succeeded in reducing PKK activities. In other words, periods of a weakened PKK threat seem to encourage the freest discourse. This fact may also explain why, over the course of last two years, a gradual, but perceptible, relaxation in the press coverage has taken place. Undoubtedly, the revelations regarding many state-related scandals that implicated senior security officials have encouraged journalists to take greater risks.

On the reporting side of the Kurdish question there is little in the form of investigative journalism, and few attempts are made to question official versions of events, even when more than one version exists. Still, there are exceptions: Even *Milliyet,* a serious paper known for its unsympathetic coverage of things southeast, in the summer of 1995 carried a week-long series on the problems of refugees from the southeast. It left little doubt about the dimensions of the human tragedy and the broad demographic extent of the problem, employing many color pictures of camps, displaced persons, and so forth, even though there was no direct analysis of the deeper roots of the Kurdish problem per se. Turkey's most serious paper today, *Yeni Yüzyil,* is bolder in its critiques of the Kurdish problem than any other mainstream paper. In August 1995 it carried a seven-day series of interviews with Yasar Kemal, Turkey's most famous novelist, himself a Kurd and long-time leftist (although he himself had not chosen to speak out much on the Kurdish issue until the last year). The interview was singularly harsh in its condemnation of state policies against the Kurds from the inception of the Turkish Republic in the 1920s, and in its demands for rights for Kurds. The Islamist press has, in general, been bolder in its criticisms of state policy, whether in its conceptualization or daily conduct of counterinsurgency operations.

There has always been an active Kurdish press, mostly in the Turkish language, although all through the 1960s and 1970s it was continuously harassed and often closed. The magazine with the longest run was one published by Kemal Burkay and his associates in the Socialist party of Turkish Kurdistan. It lasted from the end of 1974 till January 1979.[63] In the 1990s, a number of small dailies were published. These, which included *Özgür Ülke* (Free Country), *Özgür Gündem* (Free Agenda), and *Yeni Politika* (New Politics), concentrated on news from the southeast. They were subjected to judicial campaigns and even were the object of terror and arson attacks, their correspondents and distributors arrested and sometimes killed.[64] At first subjected to censorship by the state, they were later closed down by court order. This was especially true of *Yeni Politika,* which often appeared with huge empty spaces where a news story—but not its headline—had been censored and marked out by bold black lettering reading "censored," until it was closed down by court order in late fall 1995. By December 1995, a new daily, *Demokrasi,* with a decidedly more moderate tone, had emerged to replace it. (Interestingly, *Yeni Politika* is still printed in Europe under the name of *Özgür Politika* and has a broad circulation among Turkish Kurds in Europe.) Paradoxically, the emergence of Med-TV has cut into the circulation of Kurdish dailies such as *Demokrasi,* as people prefer to watch rather than read.

State control over the press, apart from self-censorship, is usually effectuated by allowing papers in principle to print what they want, but then reviewing them after the fact in the courts for revealing national secrets or distributing separatist propaganda.[65] Where security courts find violations they impose serious fines separately on both the paper and the writer of the offending article and confiscate the offending publication. In 1995, 1,443 publications (56 books, 784 journals, 602 newspapers, and 1 bulletin) were confiscated on court order.[66] These fines are generally inordinately high. The writer is also technically subject to prosecution as well. So the penalties for transgressing state policies on the Kurdish issue are considerable.[67] Papers that enjoy much advertising from state-run institutions can also be threatened with loss of advertising. The result is that most papers and most writers prefer not to move too far into the area of bold new coverage and probing analysis.[68] Indeed, many of the popular papers would not pursue such a line in any case, since they purvey a strongly anti-Kurdish line that further hardens public opinion against the Kurds and their "separatism."

The intellectual weakness of the press as an institution was further revealed with the publication of the TOBB-commissioned report conducted by Ankara University professor Dogu Ergil in the summer of 1995. This important, if flawed, report, based on extensive interviews among Kurds, revealed that most Kurds in the southeast do not want a separate Kurdish state. This "TOBB Report" was one of the first of its kind, explicitly dealing with sensitive issues. It was something of a bombshell when it hit the press, sparking widespread discussion and debate, and the potential for a deeper understanding of this sensitive issue. Despite some constructive criticism, however, the debate in the end touched very little on the substance of the issue and the implications for policy. Instead, most columnists and politicians weighed in on ad hominem attacks against the author of the report, Dogu Ergil—some of it quite scurrilous—or against the methodology, or even against the intent behind the preparation of such an analysis. Who authorized this report? What right did the Union of Chambers of Commerce have to delve into these issues, which are outside of its purview? Was not the intent of the research clearly to vindicate the PKK? Are there not some connections between the report and the CIA? In the end, the publication of the TOBB Report has been valuable in opening up, at least slightly, the arena of public debate on the Kurdish issue, even if the media and public response were disappointing.[69]

Despite the discouraging weakness of the press in Turkey, individual journalists reflect in private much greater sensitivity to the issue than is expressed in the news media, even in the more conservative papers. If the state were to change its laws and regulations, more balanced treatment would certainly emerge. The most notorious law in this respect is "Article 8" of the Anti-terrorism Law, which states that anything that serves to support separatism, *intentionally or unintentionally,* can be subject to prosecution. Such broad wording leaves almost any writer vulnerable to action. Article 8, though amended in the days prior to Turkey's accession to the European Customs Union, still allows the continued prosecution of nonviolent speech.[70]

No discussion of the media in Turkey would be complete without some mention of television. In recent years Turkish electronic media have undergone a revolution; the government monopoly of radio and television has been broken, allowing dozens of new radio and television stations to emerge, with a broad spectrum of views, independent of government control. Some of the greatest impact has come from the emergence of talk shows, typically starting around 10 P.M. and lasting until 2 A.M. or sometimes even later.[71] In addition, some of the new stations are primarily local, creating the possibility for dissemination of diverse views with a distinctly local perspective.

This kind of TV coverage has probably contributed more to creating a debate on the Kurdish problem than even the print media—and more boldly, and with a much wider following. Indeed, many commentators have pointed out that programs like "Political Forum" have become a virtual substitute for the Parliament, which has conspicuously failed to discuss this issue of such national importance. This aspect of the media's role is quite heartening, and could obviously be further encouraged by the state if it lifts some of its more restrictive legislation.

However, resisting this trend are the state-controlled media, specifically the radio and television stations. State TV has become the official purveyor of the most uncompromising line on the Kurdish issue. It still refuses to talk of Kurds. It regularly broadcasts what at best can be called crude propaganda pieces, arguing that Kurds are a Turkish tribe and that Kurdish is an invented language.[72] State TV and radio, insofar as they reflect the dominant views of the bureaucracy and military, demonstrate the gulf that exists between civil society and the state.

Ironically, many Kurds in Turkey speak with some bitterness about news media attention to the crises of the Bosnian Muslims and Chechnya.[73]

Turkish press and television coverage has been widespread on Bosnian developments, with pictures of refugees, camps, orphans, and campaigns to help in Bosnia. Yet Kurds believe that the government is encouraging the news media to focus on Bosnia as a distraction from Turkey's internal problems in the southeast. They point out—incorrectly—that the military campaign within Turkey is far greater than in Bosnia, that more Kurds have died than Bosnian Muslims; they claim that there are many millions more Kurdish refugees than Bosnian, and wretched camp conditions that at least parallel those in Bosnia. The heavy media focus on the Bosnians, while maintaining silence on the Kurds at home, is deeply angering to Kurds, who feel it is deliberate and degrading to ignore the even greater suffering of Turkey's own citizens.[74] In sum, the media have not fulfilled the kind of role in the Kurdish debate one might have hoped from a rather free press. But the possibilities for a constructive and creative press role are there, just beneath the surface, if bold and thoughtful leadership will encourage it. Turkey, in effect, is ready to evolve much more rapidly in developing the kinds of capabilities that will enable national debate and a new consensus to emerge. Rabid nationalism, to be sure, can also exploit the media, but there need not be a single voice. The news media can rapidly come to play an important new role in the solution of the Kurdish problem in Turkey—something utterly lacking in almost any other state in the Middle East in the handling of its urgent ethnic and sectarian issues.

Notes and References

1. Military interventions have occurred several times in the last three decades, but the military in each case has eventually voluntarily restored power to civilian politicians and political parties; the military also recognizes that future intervention will come at ever higher cost to itself.

2. Türkiye Büyük Millet Meclisi, *TBMM Tutanak Dergisi,* Vol. 8, (Sira Sayisi 651), October 18, 1994.

3. *Ibid.* The parliamentarian, Esat Canan, went even further by arguing that because the PKK had managed to obtain support from the population by using force, the state ought not imitate this tactic to win the population to its side.

4. See the remarks by Bahri Zengin, a member of Welfare purported to be close to Erbakan, in Helsinki Yurttaslar Meclisi, *Kürt Sorunu Için Baris Insiyatifi* (A Peace Initiative for the Kurdish Question) (Istanbul: Helsinki Yurttaslar Meclisi, n.d.), 69; also see Bahri Zengin, "Çarpiklik Nerde?" (Where is the deformity?) *Aksam,* September 21, 1994.

5. Selami Camci, "Refah Partisi ve Kürt Sorunu: Sorun, Tartismanin Disinda Tutuluyor" *Yeni Safak,* August 12, 1996.

6. Hüsnü Aktas, "Osmanli'dan Günümüze Kürt Meselesi" (The Kurdish issue from Ottoman times to today), *Akit,* July 22 and 29, 1996.

7. Ali Bulaç, "Kürtlerin Gelecegi" (The future of the Kurds), *Yeni Safak,* July 31, 1996.

8. Ali Bulaç, "Bazi Sorulara Cevaplar" (Some answers to questions), *Yeni Safak,* August 1, 1996.

9. See Bulaç's response in Metin Sever, *Kürt Sorunu: Aydinlarimiz ne Düsünüyor?* (The Kurdish question: what do our intellectuals think?) (Istanbul: Cem Yayinevi, 1992), 99–100.

10. Abdurrahman Dilipak, "Kürtler Türklerin Hangi Boyu Idi!" (The Kurds belonged to which of the Turkish tribes) *Akit,* September 18, 1996. Another author advances the same argument about the bankruptcy of the nation state, specifically the Turkish one. He points out that the Kurds who lived peacefully within the Ottoman Empire for hundreds of years are now demanding their identity in the context of the nation-state system. Sükrü Kaner, "Kürt Sorunu ve Ulus-Devlet'in Iflasi" (The Kurdish question and the bankruptcy of the nation state) *Milli Gazete,* June 27, 1994.

11. Selami Camci, "Refah Partisi ve Kürt Sorunu: Milliyetçi Egilimler Yokedilemez" (The Welfare Party and the Kurdish question: nationalist tendencies cannot be destroyed) *Yeni Safak,* August 14, 1996.

12. See for instance, Mustafa Özcan, "Kürt Enstitüsü" (Kurdish Institute), *Yeni Safak,* December 12, 1996.

13. Necmettin Erbakan, for instance, in an October 10, 1993, speech devoted mostly to the Kurdish problem, not only did not shy away from defining the problem as Kurdish (his speech was actually entitled, "Terror, the Kurdish Problem and the Southeastern Question"), but he also enumerated many of the grievances of the region's inhabitants. Rusen Çakir, *Ne Seriat, Ne Demokrasi* (Neither Shari'a nor democracy) (Istanbul: Metis Yayinlari, 1994), 156–157.

14. *Zaman,* August 25, 1994.

15. *Milli Gazete,* July 7, 1996.

16. *Yeni Yüzyil,* March 23, 1996.

17. A 1991 report of the Kurdish question that discussed the issues in an open and frank manner never saw the light of day. For a summary, see Çakir, *Ne Seriat, Ne Demokrasi,* 151–155.

18. There has, in fact, been a proliferation of reports, of different shades, from Welfare's ranks that enable Erbakan to pick and choose among them depending on circumstances. This is far more than other parties have done. In another report, prepared by a Diyarbakir parliamentarian of Kurdish origin, the emphasis was on purely economic solutions (*Milli Gazete,* November 18, 1996).

19. See for instance, Mehmet Metiner, "Refah'in Güneydogu'ya Iliskin Duyarliligi" (Welfare's sensitivity vis à vis the southeast), *Milli Gazete,* August 27, 1994; and "RP'li Heyetin Güneydogu Raporu" (Welfare Party delegation's report on the

southeast) *Milli Gazete,* August 28, 1994. Other Islamist authors have argued the same positions in other papers as well as *Milli Gazete,* which serves as Welfare's mouthpiece.

20. Hamit Bozarslan, "Political Crisis and the Kurdish Issue in Turkey."

21. For a list of the provinces, see Çakir, *Ne Seriat, Ne Demokrasi,* 218. Comparable figures for the 1989 and 1991 elections, when the party did better than in 1977, are seven and one, respectively. The poor performance in 1991 is the result of Welfare's electoral alliance with the Turkish nationalist parties and the electoral alliance formed by HEP with the Social Democrats and SHP.

22. Soon after coming to power in the summer of 1996, Welfare began exploring ways in which TV broadcasts in Kurdish could be aired in the southeast (*Yeni Yüzyil,* July 29, 1996).

23. From Fethullah Erbas's speech in a parliamentary debate. Türkiye Büyük Millet Meclisi, *TBMM Tutanak Dergisi,* Vol. 68, October 18, 1994, 394.

24. Many in Refah believe that the only reason HADEP was allowed to run the December 1995 elections despite "its known connections to the PKK" was to block the ascendancy of the Islamists. For one version of this, see the article by one of Welfare's high command, S. Ârif Emre, "HADEP Taktigi Suya Düstü" (The HADEP maneuver did not succeed) *Milli Gazete,* June 27, 1996. Also Mehmet Sertpolat, "Güneydogu'ya Bir Baska Açidan Bakmak" (The southeast from a different viewpoint) *Milli Gazete,* February 4, 1996.

25. Isin Çelebi, *Siyasette Kilitlenme ve Çözüm* (Deadlock in politics and its solution) (Istanbul: Milliyet Yayinlari, 1996), appendix 3. Bingöl is the only province in which, in 1995, Welfare obtained a majority of the votes cast, with 51.6 percent.

26. Their leader, Hasim Hasimi of Diyarbakir, exploded a small bombshell when he urged the creation of a Kurdish state in northern Iraq. something that not only the military and the mainstream parties abhor but that Erbakan and the rest of Refah also have repatedly opposed. see Hasimi's interview with Ali Bayramoglu in *Yeni Yüzyil,* July 22, 1996. Hasimi, under pressure from his party, had to later renounce some of the statements made in that interview.

27. Dissension among the Kurdish ranks became public on the eve of Welfare's 5th Congress, at which they tried to display their displeasure at the government's lack of action in the southeast (*Radikal,* October 16, 1996).

28. Ironically, when Erbakan became prime minister in June 1996, he agreed to an extension of OPC and, thereby, avoided a conflict with these parliamentarians. Eventually, the force was renewed under another name and with somewhat different characteristics, in December 1996.

29. Rusen Çakir, "Refahyol ve Güneydogu: Ummetçilikten Devletçilige" (The Welfare–TPP coalition and the southeast: From Muslim communitarianism to statism) *Milliyet,* July 28, 1996.

30. The primary protagonist in the effort was an Islamicist author and surprisingly an Alevi, Ismail Nacar, who, with an Islamist human rights organization, Mazlum-Der, was to contact the PKK (*Sabah,* August 3, 1996, *Hürriyet,* August 6, 1996).

31. *Yeni Yüzyil,* July 29, 1996.

32. This even included defending the National Security Council's controversial report, leaked to the press, in which means of reducing fertility among Kurds were debated. Given the high birth rates, the fear expressed by the NSC was that Kurds would make up 40 pecent of the population by 2010, and 50 percent by 2025. For details of the report, see, *Milliyet,* December 18, 1996.

33. Boyner resigned from the party's leadership in 1966.

34. In an April 1995 survey, 11 percent of Kurdish speakers among those polled declared their preference for the New Democracy Movement. In this poll of city dwellers, HADEP was not listed as an option. See International Republican Institute, *Turkey, Survey Results: Attitudes and Priorities of City Dwellers* (Washington, D.C.: International Republican Institute, 1995), 50.

35. They have occasionally attacked prominent establishment figures as well, such as in the case of the Sabanci family, owners of one of the two largest industrial and financial concerns.

36. Fatih Çekirge, "Özel Tim Hacaloglu'nu Tehdit Etti" (Special teams have treated Hacaloğlu) *Sabah,* August 9, 1995.

37. In the 1995 parliamentary elections, CHP enlisted the veteran Kurdish politician Serafettin Elçi to lead its list of candidates in the Kurdish province of Sirnak. Even Elçi could not save the Social Democrats; he was soundly defeated, coming in fourth.

38. *Milliyet,* July 21, 1996.

39. For him, the mere mention of the word *Kurd* has "racist" connotations, while the problem in the southeast has no ethnic or racial origin. See interview with Nilgün Cerrahoglu, *Milliyet,* February 18, 1996. The arch-nationalism of Ecevit has led many to nickname him Alparslan Ecevit, a reference to the late extreme right-wing politician Alparslan Türkes. *Ibid.* By contrast, Ecevit has been at the forefront of those arguing for the distinct rights of the Turcoman minority in northern Iraq, who are ethnically close to Turks.

40. "Demokratik Sol Partinin 'Huzur Saglama Harekati' Yerine Önerdigi Bölgesel Güvenlik Plani" (The Democratic Left party's proposed regional security plan in lieu of Operation Provide Comfort) (Ankara: Demokratik Sol Parti (mimeo), 1996).

41. In the coalition government which replaced the Welfare–True Path party one in June 1997, Ecevit not only emerged as deputy prime minister, but also as the cabinet member with overall responsibility for the southeast. The new government's overtures on the southeast have been true to Ecevit's rhetoric: The focus is completely on the economic side and requires greater involvement by state institutions.

42. See former Interior minister Nahit Mentese's remarks in Parliament regarding the southeast. Türkiye Büyük Millet Meclisi, *TBMM Tutanak Dergisi,* Vol. 68, October 18, 1994, 401.

43. Among them are Mehmet Agar, former chief of national security; Ünal Erkan, former supergovernor of the provinces ruled by emergency decree; Necdet

Menzir, former head of the security services in Istanbul; and Hayri Kozakçioglu, another former supergovernor. The latter two have resigned from the party to protest the coalition with Erbakan's Welfare party.

44. Party vice president, Mehmet Gölhan, initially signaled his approval (*Hürriyet,* August 6, 1996).

45. *Milliyet,* August 7, 1996.

46. *Yeni Yüzyil,* March 13, 1996.

47. *Yeni Yüzyil,* March 23, 1996. For a skeptical view of Yilmaz's promises, see Ali Bayramoglu, "Kürt Sorunu ve Yilmaz" (The Kurdish question and Yilmaz), *Ibid.*

48. Kurdish members, for instance, were upset that in the elections for party leadership positions, Turkish nationalists seemed to have gained at their expense (*Yeni Yüzyil,* August 27, 1996). Even Özal could not always hold his Kurdish constituency completely in line. See interview with Nurettin Yilmaz, former Mardin representative and Özal supporter, who rebelled against Özal following a Turkish military incursion into northern Iraq (*Nokta,* August 18, 1991).

49. Türkes died on April 4, 1997. It remains to be seen what influence his successor, Devlet Bahçeli, will have.

50. *Milliyet,* December 5, 1994. Türkes criticized Sakip Sabanci, the prominent industrialist who urged alternative solutions to the problem (*Milliyet,* October 6, 1995).

51. Mümtaz'er Türköne, "Kürt Kimligi: Çözüm Nerede?" (Kurdish identity: Where is the solution?) *Türkiye Günlügü* 33 (March–April 1995), 31.

52. The town of Erdemli in the province of Içel was the scene for such an intercommunal incident when a fight between two individuals ended with the death of one and a subsequent riot that saw the destruction of many businesses (*Yeni Yüzyil,* March 11, 1996).

53. There have been occasional bold attempts, such as the volume organized by Metin Sever (*Kürt Sorunu: Aydinlarimiz ne Diyor?*), in which numerous intellectuals discuss their vision of the problem. Some in that volume, such as Asaf Savas Akat, went so far as to advocate a dialogue with the PKK (see p. 13).

54. The singer Ahmet Kaya, for instance, performed on Med-TV.

55. See, for instance, the report published by the Helsinki Citizens' Assembly summarizing discussions at its February 1992 meeting (Helsinki Yurttaslar Meclisi, *Kürt Sorunu Için Baris Insiyatifi*). In addition, the Helsinki Citizen's Assembly has initiated sister city programs that link towns in the Southeast with others around the nation.

56. Metin Sever and Cem Dizdar, eds. *Ikinci Cumhuriyet Tartismalari* (Discussions on the second republic) (Ankara: Basak Yayinlari, 1993), 403–4.

57. Yilmaz Yalçiner, "Sedat Bucak'i Izlerken . . ." (Following Sedat Bucak . . .) *Akit,* November 23, 1996.

58. *Sabah,* November 7, 1994. Sedat Aloglu, who was elected as a DYP parliamentarian in the December 1995 elections as an ally of Tansu Çiller, reissued the IKV report, this time under his own name, at a DYP Istanbul party organization

meeting on April 6, 1996. In both cases he has argued that the distinctiveness of Kurdish ethnicity ought to be accepted and can no longer be questioned ("Dogu ve Güneydogu" [The east and the southeast], mimeo, 9). Dogan Güres, the former hardline chief of staff and parliamentary colleague of Aloglu, has endorsed this report; he claimed to have agreed with 90 percent of its content (Hasan Cemal, "Dogan Güres Pasa'dan: Terör Baska Kürt Baska, Bunu Görmek Lazim!" (General Doğan Güres: We must see the difference between terrorism and Kurds) *Sabah,* April 13, 1996).

59. *Hürriyet,* September 30, 1995. For his efforts, Sabanci was investigated by the State Security Court.

60. *Hürriyet,* December 22, 1995. Another influential businessman reiterated the same thoughts in an interview with the English daily, in which he blames the high rate of inflation on two factors, one of which is the quasi-war in the southeast, and urges the state to seek nonmilitary solutions. Interview with Can Paker, CEO of Türk Henkel, *Turkish Daily News,* December 23, 1995, B1.

61. The report went well beyond the Kurdish issue. While TÜSIAD called on the state to allow people to freely name their children, teach Kurdish and broadcast in Kurdish it also questioned the democratic legitimacy of military-based institutions, such as the National Security Council. TÜSIAD, *Türkiye'de Demokratikleşme Perspektileri* (Istanbul: TÜSIAD, 1997).

62. Murat Bekdik, "Güneydoguda Çözüm Için 'Anlayis Reformu' Gerekli" (A solution to the Southeast is only possible through a reform of the mindset), *Zaman,* December 6, 1996. Also see *Millyet,* September 3, 1996.

63. For a discussion of the Kurdish press, see Kemal Burkay, *Geçmisten Bugüne Kürtler ve Kürdistan* (The Kurds and Kurdistan: From the past to today), Vol. 1 (Istanbul: Deng Yayinlari, 1992), 267–73.

64. Mark Muller, "Nationalism and the Rule of Law in Turkey: The Elimination of Kurdish Representation during the 1990s," in *The Kurdish Nationalist Movement in the 1990s,* ed. Olson, 184.

65. The National Security Council decided in 1995 to increase the pressure on extreme left-wing and right-wing, as well as separatist, publications, so much so that it was decried by an influential and moderate columnist as nothing but censorship. See Oktay Eksi, "MGK, yoksa aklini mi yitirdi?" (Has the National Security Council lost its mind?) *Hürriyet,* July 27, 1995.

66. U.S. State Department, *Turkey: Human Rights Report, 1996.*

67. Nothing seems to escape the notice of the State Security Courts. On April 4, 1997, the presenter on Environment Radio (Çevre Radyosu) was sentenced to a prison term for a program aired on that radio station that questioned the state's version of a massacre in which a number of village guards had been killed. The station had interviewed the families of the dead men (*Anadolu Ajansi,* April 4, 1997).

68. Another worrisome development is the extent to which large corporations in control of media empires have used their assets in pursuit of political and economic gains. This became painfully apparent during the 1995 election campaign

when *Sabah,* reputed to have received a large infusion of credit from the Çiller government, unabashedly supported the government, while *Milliyet* and *Hürriyet* did exactly the opposite, backing the ANAP. Lost in the heat of the debate was the fact that both sets of newspapers, as well as others, twisted the facts and engaged in exceedingly biased coverage, further damaging the little credibility they may have had on these issues.

69. One interesting aspect of the TOBB Report was that it was commissioned by TOBB Chairman Yalim Erez, a close confidant of Prime Minister Çiller, and elected as a member of Parliament from Mugla in the December 24, 1995, election. It is inconceivable to think that the report was commissioned and published without her advance knowledge. Yet the prime minister denied any knowledge and expressed her own doubts about the methodology behind the report. Still, the report proved to be a useful—if only temporary—vehicle to start a national discussion on the issue.

70. Human Rights Watch/Helsinki, *Turkey: Torture and Mistreatment in Pre-Trial Detention by Anti-Terror Police* (New York: Human Rights Watch, 1997), 40.

71. In late 1994, the weekly discussion program "Siyaset Meydani" (Political Arena) devoted a session to problems in the southeast that commanded immense public attention and lasted until seven in the morning. It was seen across Turkey, including a massive viewership all over the southeast. Other programs have talked about various aspects of the Kurdish problem, with some caution but nonetheless quite openly, with many points of view represented in the debate. The on-again, off-again *Siyaset Meydani* is watched regularly by 34 percent of city dwellers according to one survey. International Republican Institute, *Turkey, Survey Results: Attitudes and Priorities of City Dwellers,* 59.

72. Ertürk Yöndem on "Perde Arkasi," October 12, 1994, quoted in Koray Düzgören, "Türkiye'nin Kürt Çikmazi: Sorunun Tanimi ve Gerçekler" (Turkey's Kurdish dead-end: Its definition and realities) in Seyfettin Gürsel et al., *Türkiye'nin Kürt Sorunu,* 13.

73. For instance, see Alinak, *HEP, DEP, ve Devlet: Parlamento'dan 9. Kogusa,* 220.

74. Similarly, Kurds were very affected by the Turkish response to the Bulgarian government's attempts at eradicating any semblance of Turkish culture in Bulgaria. Ankara understandably began a campaign against the communist rulers in Sofia, who forcibly tried to slavicize place and even family names in order to compel assimilation. Yet, for Turkish Kurds, the Bulgarian policies were no different than those they had been experiencing. The same applies to harsh Turkish government and press criticism of assimilationist policies against ethnic Turks in Greece—often paralleling Turkish assimilationist policies in the southeast. On a parallel with the Turks of Cyprus, see Server Tanilli, "Kürt Gerçekligi ' ni Tanimanin Anayasal ve Yasal Gerekleri Üstüne bir Taslak" (A proposal on the legal and constitutional requirements for the Kurdish reality) in Türk-Kürt Dostluk Girisimi, *Kürt Sorunu: Aydinlar ne Diyor?* (The Kurdish question: What do intellectuals say?) (Istanbul: Belge Yayinlari, 1994), 102. After reciting Kurdish population figures, Tanilli pointedly asks, "Should such a population not have the same rights as those 100,000 Turks on Cyprus?"

5

Turkish Government Policies in the Southeast

I T IS IMPOSSIBLE TO identify a single locus of Kurdish policymaking within the Turkish state, although the National Security Council is the single most important institution. The policy grows out of a long-time elite circle of Turkish politicians and statesmen imbued with the conviction that this is a unitary state with a uniform national identity: It has had a hard time admitting the presence of alternative national identities. This Kemalist consensus is strengthened by an ever-vigilant army that, in the past, has not shied away from expressing its preferences or intervening. These policies continue to be fostered by the silence or noninvolvement of most of the press, intellectuals, civil society, and political parties. This is not to say that the Kemalist consensus is immutable: During his presidency, Özal managed to challenge it and introduce new ideas and open new realms of inquiry and thinking. He did this almost single-handedly, and often with members of his own party opposing him.

Policy in the southeast has relied almost exclusively on the military option. As we note below, with massive infusions of manpower in tandem with better tactics and weaponry and sheer brute force, the state has managed to reclaim some if not most of the areas once under PKK control (especially at night, when the PKK would roam unimpeded). This has been achieved at a tremendous cost: large-scale village evacuations and increasing refugee population, widespread human rights abuses, and the like. Still, despite this infusion of manpower and matériel, the military option has not produced the ultimate desired result: the permanent eradication of the PKK and the insurgency, even if it is currently contained within some acceptable limit of violence for the time being. More important, it is unlikely to achieve it in the foreseeable future.

As with the PLO and other nationalist organizations, the PKK does not need to score a military victory—indeed, it cannot ever do so—against the Turkish army. There is no hope for a PKK "revolution" in Turkey that could change the facts on the ground. But the PKK does not need a military victory to have major impact; all it requires is to survive and continue to propagate the cause. It may well be that the PKK itself will not even be the beneficiary of its guerrilla and political activities, but that it will create the groundwork whereby future political activities by other Kurdish parties (possibly including a transformed PKK) will be able to take place. By merely surviving, the PKK defies defeat and must still be considered to be making political progress as the process of consciousness-raising goes on among Kurds.

Kurdish policy resides primarily in several key institutions: the president, prime minister, the military high command, and the National Security Council. The implementation of the policy falls to the armed forces National Intelligence Organization (MIT), the judicial system, the gendarmerie, and a variety of security services, such as the National Security Organization. The instruments and institutions employed by the state to handle the Kurdish problem clearly reflect the state's conviction that the problem is primarily one of security, law and order, and violence promoted by external powers. Hence, if the violence can be suppressed, then most of the problem will have been taken care of. More thoughtful policymakers certainly recognize that other problems exist in the southeast as well—they are primarily economic—but these difficulties are to be put on hold until the "terrorism" comes to an end. There is no question that the PKK regularly engages in political violence, by which we mean attacks against state security forces and institutions, and also in terror—that is, violence against innocent civilians. The real problem for the state is not just the PKK, however, but, as argued earlier, one of rising Kurdish consciousness and identity.

The way the problem is defined also tends to define the methods employed in the solution; in this case, given the prevailing consensus that the problem is basically one of "terror," many elements of the state act along these same lines. The courts, and especially the State Security Courts, do not have to get directions from political higher-ups in order to launch investigations of potential suspects or to close down parties. Precisely because there is no central coordinating body—the closest to this is the National Security Council—at times these institutions may even appear to be operating at cross purposes. Still, they rarely stray too far from the consensus, even though it is possible, as Özal demonstrated in the final years of his life, to challenge this consensus.

The President and the Prime Minister

The 1982 constitution, adopted during the 1980–83 military interregnum, increased the powers of the presidency over the very nominal ones that had existed previously. But in functional terms, the power of the president remains that of a bulwark—that is, containing rather than initiating change. It is the prime minister who is responsible for originating policy. Despite such constraints, the era of Turgut Özal, first as prime minister and later as president, represented the high point of political leadership. In the hands of Özal, the presidency was transformed into an activist office, not just on the Kurdish issue but also on foreign and economic policy.

Faced with a world order, especially a regional order, transformed in the onset of the 1990–91 Gulf Crisis, Özal maneuvered his country's domestic and foreign policy away from its intransigent attitude vis-à-vis the Kurds. Having established some of the institutional mechanisms of repression in the southeast himself, such as the village guards and the emergency rule system, he decided to relax domestic restrictions on the use of Kurdish, engaged in the Iraqi Kurdish factions in a dialogue, and, instead of excluding the HEP members of parliament, he made use of them to push the PKK to moderate its views.[1]

Özal, who claimed partial Kurdish ancestry himself, carried out the major breakthroughs in lifting the veil of secrecy and silence on the Kurdish problem and began to treat it as a reality and as a problem requiring concentrated reform, not just suppression. What we have termed "progress" here in recognizing realities was viewed by many within the state structure as opening Pandora's box and exacerbating the problem. Indeed, there can be little doubt that Özal's policies of open recognition of the problem and of the need for cultural concessions to the Kurds has in fact accelerated the process of building expectations, if not demands, by the Kurdish public, and of heightening the ethnic consciousness-raising process. These processes were certain to come in any case—it has been only a question of when and how. Özal was quite conscious of what he was doing; he told an interviewer that Turkey was being held back from progress by a series of taboos and that he was intent on challenging them.[2] He even mused that he was ready to discuss everything, including a federation.

In effect, Özal was successful in shifting the terms of the debate within the state and in introducing alternative approaches. Thus the real question became how long suppression of the Kurdish problem could "work" as the key government policy. Hard-liners within the Turkish establishment argue to this day that concessions serve only to exacerbate the problem; liberals argue—primarily behind closed doors—that a broad policy review and reform are the only means of coping with long-range Kurdish expectations, especially if the problem is to be solved before separatism becomes the only remaining answer. Özal's success came despite the opposition from powerful institutional interests within the state, including, from late 1991 to April 1993, his prime minister, Demirel.

Upon Özal's untimely death in April 1993, Demirel assumed the presidency. Despite his declarations upon his election in 1991 as prime minister that he "now recognized Turkey's Kurdish reality," Demirel proceeded to reverse Özal's reforms and permitted relations with the Iraqi Kurdish factions to deteriorate. He brought no new thinking to the problem and sided with the hard-liners as he increasingly expressed the view that Turkey did not have a Kurdish problem, but a terrorism one. For Demirel, any talk of cultural rights is tantamount to dividing the country, and foreign criticisms of the government's policy along these lines represent a return to Sèvres.[3] In the absence of someone like Özal, who either prodded the bureaucracy to come up with new ideas or simply bypassed it, Turkish policy settled back into its comfortable Kemalist niche of denial of the Kurdish identity.[4] And when in 1996 a new prime minister, Necmettin Erbakan, sought to engage the PKK in an indirect dialogue to explore the possibilities that the Kurdish militants might lay down their arms, it was Demirel who interceded to impede the contacts from going forward. He publicly acknowledged and took credit for his role in this affair and justified it by arguing that "if he was made to feel uncomfortable by the whole episode then everyone in society and state, including the military, would feel uneasy at such a prospect."[5]

Demirel, never comfortable with Özal's entreaties, was quick to change course upon assuming the presidency. As one of the political leaders who had dominated Turkish politics since the early 1960s, Demirel had never demonstrated any sensitivity to the Kurdish question. With Özal out of the way he reverted to his old stand; the "Kurdish reality" sentence that had caused the expectations of Kurds to soar simply became moot. Between the 1991 elections and his assumption of the presidency in 1993, Demirel also witnessed the rise and fall of HEP and all the attendant problems that party had given rise to. Hence, in addition to his conservative instincts on this issue and in spite of all his promises of restoring real democracy to Turkey, Demirel had become uneasy about the issue. This uneasiness enabled the hard-liners, especially those in the armed forces, to convince him that reform would ultimately entail separation.

With Demirel's ascendance to the presidency, the new prime minister, Tansu Çiller, a novice when it came to policymaking, was nonetheless determined not to be dominated by a president with decades of experience in Turkish politics. The resulting testy working relationship, unlike Özal's with his own prime minister, more closely resembled what the constitution had envisaged. Whether it was because of her desire to differentiate herself from the president whose party she had just taken over or naïveté, Çiller's initial reaction was to seek the means for quick reconciliation. She floated a number of ideas: The first was a suggestion to create a civilian and parliament-based National Security Council that could investigate the Kurdish issue; second, she proposed Kurdish broadcasts on state-owned television as well as optional classes in Kurdish. All of these ideas, including the "Basque model" as a potential formula for resolving Turkey's ethnic problem—a suggestion made following a meeting in Vienna with Spanish prime minister Felipe Gonzales—were shot down. Demirel, by arguing that concessions could not be made while terrorism was rampant, and the chief of the general staff, Dogan Güres, by pointing out that the proper place to discuss these issues was the National Security Council, put an end to these discussions.[6] In fact, what Çiller proposed was to civilianize the regime further and to reduce the influence of the military high command; as such, it was quite revolutionary. Yet, faced with these criticisms, Çiller rapidly backed off further personal interest in the problem and turned over conduct of the Kurdish policy to the military. Underlying Çiller's quick change in policy was her need to consolidate her position within her party; she had been elected as a surprise candidate over two better established political leaders. The party was replete with cliques that owed their allegiance to different personalities, ranging from President Demirel to the former speaker of parliament, Hüsamettin Cindoruk. Her proposals were clearly undermining her hold on the party and endangering her position. It was to safeguard them that she executed a complete turnaround in policy.

Having committed herself to a hard line, Çiller embraced the policy of equating all things Kurdish with the PKK. In the process, she used her newly gained steadfastness to her political advantage. She engineered the closing down of the DEP and the imprisonment of its deputies in the weeks leading to the 1994 municipal elections, and then based her electoral campaign almost wholly on that issue.[7] As a policy issue, the Kurdish question was reduced to eliminating the PKK, body counts, and cross-border raids, leading to a significant increase in human rights violations. Few believed her annual announcements of proposed expenditures to improve the conditions in the southeast.[8] She was pragmatic enough to know when to make, or at least appear to make, concessions: Pressed by the Europeans and the U.S. to remove or reform some of the more egregious and antidemocratic aspects of the penal code and the constitution, she complied to ensure Turkey's accession to the European Customs Union. Despite Turkey's return to coalition politics after the 1991 elections, Çiller had considerable room to maneuver on the Kurdish issue precisely because the Republicans in her coalition government were already committed to a "softer" line on the southeast. In other words, just like Özal, she did command a majority in Parliament.

Her strategy worked: By the onset of the 1995 national elections, she had eviscerated the party apparatus and replaced many of its members with her loyalists. In a remarkable testimony to her abilities, she succeeded in recruiting many of the hard-liners on the Kurdish question as parliamentary candidates, including the former chief of staff who had bitterly opposed her initial overtures to the Kurds. Few of these new members of Parliament had local constituencies of their own and they were, therefore, expected to be totally dependent on her for their position. In effect, by aligning herself with the military chiefs and winning their confidence, Çiller outmaneuvered them and the president.[9] At the end of her tenure as prime minister, the possibility of meaningful change in Kurdish policy appeared unlikely, even though with her credentials as a hard-liner, U.S.

support, and Turkey's successful adhesion to the customs union, Çiller had built up enough political capital to initiate creative change had she won a mandate on her own.[10]

In general, the office of the prime minister in Turkey, as in many parliamentary systems, is equipped with significant powers, setting and dominating the country's daily agenda. As Özal demonstrated when prime minister and facing a military president, it was possible to shape and direct the nature and direction of the national debate. In fact, part of Özal's agenda was to "civilianize" Turkish politics by reducing military prerogatives and making the institution more responsive to the civilian leadership.[11] Nevertheless, the general perception among Turkish politicians is that the "state" is more powerful than an elected government.[12] By appearing to go along with the established view on the Kurdish question during his premiership, Erbakan has given credence to this notion. Unable to make overtures to the likes of Syria and constrained from deepening the relationship with Iran, Erbakan found that his preferred way of resolving the Kurdish question, by engaging Turkey's neighbors actively involved in supporting the PKK, was blocked.[13]

Because he already represented a challenge to the country's secular makeup and was, therefore, viewed with suspicion by the country's civilian and military elites, Erbakan was handicapped in his ability to approach the Kurdish question. Arguing that significant successes had been scored against terrorism, Erbakan in April 1997 announced yet another plan that emphasized the economic development of the southeast. It envisaged a seven-year, $32 billion investment initiative encompassing twenty-five provinces.[14] Not surprisingly, the plan was devoid of any of the social and cultural initiatives he and his party had hitherto emphasized.

The Military

For over a decade now, the military has borne the main burden of fighting the Kurdish uprising. As the traditional guardian since Atatürk, of Turkish security in the broadest sense, the military naturally plays a dominant role in not just the execution but also the shaping of policy in the Kurdish situation as well. Since president Özal's death, however, the civilian leadership has abdicated its share of the responsibility for devising and implementing policies toward the southeast. By directing the army to spearhead policies to cope with the problem, the civilian leadership has abandoned other policy instruments, leaving armed force the sole implement for dealing with the southeast problem.

The military's effectiveness in the southeast has increased considerably as it gained experience fighting an unconventional enemy. First and foremost, the region was saturated with conventional army troops. The total deployment of Turkish troops in the southeast dedicated to the defeat of the PKK is around 220,000,[15] not including the special forces and village guards. Second, considerable efforts were expended to acquire better intelligence and mobility. Over time, well-conditioned troops have been able to take the fight to the PKK, rather than conducting a static defense. The night, which used to belong to the PKK in the region, is increasingly contested and won by better trained and, more important, mobile troops. The army has also integrated the use of helicopters that provide it with faster response time and are able to take soldiers into areas difficult to reach by conventional methods. It also engages in large cross-border operations in addition to what are now routine small-scale raids into Iraq and aerial bombings. The largest such operation was conducted in March and April of 1995, when 35,000 troops crossed the border to push back the PKK and disrupt its logistical capabilities. Another, begun in May of 1997, was rumored to have entailed as many as 50,000 troops.

The policy of saturating the region with regular troops has meant that "the war has become an army responsibility."[16] These efforts have paid off in many respects. The PKK is now on the defensive throughout the region, its ability to strike at will has diminished considerably, and the tactical initiative belongs to the military. In Tunceli, for instance, "terrorist" incidents have declined by 75 percent since 1995.[17] The military high command is sufficiently confident of the progress it has achieved to suggest, as the chief of the Navy, Admiral Güven Erkaya, did, that "radical Islamic movements pose[d] a bigger threat today than the PKK."[18] Still, despite all these efforts, the military has yet to deliver a blow strong enough to destroy the PKK. In the medium and long run, the army will, in all likelihood, continue to maintain a very large presence in the region, to fend off a PKK comeback and preserve the new status quo.

It would be a mistake to assume that the military has unilaterally and enthusiastically taken charge of the Kurdish problem. The armed forces, as one of Turkey's elite institutions, contain a broad spectrum of thinking. The army, furthermore, has a better grasp of the realities of the southeast than almost any other government entity. It has tens of thousands of soldiers in the field who daily witness the conditions of life, the sufferings of the civilian population, the terrible social dislocations that emerge from the wholesale razing of villages, the sufferings in the refugee camps, and the peremptory and often arbitrary treatment that the local population regularly encounters in most of the southeast.[19] To some extent, the army has been tarnished by the behavior of the gendarmerie (jandarma), the special teams, and village guards. The gendarmerie, the rural soldiers, have historically played a key role in the internal security of the country. It is especially in the Kurdish areas that it has been most prominent. Unlike regular troops, gendarmerie conscripts are not well trained. They are more susceptible to committing human rights violations and, as a result, have been traditionally detested by the local populations.[20] Nor has the regular army been immune from allegations of the mistreatment of local inhabitants. In addition, the emergence of "gangs" within the armed forces with connections to Mafia-type criminal organizations is likely to have a deleterious impact on both morale and the military's reputation.[21]

Cognizant of this, and in order to combat any deepening alienation of the local population, the military high command has also taken steps to reduce human rights abuses committed by its soldiers. The Chief of the General Staff Directorate published a small booklet in 1995 to be carried by every soldier. It calls on them to get to know the local population, to be respectful of their customs and needs, and, most important, not to abuse them physically or otherwise.[22]

The military also knows the number of casualties that this conflict is inflicting upon its troops, and the growing concern among the population for these losses. It is aware that the use of the army for such internal security reasons is not really the first duty of the armed forces and that it damages its standing among broad elements of the population. The heavy costs of the campaign prevent the army from carrying out the modernization program that it had planned a long time ago. The requirements of the Kurdish campaign forced the military to do an about-face and extend the period of conscription, after having reduced it.[23] It has also suffered from a credibility problem: It has annually assured the public of its imminent victory over the PKK, only to announce another final offensive the following year.[24] The army knows, too, that Turkey's relations with Western Europe and the U.S. are being affected in ways that bear directly on the military budget: Its image has been tarnished abroad; several countries have warned Turkey about the use of NATO equipment against the Kurdish population; and the anti-Kurdish campaign provides excuses for the U.S. military aid budget to be cut by Congress. Clearly, however, other considerations play a more important role in their thinking.

The internal deliberations of the top military leadership are not generally made public, so it is difficult for the outside observer to comment with any authority on its thinking. But from available evidence it seems apparent—and logical—that the top military leadership cannot be of one mind on this conflict. After thirteen years of conflict in the southeast, the military itself may recognize the need for some kind of broader political solution than the civilian leadership has been able to formulate. The retired chief of staff, Dogan Güres, who has had time to reflect on his experiences, has suggested that the art of governance is to find or, more important, to create the right moment, conditions, and opportunities to move public opinion in the direction of a solution that is not totally military in content.[25]

The strict hierarchical system does not allow for a great deal of questioning of policy within the institution. The dilemma for the military, as the most Kemalist of Turkish institutions, lies in the recognition of a Kurdish reality that violates the very essence of their "Kemalist ideology" in its latter-day form.[26] This is especially true of the higher-ranking officers whose careers were made not in the southeast but in traditional posts well before the intensification of the Kurdish question.

Moreover, the military hierarchy cannot publicly muse about "political solutions" while it simultaneously seeks to send young recruits into the difficult terrain of the southeast. Unlike a struggle against a foreign enemy, this one is made more difficult by the very fact that it is a domestic insurrection in which the opposing side is characterized as traitorous.[27] The difficult geopolitical position Turkey has found itself in since independence, on the edge of a strategically vital region with plenty of real and potential enemies surrounding it, also explains why it has approached this particular conflict from the perspective of the nineteenth century. The fear of losing any more territory is inculcated into not just the military mind but also into those of civilians (all Demirel has to do to refute an argument is use the magical word *Sèvres,* invoking the memory of the now infamous 1920 treaty, which sought to dismember much of Anatolia itself). Most disturbing, some upper echelons of the military have even gone to great length to claim that Kurds do not, in fact, exist.[28]

Thus, whatever examples there are of both enlightened and unenlightened thinking within the military, and no matter what individual officers may think about the conflict, the military as an institution has weighed in heavily against any kind of political accommodation. A key factor may be that top officers have found Turkey's democratic institutions all to be wanting, and hence they don't trust them to find a solution. They have been made unhappy by the continuous political infighting in Ankara, the media (and especially the private television channels), the Parliament's inability to act quickly, the number of inexperienced politicians, and loose talk of a political solution to the Kurdish question. Many of them therefore expect the civilian leadership to give them a carte blanche in fighting terrorism.[29] In the final analysis it will require recognition by thoughtful top leadership of the military that a political solution is the only answer before progress can be made. We do not view such a development as far-fetched, but we are concerned that things may have to get worse before such recognition emerges, much less before it is politically acceptable within the security structure.

The National Security Council

When it comes to the Kurdish question, the National Security Council (NSC) is the most influential state body. It is a civilian-military institution first created in the aftermath of the 1960 coup, designed as an overseer of civilian authority. It was revamped following the 1980 military intervention.[30] It was a reflection of the deep misgivings the soldiers have had of civilian leadership.[31] While its powers are officially limited to an advisory capacity, its composition potentially makes it the most important body in the country. Presided over by the president of the republic, the body contains as permanent members the prime minister, the ministers of defense, foreign affairs, and interior, as well as the chief of staff and the heads of all the services including the gendarmarie. In addition, the undersecretaries for the MIT and foreign ministry are always present in the deliberations. Other cabinet members can be invited if their expertise is needed. The careful balance between the military and the civilians was expected to work in favor of the military, since the 1980 coup-makers assumed that the president would come from their ranks, as he has done so often in modern Turkish history.

The 1982 constitution envisages that the council of ministers give priority to the NSC's suggestions, and it does not limit the scope of the council's interest: Anything that is considered threatening to the unity and existence of the state is fair game. In practice, the NSC has proffered opinions ranging from renewing Operation Provide Comfort (despite the overwhelming sentiment in Parliament that it be terminated) to renewing the state of emergency in the southeast to deciding the curriculum in schools.[32] It is not clear how much dissent the NSC tolerates in its proceedings; according to one former chief of staff, decisions are taken on the basis of consensus.[33]

For all its powers the NSC is not omnipotent, and its automatic pro-military majority was upset when Özal managed to get himself elected president in 1989. He also showed how the NSC could be led by one individual, a civilian, if that person proves to be forceful enough to marshal the resources available to him. When the Gulf conflict erupted, Özal took command of the NSC and single-handedly shaped a new foreign policy for Turkey, despite the objections of the military, which caused a crisis within the military establishment.[34] If Özal could push the NSC in the direction he wanted, it was because, against a unified military, he too could put together a coalition of civilians—as president. Initially, he had a compliant prime minister from his own political party, which, in turn, controlled a majority of the seats in parliament. With them he had control over vast sections of the civilian, political, and bureaucratic forces needed to support him. This is not to say that he got his way every time and, in fact, he did face some opposition after 1991, when his party lost the elections.

This differs greatly from the situation following his death, when intraparty bickering and conflict, weak leaders in search of allies, and, by and large, leaders without a vision could not propose alternative policies to the NSC's military contingent. It is therefore easy to see, in the post-Özal deliberations of the NSC, how both president Demirel and Prime Minister Çiller, neither of whom were strongly committed to reform on the Kurdish policy, readily agreed to go along with the least common denominator—that is, the continuation of the military policy. In 1994, the NSC suggested its own "solution" to the problem of the southeast: It requested significant increases in the firepower available to the armed forces, rejected any suggestion of concessions on Kurdish language rights, and, on the contrary, insisted that education in the region focus on "Turkish culture and identity."[35] As far as the government at the time was concerned, the junior coalition member, SHP, was on record with ideas in direct opposition to the NSC's suggestions. Clearly, the SHP, at the time represented by the foreign minister in the NSC, had little or no impact on the final outcome.

In the final analysis, the NSC derives a great deal of its power from the divisions among the civilians: For instance, when, early on, Çiller suggested the creation of a civilian body within Parliament that would parallel the NSC, she was stopped in her tracks by the president, the speaker of Parliament, opposition from other quarters in her own party, and the main opposition leader.[36] Hence, if the NSC is to take the lead on reformulating policy on the Kurdish question, the initiative will have to come either from a unified civilian leadership that has thought through the consequences of its actions, or from the military high command. Erbakan, who did not face the constraints Çiller did, could have challenged the NSC on this issue, but the increasing acrimony between the Welfare party and the officers over supposed violations of secularist principles has dampened any enthusiasm Erbakan may have had for tackling the volatile Kurdish issue. The success that the NSC has had in forcing out the Erbakan-led government—through a process begun with a February 28, 1997, NSC meeting, in which the military hierarchy dictated some twenty demands to the civilians—has clearly reaffirmed the power of this quasi-military institution in all aspects of Turkish political life, including the future of the Kurdish issue. Having said this, it is also important to note that the NSC has, for the first time, hinted at the possibility that measures other than military and economic ought to be considered: A statement after the March 31, 1997, NSC meeting stated that "in the east and southeast, economic, social, cultural, and psychological measures ought to be speeded up."[37]

The National Intelligence Organization

The National Intelligence Organization, MIT, like the military, is deeply involved in security operations in the southeast. Traditionally, it has followed the activities of all those suspected of what the state calls *Kürtçülük*, or Kurdish nationalist activities. MIT has been increasingly active in Europe and in northern Iraq, where three of its operatives, working under the cover of the Turkish Red Crescent, were murdered by Iraqi Kurds angered at the killing of their brethren by Turkish army troops during the incursion into Iraq in March and April of 1995.

The organization, while "attached" to the office of the prime minister, is, in fact, more influenced by the armed forces. The present undersecretary of the MIT is a civilian, which is a departure from the norm. His appointment is decided by the NSC with the prime minister's consent and the president's approval. The bulk of the MIT's officers come from the military, and all decisions concerning their promotion, retirement, and assignment are decided by the armed forces.[38] The MIT is not heavily involved in the broad charting of government policy on the Kurds, even though it is deeply involved in the routine collection of intelligence and the implementation of government policy. As with many intelligence organizations, the MIT probably has a good feel for the situation in the southeast and reportedly does not as an institution hold necessarily hard-line views on a solution to the problem. Still, the disproportionate influence of the military can bias its information-gathering capabilities.[39]

Other Security Forces

With the Kurdish insurrection and the proliferation of other illegal and violent groups, there has been a commensurate increase in the recruitment of the internal security services. The National Security Organization (Milli Emniyet Teskilati) is responsible for maintaining security. Reporting to the Interior Ministry, this organization has developed new cadres to combat terrorism. With its burgeoning staff, the police organization has increasingly come under attack for extrajudicial killings, disappearances of prisoners, and other human rights violations. Although responsibility was denied by the police, the murder in police custody of a left-wing journalist, Metin Göktepe, early in 1996—his body was dumped not far from the station—once more embarrassed the security apparatus and refocused attention on the behavior of its personnel. The police have also become more autonomous, or even completely autonomous, and more violent; it is not uncommon to see ordinary and peaceful demonstrators badly beaten up. Additionally, the police in the large cities have become increasingly frustrated by a significant increase in deadly attacks against them by militant and armed left-wing elements.

But of greater concern with respect to the Kurdish question is the emergence and strengthening of two new security forces in the southeast that do not fit into the institutional makeup of the state. These have given rise to fears that they have become a "war lobby" of sorts, which complicates yet further any arrival at a solution. This "war lobby"—a simplistic and prejudicial term—consists of those elements that seem to have some vested interest in the perpetuation of the conflict. Elements of the "war lobby" include the village guards, the special teams, and activist elements of the Turkish right-wing nationalist party, the Nationalist Action party (MHP), who make up a significant portion of the special terms.

The Village Guards (Köy Koruculari)

We have already discussed the question of village guards in the context of intra-Kurdish divisions. Initially designed to help combat the PKK by providing security officials with intelligence otherwise inaccessible to the army, the village guards as an institution—themselves invariably Kurds— also help divide the Kurdish community. The state's divide-and-rule policy relied heavily on the landlords who control whole villages, and who were also more likely to support the status quo. There are reportedly some 62,000 village guards in the southeast. As much as the state claims it abhors the violence of the PKK, it has never shrunk from employing village guards who are ferociously anti-PKK, possess an economic incentive to perpetuate the struggle, and who have less than professional skills.[40]

Early on, the PKK targeted village guards as representing the ultimately traitorous elements within the Kurdish population. Fighting between the PKK and the village guards is probably the single bloodiest aspect of the struggle in the southeast, and the situation in which the term "terrorist" is most readily invoked. In the past, roving PKK teams routinely wiped out village guards, often including their entire families. Village guards, in turn, took action against suspected PKK activists or sympathizers in the villages, and they too included their opponents' families. In the general context of the conflict in the southeast, traditional enmities and blood feuds among Kurdish tribal clans have often been revisited and redefined as being part of the broader "anti-PKK struggle." The village guards are well paid for their work, receiving approximately $100 a month, and, with this representing their only source of income, they have reason to want to see the conflict perpetuated.[41] Hence the guards have been known to manufacture clashes with the PKK in order to impress authorities with the continuing need for their services.

On the other hand, the guards also resent the security forces, who use them in the most forward lines in the combat against the PKK. The guards, or the villages they come from, feel sometimes doubly victimized: by the state that forces them to join—since the security forces often threaten villages with evacuations if they do not collaborate—and by the PKK, which then targets them. Among those villagers evacuated, some who wanted to return to their villages were allowed back only when they volunteered to become village guards.[42] Some of the village guards work for both sides in this conflict; the TOBB Report suggested that some of the guards "volunteered" by the state have also been trafficking in arms.[43]

Special Teams (Özel Timler)

The special teams were organized to take the combat directly to the PKK, as a form of unofficial "special forces."[44] They operate in small groups and are specially trained in counterinsurgency tactics. They dress in civilian clothes and sometimes even in PKK-style uniforms, such as they are, and are nominally under the control of the Ministry of Interior. They have been heavily recruited from the members of the Nationalist Action Party, and they often wear the gray wolf insignias that are the symbol of the nationalists and of the MHP.[45] They are very well paid (between $800 and $1,100 a month), and are often signed up for contracts of six years or so, rotating in and out of the region periodically. There are an estimated 22,000 to 23,000 of these team members.[46]

There are two types of special teams: those that are part of the gendarmerie, and those that belong to police units. While the former go by the name Special Team, the police units are known as Special Action Teams (Özel Hareket Timleri).[47] The special teams have gained a reputation for brutality, killings, and vigilante-type violence. As such, they have earned the enmity of Kurds, and their removal from the area is one of the key demands of all Kurds in the region. Despite their nominal subservience to civilian authorities, they have often flouted those authorities if they have proven less than willing to cooperate with the special teams in brutalizing the population. In the summer of 1995, many such incidents came to light. As a result of some reportedly highly provocative acts by the special teams in Tunceli in 1995, the minister of interior was forced to withdraw them and apologize for their conduct in terrorizing local citizens.[48] After withdrawal, however, they often serve tours of duty in western Turkey.

There is increasing concern among many Turks that the special teams are gaining a vested interest in violence, that they will be difficult to disband because of the MHP party affiliation of many of them, and that they will represent the kernel of future vigilante groups in the large cities who may operate against Kurds there in general. Already there have been reports of troubled special team members rotated to other parts of the country getting involved in acts of violence and retribution against Kurds.[49] They have clearly gained a degree of autonomy from the army and the civilian authorities. They are tolerated because they have proven to be effective against the civilian support system the PKK has established. The special teams have also been sanctioned by the military because they, in effect, do the "dirty work" of the army. In the long run, the adverse conditions under which they work and the training they have received make them prone not just to psychological difficulties but also to the kinds of problems faced by the "Afghans," the trained Muslim anti-Soviet fighters who, with the end of the Afghan war, have sold or volunteered their services for other militant causes. A former Istanbul chief of police blames the violent and unlawful behavior of police officers in the big cities on their experiences in the southeast and their attendant psychological problems.[50] In late 1996, concerns over the behavior of the special teams reached the military hierarchy as well. The NSC, in a document leaked to the press, not only criticized them for their brutal behavior but also went so far as to question their long-run utility. The NSC suggested that the teams be put under the overall control of military commanders, including during their training periods.[51]

Other Institutions

The judicial system has also played a major role in the deepening of the conflict. The Turkish political system has always paid a great deal of attention to its legalistic side. Many laws, whether pertaining to political parties or associations, are restrictive enough to easily invite investigations by state prosecutors. Because the Kurdish question is defined by the Kurds themselves in terms of a separate ethnic identity, almost any type of political activity runs afoul of the law. As a result, if state institutions are to function according to their mandate, they have no choice but to prosecute.

With respect to the Kurdish question, two institutions have played an important role: the Constitutional Court and the State Security Courts. While the Constitutional Court decides questions such as the banning of political parties, the National Security Courts, as mandated by the constitution, try cases that deal with sedition and attempts to destroy the unity of the state. The president of the Constitutional Court, Yekta Güngör Özden, for instance, chided President Demirel when he floated the trial balloon that the government ought to consider the notion of "constitutional citizenship.' Özden thought that such a concept contradicted the constitutional premise of a unified state and the notion that all citizens of the Turkish Republic are Turks.[52]

The State Security Courts are unusual in that they are composed of a president and four members, two of whom come from the military. Set up in different parts of the country depending on need, these courts have taken the lead in pursuing Kurdish activists—both violent and nonviolent—thus stifling dissent. The state security courts have also taken the lead in the closing down of newspapers and in narrowly interpreting the limits of free speech. The courts have provided the regime with a veneer of legality in the pursuit of Kurdish nationalist thought and behavior. The judicial system as a whole and these institutions in particular are at the core of defending the ideological purity of the state. And no one was more at the front of this ideological fight than Nusret Demiral, the former head of the Ankara State Security Court, who zealously prosecuted Kurds, and especially the members of the pro-Kurdish political parties, and who once jailed people for sedition after a noisy celebration in his building. But he divulged his true political sympathies when he presented himself as a candidate of Türkes's Nationalist Action party in the December 1995 elections.

In sum, the heart of present state policy toward the Kurds seems to reside primarily in the security organizations and institutions of the state, which have been given a free hand by the civilian leadership to deal with the "terror problem" as the heart of the Kurdish problem. The bureaucracy has always regarded the southeast and east as undesirable regions—areas to which bureaucrats and ordinary civil servants could be exiled for punishment, or simply a temporary way station in pursuit of career advancement. Today, many state employees who work there receive danger pay. Hence the state's attitude, down through the lower ranks, has never been one of great sympathy or understanding. Few if any of the high-ranking administrators of the state, whether in foreign affairs or domestic security branches, have an understanding of the problems confronted daily by Turkey's Kurdish citizens. In part because of misinformation and deliberate distortion of facts, or simply a refusal to recognize these facts—a "cognitive dissonance" of sorts—the gap between the two sides is enormous. The present Turkish state, while not monolithic, is dominated by a core for whom the southeast and the Kurds are more an ideological abstraction than a complex reality.

Notes and References

1. Derya Sazak, "Özal, HEP, PKK," *Milliyet,* March 14, 1993. For a discussion of this period and Turkish policy in the area, see Gürbey, "Options for and Hindrances to a Resolution of the Kurdish Issue in Turkey"; Barkey, "Turkey's Kurdish Dilemma" and Philip Robins, "The Overlord State: Turkish Policy and the Kurdish Issue," *International Affairs* 69, no. 4 (1993). Özal also made sure that the Kurdish-based party HEP would not be cut off from the state funds it was legally entitled to, despite the controversies surrounding it.

2. *Hürriyet,* April 28, 1992.

3. Interview with President Demirel, *Yeni Yüzyil,* May 22, 1995.

4. Some have ascribed Demirel's turnabout to the army's opposition. Three hard-line parliamentary deputies were reportedly dispatched to him with a warning from the generals.

5. *Sabah,* August 9, 1996.

6. Kemali Saybasili, *DYP-SHP Koalisyonu'nun Üç Yili* (Three years of the DYP-SHP coalition) (Istanbul: Baglam Yayinciliik, 1995), 62–63. The "Basque model" proposal was subjected to severe criticisms. For a published attack on the Basque model's applicability to Turkey, see former minister Mehmet Turgut's *Türkiye Gerçegi ve Bask Modeli* (The Turkish reality and the Basque model) (Istanbul: Bogaziçi Yayinlari, 1994). Many of our interviewees suggested that Çiller, by virtue of the fact that she was ill-informed about the subject matter, allowed the military, specifically Chief of Staff General Dogan Güres, to sway her in favor of the hard-line position.

7. In her 1994 campaign she often stressed that a vote for her was a vote against the PKK, which, as a tactic, may have been self-serving, but it also indirectly elevated the stature of the organization.

8. As Oktay Eksi argued, her 1995 proposal was almost identical to her 1994 one, which, in turn, was a copy of the 1993 one. In effect, no moneys were spent, despite the allocations, and few believed Çiller, as the government had been experi-

encing severe revenue shortages. "Müjde Çok da Sonucu Bilen Yok" (There is plenty of good news but no one knows the final results) *Hürriyet,* July 16, 1995.

9. Güres admitted in an interview before the 1995 elections that Çiller had improved the morale of the armed forces (*Milliyet,* November 19, 1995).

10. Mehmet Turgut argued that it was not inconceivable—just as with Nixon's initiating contact with China or de Gaulle's resolving the Algerian crisis—for Çiller to execute another turnabout in policy. In fact, Turgut suspected that the controversial 1995 TOBB report was the first salvo along this course. "*Dogu Sorunu Raporu*" *Üzerine,* 176–77.

11. For more on this issue, see Henri J. Barkey, "Why Military Regimes Fail: The Perils of Transition," *Armed Forces and Society* 16, no. 2 (February 1990); George S. Harris, "The Role of the Military in Turkey in the 1980s: Guardians or Decision-Makers?" in *State, Democracy and the Military: Turkey in the 1980s,* ed. Metin Heper and Ahmet Evin (Berlin: deGruyter, 1988); and Ümit Cizre Sakallioglu, "The Anatomy of the Turkish Military's Political Autonomy," *Comparative Politics* 29, no. 2 (January 1997).

12. Hasan Cemal, "Yasar Kemal, Mesut Yilmaz, Kürt Sorunu . . ." (Yasar Kemal, Mesut Yilmaz, and the Kurdish question . . .) *Sabah,* March 10, 1996.

13. Welfare Party MP and chair of the parliamentary commission on border security, Hanifi Demirkol, argues that the problem of "terror" can be solved only with the cooperation of Turkey's neighbors (*Zaman,* December 13, 1996).

14. *Milliyet,* April 21, 1997. The plan also included "psychological" measures designed to improve the image of the region domestically and internationally.

15. Former Defense Minister Mehmet Gölhan's figures quoted by Christopher Panico, "Turkey's Kurdish Conflict," *Jane's Intelligence Review,* 7, no. 4 (April 1995). Human Rights Watch Arms Project estimates that there are approximately 300,000 security forces in the southeast, of which 140,000 to 150,000 are regular army troops, 50,000 are part of the Jandarma (Gendarmerie), 40,000 are police, and 67,000 are village guards. Human Rights Watch, *Weapons Transfers and Violations of the Laws of War in Turkey* (New York: Human Rights Watch, 1995), 44.

16. Tammy Arbuckle, "Stalemate in the Mountains," *Jane's International Defense Review* (January) 1997, 49.

17. *Le Figaro,* March 25, 1997. Tunceli was also the location of one the deadliest suicide bombings of the summer of 1996.

18. *Associated Press,* March 8, 1997. In fact, in the public campaign initiated by the military high command against the Welfare party–led government in the spring of 1997, the message was that the Islamists had replaced the PKK as the most serious threat forcing the state to become a dominant theme.

19. This is not to say that the army is blameless when it comes to human rights abuses. For details and case studies, see the Human Rights Watch report, cited above.

20. A gendarmerie officer who testified at a parliamentary investigation committee reportedly pointed out that "in the southeast one need not be a sympathizer of the [PKK] to warrant his execution. It is sufficient that he be close to its ideol-

ogy." He also recounted how mass and indiscriminate retaliation was conducted on a pro-government village that was unfortunate enough to lie close to the location of a firefight between the PKK and the security forces. Osman Güzelgöz, "Güneydogu Gerçekleri" (Realities of the southeast), *Zaman,* March 1, 1997.

21. *Cumhuriyet,* June 14, 1996.

22. T. C. Genelkurmay Baskanligi, *İç Güvenlikte Halkla Iliskiler ve Halkin Kazanilmasi: Davranis Ilkeleri Rehberi* (Public relations and winning the public in internal security: A behavioral guide) (Ankara: T. C. Genelkurmay Baskanligi, 1995). The chief of staff of the armed forces, Ismail Karadayi, is reported to have taken over completely the totality of the military operations in the southeast, eclipsing the supergovernor of the area. See Stephen Button, "Turkey Struggles with Kurdish Separatism," *Military Review* (December 1994–January/February 1995), 76.

23. The military leadership has also been sensitive to any discussion of increased draft resistance. In its most extreme form, this was displayed during the prosecution of a well-known TV and print journalist for having aired a program that featured draft dodgers.

24. In one of the few criticisms levied at the army by journalists, former chief of staff Dogan Güres received much ridicule for his statement that the "Turkish flag was again flying in the Cudi mountains"—hardly an accomplishment on Turkey's own soil, even if the area was a stronghold of the PKK.

25. Hasan Cemal, "Dogan Güres Pasa'dan: Terör Baska Kürt Baska, Bunu Görmek Lazim!" *Sabah,* April 13, 1996.

26. A retired general interviewed by Mehmet Ali Birand argued that the military cannot accept the notion of "Kurdishness." According to long-held official views, now largely discredited in most people's eyes, the Kurds are descendants from a Central Asian Turkish tribe. The military never uses the word *Kurd* because if it does it will have indirectly accepted the existence of the Kurds. Mehmet Ali Birand, *APO ve PKK* (APO and the PKK) (Istanbul: Milliyet Yayinlari, 1992), 102.

27. An added worry is potential PKK infiltration of military ranks. In the summer of 1996, the army initiated an operation against the PKK after discovering that two master sergeants had been passing information to the insurgents (*Yeni Yüzyil,* August 19, 1996).

28. A recently published lengthy volume by the general staff argues that Kurds are nothing but the creation of imperialists, including the U.S., whose main purpose is to create a Kurdish state, destabilize Turkey, and eliminate it from future competition in Central Asia. Mehmet Kocaoglu, *Uluslararasi Iliskiler Isiginda Ortadogu,* 263–332. While the author claims that these are his ideas and not the general staff's, the publication is accompanied by a recommendation from the commander of the air force that it be used as a source. These ideas are not atypical, and they are shared by civilians and military alike. For an important civilian's rendition of the same idea, see former interior minister and speaker of the parliament Ismet Sezgin, who, in a March 1992 interview, simply stated that in the southeast "the

West is trying to achieve what it could not with Sèvres [the 1920 Sèvres Treaty that partitioned Turkey among the allies]. The aim is to create a Marxist-Leninist autonomous Kurdish state" [sic] reprinted in Ahmet Taner Kislali, *Atatürk'e Sald-irmanin Dayanilmaz Hafifligi* (The incredible lightness of attacking Atatürke) (Ankara: Imge Kitabevi, 1994), 295.

29. Analysis by the weekly magazine *Tempo,* November 10, 1993, quoted in Saybasili, *DYP-SHP Koalisyonu'nun Üç Yili,* 75.

30. Prior to 1960, there existed a body entitled the Supreme National Defense Council. The coup members not only changed the emphasis from national defense to security, but they also elevated it and made it a constitutional body. See TÜSIAD, *Türkiye'de Demokratikleşme Perspeklifleri,* p. 72.

31. For an analysis of this institution, see Hikmet Özdemir, *Rejm ve Asker* (Soldiers and the regime) (Istanbul: Iz Yayincilik, 1993), 99–140.

32. Ali Bayramoglu, "Asker Yetkili Olunca . . ." (When soldiers have the authority) *Yeni Yüzyil,* June 15, 1996. Bayramoglu, a critic of the NSC, also argues that the NSC decides what kind of programs are aired on state-run TV and changes in the penal code, and that it interprets the meaning of citizenship. According to existing law, the Council of Ministers may approve instruction in a foreign language only at the recommendation of the National Security Council. Presently, in middle schools throughout Turkey, only English, French, German, and Japanese can legally be taught. The NSC in 1994 recommended that instruction in Russian, Arabic, Spanish, and Italian could be considered by the Council of Ministers (*Cumhuriyet,* August 23, 1996).

33. *Tempo,* September 6–13, 1993, quoted in Saybasili, *DYP-SHP Koalisyonu'-nun Üc Yili,* 55. One exception to this consensus rule occurred on February 28, 1997, when the military, over the objections of Prime Minister Erbakan, pushed through a list of twenty demands on de-Islamizing Turkish society.

34. In his memoirs, General Necip Torumtay, the chief of staff who resigned during the Gulf Crisis because he disagreed with Özal on the nature and method of the foreign policy being followed, describes how the president almost from the beginning set out to impose his vision on the NSC. *Orgeneral Necip Torumtay'in Anilari* (The memoirs of General Necip Torumtay) (Istanbul: Milliyet Yayinlari, 1993), 111.

35. *Milliyet,* August 17, 1994.

36. Saybasili, *DYP-SHP Koalisyonu'nun Üç Yili,* 62–65. Çiller's idea resembled one offered by Ecevit a year earlier. While he too wanted to reduce the role of the military, his ultimate aim was different from hers. *Nokta,* March 29, 1992, 22–23.

37. For a full statement, see *Anadolu Ajansi,* April 1, 1997, and the daily papers.

38. For more on the MIT, see, Cüneyt Arcayürek, *Darbeler ve Gizli Servisler* (Coups d'etats and secret services) (Istanbul: Bilgi Yayinevi, 1989), 59–65; Saybasili, *DYP-SHP Koalisyonu'nun Üç Yili,* 56; and Özdemir, *Rejim ve Asker,* 189–209.

39. So far, however, the behavior of the intelligence organization has been mixed. There are indications that at least during Demirel's prime ministership, the

MIT as well as the armed forces may have deliberately withheld crucial information from him about their own activities in the southeast.

40. The most often cited example is of one notorious non-Turkish-speaking village guard leader, Tahir Adiyaman, who is reputed to have killed seven gendarmerie soldiers before being amnestied in return for his services.

41. Sedat Bucak, the DYP parliamentarian who also commands large numbers of village guards, for instance, argues that the only solution is to fight the PKK to the bitter end (*Yeni Yüzyil*, August 23, 1996).

42. *Milliyet*, July 28, 1995.

43. Türkiye Odalar Birligi, *Dogu Sorunu: Teshisler ve Tespitler*, 63.

44. Credit for this innovation goes to Mehmet Agar who, in 1993, became the chief of the National Security Organization and later minister of Justice Interior. Accordingly, the special teams were to fight the PKK with tactics borrowed from the PKK and treat all PKK sympathziers as terrorists (*Show-TV*, December 24, 1996).

45. A number of parliamentarians from different parties have complained about the relationship between these teams and MHP, including one DYP member, Mustafa Zeydan, who comes from a tribal family with many village guards. See *Yeni Yüzil*, July 21, 1995.

46. Estimate by former CHP parliamentarian Sinan Yerlikaya, *Ibid*. Other estimates have put the number as low as 10,000.

47. For more on the special teams, see Tammy Arbuckle, "Winter Campaign in Kurdistan," *International Defense Review* 28, no. 2 (February 1995).

48. These events came to light after special team members, incensed at the killing of three of their own, dumped the naked and mutilated bodies of seven alleged PKK members at the city center and also attacked a variety of public officials, including medical personnel. Eventually, the perseverance of some parliamentarians paid off (*Yeni Yüzyil*, July 23, 1995).

49. One such example is Antalya, where the team members have harassed Kurds who have recently migrated to that city from the southeast. "Özel time Antalya'da 'tedavi' tatili" (A "treatment" holiday in Antalya for members of the special team) *Cumhuriyet*, August 8, 1995.

50. *Sabah*, June 25, 1996.

51. *Milliyet*, December 18, 1996. The NSC's criticisms of the teams are also part of a widening concern by the military over the competition for resources between themselves and the internal security services controlled by the Ministry of the Interior.

52. *Hürriyet*, April 26, 1994. Özden qualified his remarks by pointing out that the "constitution did not base itself on a racialist notion of Turkishness."

6

The Kurds and Turkish Foreign Policy

THE KURDISH QUESTION has increasingly come to cast a long shadow on all of Ankara's foreign policy concerns, ranging from relations with the U.S. and Europe to the Middle East and even Russia and the Caucasus.[1] This is largely by Ankara's own choice, for it has decided to extend its usual domestic practice of associating anything Kurdish with the PKK, including in the realm of foreign policy. While Turkey has succeeded in equating the PKK primarily with terrorism and other ills in the minds of Americans and most Europeans, it has also steadfastly refused to acknowledge the existence of moderate Kurdish groups. As the Kurdish issue gains more currency internationally, this may become a problem that will yet haunt the government, because it risks alienating international opinion. Turkey will go on instructing its Turkish diplomatic legations abroad to continue the policy of countering the slightest criticisms of Ankara's Kurdish policy in the press or elsewhere with unyielding responses—however unconvincing and even damaging such stereotyped responses may be.

From Russia, Syria, Iran, and Greece—who are ready to use the issue against Ankara—to Ankara's friends in Europe and the U.S., who increasingly perceive the Kurds as underdogs and are embarrassed by Ankara's policies, the government's strategy has enabled a multitude of states to become involved in Turkish and Kurdish politics. In so doing, Ankara has transformed the Kurdish issue into Turkey's greatest vulnerability. In effect, Ankara is increasingly facing the possibility of being imprisoned in a cage of its own making. The day-to-day activities of the Turkish Foreign Ministry appear to be guided by its desire to combat the PKK and the Kurdish issue internationally.[2] Even Libyan leader Mu'ammar Qaddafi's intemperate comments during Prime Minister Erbakan's visit to Libya in October 1996 was cause for a domestic political storm rarely experienced in Ankara.

We turn to a closer examination of three principal areas of Turkish foreign policy interest in order to assess the full impact of the Kurdish question. The three are Turkey's relations with the United States, its relations with Europe, and its regional role and standing. Finally, we will also explore the potential impact of the Kurdish problem on geopolitics in the Caucasus and relations with Russia that preoccupy the Ankara government.

Relations with the United States

In the long run, the most critical factor in Turkey's geopolitical standing is its relations with the United States. President Özal was the first to clearly chart a new course in Turkish-American relations when he aligned his country, despite intense domestic opposition, along with the multinational coalition facing Saddam Hussein. Özal, just as in the Kurdish question, was more willing to pursue policy choices outside the conventional and— perhaps because he had resided in the U.S.—was less willing to demonize the United States and the West. However, with his death, Turkish foreign policy assumed its previous stance of close and yet "distant" friendship.

Despite the appearance of the Soviet Union, U.S. policy toward Turkey has remained very supportive, reflecting an appreciation not only of Özal's contribution but also of Turkey's key strategic location at the junction of many different economic and political zones of concern.[3] Following the Gulf War, the United States pushed Kuwait and Saudi Arabia to compensate Ankara for the losses it had incurred during the war as a result of the shutdown of the Iraqi oil pipeline traversing Turkish territory and the collapse of transit traffic in the southeast. The United States provided significant military supplies to Turkey for free as it ran down its European stocks (Greece was another beneficiary of this policy) and, perhaps most important, it vigorously and successfully lobbied the European Union members to facilitate conditions for Turkey's accession to the customs union. The U.S. Commerce Department has included Turkey in its list of the ten Big Emerging Markets that warrant special attention because of their potential for expanding trade relations. Recently, the U.S. has moved away from its pro-Russian policy and supported Turkish demands that Azeri oil be transported not through the Russian Black Sea port of Novorossiisk but rather through the Anatolian mainland to the Mediterranean.

Paradoxically, the Kurdish question may have helped Turkey's relations with the United States in the short run. The birth of the PKK in the late 1970s as a clearly Marxist-Leninist organization at that time positioned it on the wrong side of the Cold War from the U.S. point of view. Over time then, U.S. policy has mimicked Turkey's views of the PKK: in branding the PKK a terrorist organization at every possible occasion, the United States has demonstrated its unwavering support for Turkey's basic position in this regard. In the absence of the Kurdish insurrection, it is also unlikely that Ankara would have faced such difficulties in its attempt to join the European Customs Union and, therefore, the intensive and successful U.S. lobbying would have been unnecessary. Despite the decidedly pro-Turkish positions of recent U.S. administrations, the Kurdish question intrudes on the U.S.-Turkish dialogue in three areas: policy toward Iraq, and northern Iraq in particular; human rights violations in Turkey; and concern for Turkey's long-term stability in the face of potential civil war there.

It was the U.S.'s sense of obligation to Özal's Gulf War stance that ultimately led to what came to be called Operation Provide Comfort (OPC), a round-the-clock military protective shield for the Kurds of northern Iraq that averted the prospect of half a million Iraqi Kurdish refugees fleeing into Turkey.[4] The joint military task force—composed of U.S., British, and French aircraft as well as a small contingent of ground troops that includes Turks—enabled these Kurdish refugees to return to their homes after their flight at the end of the Gulf War. Subject to six-month renewals by the Turkish Parliament, OPC has become one of the more contentious issues in the bilateral relations with the U.S. In 1996, the renewals followed very contentious debates in Parliament, which was reflected in the irregular extension periods.

Turkish unease over the de facto autonomous entity in northern Iraq run by the Kurds was at the source of the resentment felt toward OPC. Primarily because the entity in northern Iraq is perceived to have acquired statelike attributes that can potentially influence Kurds living in Turkey, the continued presence of OPC gets only grudging approval from the Turkish establishment. In fact, many, including the former head of state and junta leader Kenan Evren, political parties, and journalists had openly advocated the removal of the force. Bülent Ecevit and Necmettin Erbakan, as noted earlier, had vociferously argued against the continued renewal of OPC. In fact, a majority of the Turkish Parliament would have voted against a renewal of OPC if a truly free vote were allowed on the subject. The military itself had done little to bolster the fortunes of OPC, preferring to let the mission hang in the balance until the parliamentary vote, thereby increasing its own leverage with Washington to extract more concessions for further extensions of the operation.

By contrast, the foreign ministry has always been cognizant of the negative repercussions the cancellation of OPC would have on U.S.-Turkish relations, especially if it were followed by an Iraqi advance toward the north. The ministry also understood that the removal of the umbrella over northern Iraq could result in a significant refugee flow, duplicating the conditions that gave rise to OPC in the first place. Still, in the August/ September 1996 crisis, when Saddam Hussein's forces collaborated with Massoud Barzani's KDP to attack their rival, the Turkish government led by Erbakan/Çiller made it abundantly clear that it would not sanction the use of OPC forces at Incirlik to punish the Iraqis. This crisis ultimately forced a rethinking of OPC and its replacement by a reformulated command renamed Northern Watch, from which the French opted out. Without a ground presence in the northern Iraqi town of Zakho and with more restricted overflight rules, Operation Northern Watch is more in line with the Turkish military's preferences, and it is also an arrangement that allowed Erbakan to claim that he had succeeded in eliminating OPC.

The U.S. has been careful to continually reiterate its policy that it respects the territorial integrity of Iraq; with the exception of senior diplomats and others well acquainted with U.S. politics, this is a claim that convinces few in Turkey. The upsurge in fighting between the two Kurdish factions in northern Iraq has somewhat reduced Turkish anxieties, since it serves to demonstrate the "inability of the Kurds to run their own affairs."[5] The U.S. has made sure that Turkey was directly involved in the negotiations it sponsored in Ireland in the fall of 1995 to reconcile the Iraqi Kurdish factions. Nevertheless, the lack of cooperation between the two Kurdish parties in northern Iraq provides an opening to the PKK to operate with greater impunity.

It is also this fear of a deepening of PKK support in northern Iraq that fuels Ankara's continued unease with the Iraqi autonomous region, and, therefore, until recently it had openly advocated a return to the status quo ante that prevailed before the Gulf War. In fact, Ankara, on more than one occasion, has made its displeasure obvious at any arrangement that would secure a federal or even an autonomous region for the Kurds in a post-Saddam Iraq. Also claiming that the embargo on Iraq has disproportion-ately harmed its own citizens of the southeast—an argument simultane-ously used to explain away some of the support for the PKK—Ankara has demanded that it be eased. While Turkey has somewhat pulled back from an open disagreement with U.S. positions on Iraq, it is clear that it would prefer reassertion of Iraqi control over northern Iraq. Ankara remains am-bivalent, however, since it is also aware that a return of Saddam by force to the north could again spark an exodus of Kurdish refugees, and that Saddam could at any time turn against Turkey, exact revenge, or exploit Turkey's Kurds against Ankara. In addition to asking the Gulf countries to help Turkey, the U.S. has also agreed, within the limits of the U.N. Secur-ity Council Resolution 986, to the limited use of the Kirkuk-Yumurtalik pipeline for Iraqi exports of oil to the Mediterranean. In order to help Turkey meet its domestic oil needs and alleviate some of the losses incurred because of sanctions on Iraq, the U.S., in the negotiations leading to the passage of UNSC 986, insisted that a majority of Iraqi oil be transshipped through the pipelines to the Mediterranean port of Ceyhan.

Unlike some of the Europeans, the U.S. has been more tolerant of Turk-ish incursions into northern Iraq in pursuit of the PKK, including the large one in March and April of 1995, noted for its duration and the extent of the operation (35,000 men).[6] Ankara's appreciation for the U.S. position notwithstanding, the basic interests of the U.S. and Turkey in Iraq are difficult to reconcile; for the U.S., Saddam Hussein remains the primary threat to the region and its interests, whereas from Turkey's perspective it is the existence of the Kurdish entity that poses the greatest threat. At the heart of this divergence lies two different interpretations of the Kurdish problem in Turkey.

As reflected in State Department reports on human rights violations, the U.S. has become increasingly concerned by Ankara's repression and the magnitude of the Kurdish problem. The Kurdish question was first mentioned in the department's 1988 report.[7] Since then its reports have chronicled Ankara's human rights violations in greater detail, all the while criticizing the PKK for its share of atrocities. Nevertheless, the State Department reports have become an important tool for those in Congress eager to reduce the level of aid to Turkey, or those opposed to Turkey because of its 1974 invasion of Cyprus, or those simply uncomfortable being associated with levels of repression unbecoming of a U.S. ally and NATO member.

Similarly, nongovernmental human rights groups have accelerated their criticism of Turkish policies. The beginning of the Arab-Israeli peace process and the dissolution of the Soviet Union have also allowed human rights activists to focus more on previously neglected questions, such as that of Turkey's Kurds. One of the human rights groups' more notable successes was achieved when it managed to block the sale of cluster bombs to Turkey. Although unsuccessful at other times, as in the case of short-range missiles or helicopters, these groups are nonetheless maintaining an unwelcome level of pressure on Ankara. This pressure has become intense enough that even the Ministry of Foreign Affairs, known for its cooler approach, took the initiative in the summer of 1996 to virtually "declare war" on the Turkish Human Rights Foundation. It circulated a letter to all relevant ministries, including Defense, Health, Interior, Justice, and the MIT, asking them to impede the activities of the foundation.[8]

Because the Kurdish issue evokes the worst fears among the Turkish public and leadership, the current U.S. administration has chosen to pursue a policy intended to bolster Turkey's confidence in the post–Cold War environment with the hope that a Turkey more firmly rooted in both NATO and the European Union—even if only a customs union—will be able to take steps to accommodate some of the Kurdish demands. The threat of destabilization that the prolongation of the Kurdish question poses for Turkey is particularly worrisome to the U.S. With its shifting and renewed strategic importance, Turkey remains a valued ally; given the costs of the long-standing Arab-Israeli conflict, the U.S. does not want the emergence of yet another long-standing ethnic conflict that could encompass other regional actors. Any weakening of Turkey as a result of its Kurdish imbroglio does not bode well for NATO, even if the primary enemy against which it was constituted has left the scene.

Can the U.S. indirectly create the conditions conducive to Turkey's leadership undertaking political reforms that are inclusive in character and therefore accommodative of moderate Kurdish demands? Despite U.S. efforts in Turkey's behalf, Turkish suspicions linger that the U.S. may be harboring a secret agenda; this unease is bolstered by the conflicting messages that emanate from Washington, especially during periods of intense legislature/executive squabbling. This conflictual attitude is best captured by a foreign policy watcher: "If we put aside the improvement in our relations with the U.S. since 1991 . . . Western European and U.S. policies have given rise to the isolation of Turkey on the international scene."[9]

What is the source of this sense of isolation? On the one hand, this is not a new phenomenon; Turkey has always felt that it does not receive its fair share of attention in the West. On the other hand, Ankara has interpreted Western passivity to both the Armenian-Azeri and the Bosnian conflict as the abandonment of Turkey's own core interest, and it has also failed to demonstrate any awareness of inherent contradictions between Ankara's Kurdish policy and its concerns for the fate of ethnic Turks in Bulgaria or Greece. Surrounded by states that have troublesome relations with Turkey, Ankara has a demonstrated ability to exaggerate its own vulnerabilities.

The results of the 1995 parliamentary elections tend to reinforce this growing sense of isolation, since the only two parties and leaders who have scored any gains were those most opposed to the United States. Erbakan and Ecevit have continuously reiterated their opposition to principal U.S. interests in the region and in Turkey. Ecevit has never hidden his sympathy for Saddam, and Erbakan spares no opportunity to argue for a disengagement from the West. At the very least, opposition to the U.S. and the West will be even more vigorous than before in Turkey, irrespective of the composition of the Turkish government. Whereas U.S. vital interests in the region surrounding Turkey have diminished somewhat with the end of the Cold War, Turkey's own interests have grown and expanded across a much broader region and have become more vital. Ankara under almost any prime minister in the future is more likely than ever before to pursue its own interests more vigorously, with less attention accorded to U.S. preferences. This new reality diminishes Washington's ability to influence Ankara's policy toward the Kurds.

For the U.S., Turkey's Kurdish predicament poses a stark dilemma. Ankara is too valuable a strategic ally to pursue a policy that it will interpret as being hostile. On the other hand, Washington faces a moral and practical quandary if the repression in the southeast continues unabated: While the moral problems are obvious and exacerbated by the fact that the Turkish military is primarily equipped with U.S.-made matériel, at the practical level two issues emerge. The first is the distinct possibility that continued

conflict could result either in chronic political instability or in severe domestic unrest. Second, Turkey has been a linchpin of U.S. policy in all the
areas bordering this country, not just as an actor but also as an example of
democratic and economic success. Both of these factors would be endangered by a prolongation or intensification of the conflict with the Kurds.

Relations with Europe

Turkey's most important economic relations are with the European
Union.[10] By abandoning its inward-oriented economic policies in the early
1980s, Turkey has succeeded in not only diversifying its exports but also
in becoming an important market for direct foreign investment. Turkey's
economic progress and its proximate location to Europe have given an
added impetus to its primary and blossoming trade links with Europe.

At a time when trade blocs account for an increasing share of world
trade, Turkey needs to locate itself firmly in one. This is why the achievement of a customs union agreement with Europe has been such a priority
for recent Turkish governments—even though they would have preferred
to become full members of the European Union. Yet it is in the realization
of the customs union agreement that the Kurdish issue has made itself felt
most acutely. The European Parliament made it clear that it would not
sanction Turkey's accession to the customs union until certain basic modifications were made to the laws governing the criminalization of speech
and constitutional provisions that represent roadblocks to furthering the
democratization process. While some members of the European Parliament would prefer to push Turkey to make more concessions, such as the
release of jailed DEP parliamentarians, others are clearly satisfied with the
minor constitutional changes and the modification of the infamous Article
8 of the penal code.

However minor the European demands, they represent an obvious interference in the domestic affairs of Turkey—despite Europe's extensive
military relations with Ankara. Still, given the importance of the customs
union, Ankara was willing to pay the price to join. While there were Turkish parliamentarians and others who advocated deeper changes in these
provisions in the name of greater democratization, Ankara's recalcitrance
over altering them definitively lasted until the very last moment.

Will admission into the customs union increase or decrease the pressure Turkey will feel from the European Union member states with regard to democratization and the Kurdish issue? Although the Europeans no longer have the customs union as a carrot to dangle in front of Ankara, the fact remains that for Turkey this is an interim step: The ultimate goal is full membership. This very desire for membership in the customs union will render Ankara vulnerable to continued criticisms and pressure for human rights violations.[11] Already, Germany has been forced by domestic critics to suspend arms deliveries to Turkey; while these were eventually resumed, the suspension itself demonstrated the capabilities of domestic lobbies.

While Turkey was actively pushing for inclusion into the customs union, it did not shy away from confrontations with European Union member states over the Kurdish issue. As noted earlier, both Belgium and the Netherlands were severely criticized for allowing the Kurdish parliament in exile to gather for meetings in their respective capitals. Turkey placed The Hague on its "red list," presumably as retaliation and as a sign that arms purchases from the Netherlands would be reduced. Ankara has overreacted to the parliament in exile, which has subsequently met in Austria and most recently in Moscow. The great consternation with which these meetings are received in Ankara has obliged Turkish leaders to initiate political démarches that far exceed the severity of the political embarrassment that may be caused by these meetings of the parliament in exile.[12] Ironically, these démarches have served to attract far greater attention to the question.

The presence of a Kurdish diaspora in Europe has increased the involvement of European governments because, once politically mobilized, Kurdish activities will help sustain the pressure on Ankara. Although there are a far larger number of Turks residing in Europe than there are Kurds, the latter have the advantage of being an underdog and mobilizing in support of a cause. The PKK, despite the fact that it has been banned in Germany, has been far more successful in organizing the Kurds of Germany, who perhaps number 500,000 out of a total Turkish/Kurdish community that approaches 2 million, than it has the Kurds of Turkey.[13] With the rise in intercommunal conflict between Kurds and Turks in Germany itself, including the bombings of Turkish businesses, the Kurdish question increasingly assumes a domestic aspect for the German government that it finds itself powerless to resolve. Therefore, in the long run, it is likely that the German government will seek to influence Ankara to adopt a more accommodationist stance at home. In the short run, to curb the spread of intercommunal violence, Bonn even dispatched a high-ranking intelligence advisor to Chancellor Kohl to meet with PKK leader Abdullah Öcalan in Syria.[14]

The Regional Role

The elimination of Cold War–era inhibitions on state action and the proliferation of new actors on its borders has further complicated Ankara's task. In fact, Turkey has discovered that its Kurdish problem has rendered it vulnerable to those neighbors with which it has had long-standing disputes by providing them with an opportunity to embarrass or even harass Ankara.[15] The most obvious such case is Syria, which has actively supported the PKK and specifically given shelter to its leader, Abdullah Öcalan. Greece, which fears Turkey's growing regional importance, has long sought to contain Ankara's military power and contested it on the divided island of Cyprus; for Athens, the Kurds represent a welcome source of Turkish weakness that can readily be exploited.[16] Similarly for Iran, which regards Turkey as a Muslim state in the service of Tehran's American nemesis, the Kurdish insurrection not only distracts Ankara but also makes it solicitous of Tehran's cooperation for border security. Armenia has also had unofficial contacts with the PKK to remind Turkey that it too can play at the Kurdish game if necessary.

The temptation for the different states to use their neighbors' Kurds in pursuit of their regional ambitions is matched only by the willingness with which the Kurds have accepted assistance from neighboring states as a means of eluding the limits imposed by state boundaries.[17] Nearly all Kurdish leaders, when queried about the wisdom of consorting publicly with Turkey's enemies, reply that what Turkey is doing to the Kurds is so damaging to the Kurds as a people that they are determined to let Ankara know that the Kurds can hurt Turkey, too, if necessary.

In the long run, the impact of the Turkish-Syrian divide is particularly damaging to Turkey's role in the region. In addition to harboring a long-held resentment over the loss of Alexandretta (Hatay Province) to Turkey in 1939, Syria has increasingly worried about Turkish attempts to develop the southeast through the GAP, the Southeastern Anatolia Project, which envisages the construction of dams and irrigation networks on both the

Euphrates and the Tigris. This project has already diminished the downstream flow of water into Syria and in the future will affect the quality of the water as the use of fertilizer increases, thereby contaminating the river. Syrian support for the PKK has been interpreted by Ankara and many others as a card to use against the extension of the GAP project. Despite their long-standing differences, Syria and Iraq are united by the issue of water, since Iraq too is at risk, given its dependence on both of these rivers. The water problem resonates elsewhere in the Arab world, where the issue has the potential of uniting a number of states behind Syria and Iraq.[18] Egypt, for one, faces exactly the same dilemma with the river Nile and its upstream control by a hostile Sudan or an untrustworthy Ethiopia.

Although Syria and Iran have periodically cooperated with Turkey over northern Iraq, they are deeply distrustful of each others' intentions.[19] Even though neither of these states would like to see an independent Kurdish state in northern Iraq and both cooperate with Turkey through regular tripartite meetings, Saddam's adventurousness allows for the realization of multiple scenarios. Even Erbakan's ascendancy has not helped matters much. Despite the Islamist Turkish prime minister's desire to improve relations with all three of Turkey's neighbors, Syria, Iraq, and Iran, his efforts in this regard appear to have been blocked by the military and other state institutions. Although Erbakan and his party members went so far as to question the validity of the intelligence services' assessment of Iranian intentions and the existence of PKK camps in Iran, Turkey's Muslim neighbors are not confident of the durability of this government. Quite to the contrary, not only are PKK camps in Iran visible from the Turkish side of the border, but the Syrians also helped the PKK circumvent the "blocked routes from Iraq" by opening two PKK camps near the border with Hatay (Alexandretta).[20]

With the emerging divisions among the Kurds of northern Iraq, Turkey has increasingly relied on Barzani's faction, the KDP, whose territory abuts the Turkish frontier, to contain PKK activities. The subtle shift in Turkey's post-Özal strategy away from a refusal to cooperate with the Kurds of Iraq to one of almost exclusive reliance on the KDP may have initiated a new conflict of proxies in the region. The outburst of severe PKK-KDP fighting in northern Iraq in the fall of 1995 may be an attempt by both the Syrians, who have a great deal of sway over the PKK, and the Iranians to check the growing influence of Turkey in the area.[21]

Syrian support for the PKK has resulted in shifting Turkish perceptions of security threats toward its southern borders and has brought numerous calls for a harsher policy vis à vis Damascus from the Turkish press as well as parliamentarians. Turkey undertook one action in January 1994 when a small force of commandos attacked a PKK installation in Kamishli across the border in Syria. A series of bombings plagued Syria in the early summer of 1996; although they did not result in any casualties, they were assumed by many in the Arab world to have been instigated by the Turkish security services. Two factors have constrained the potential for a wider conflict with Syria: the fear of creating an anti-Turkish backlash in the Arab world, and the impact such a course of action would have on the Syrian leg of the U.S.-sponsored Arab-Israeli peace process. On the other hand, the peace process has allowed Turkey to effect a rapprochement with Israel and seek to balance Syria. A military training and exchange agreement signed by the Turkish military with its Israeli counterparts in February 1996 provided Israeli aircraft with training facilities in Turkey. This was followed by a series of high-level exchanges that continued during the Erbakan-led government, although Erbakan himself has tried his utmost to scuttle the deals between Israel and Turkey.[22]

Not surprisingly, the whole of the Arab world perceived this agreement as an attempt by the two countries to encircle Syria. Whatever the agreement's intent, the Arab reaction to the agreement from the point of view of the Turkish military demonstrated that they had succeeded in sending the desired message to Damascus. The Syrians may be playing a similar game with Ankara by improving their relations with Greece. Turkey warned Damascus not to enter into an alliance with Greece and was reported not to have found convincing Syrian assurances that it would not give Greece any bases on its territory.[23] An unintended consequence of the Israeli-Turkish rapprochement may be a realignment of Arab politics. Syria may seek "to create conditions and balances in the region that can deter or resist the Israeli/Turkish threat, and the two most important Arab partners in this respect are Egypt and Iraq." Similarly, the Israeli-Turkish relationship may give rise to further support for the PKK among Arabs in general.[24]

The Turkish-Iraqi relationship deteriorated with the onset of the Gulf crisis as pipelines carrying Iraqi crude to the Mediterranean were ordered shut down by Özal, who correctly anticipated U.N. Security Council resolutions. In fact, Özal may have accelerated a process of estrangement that began in the waning days of the Iran-Iraq war when Iraqis bitterly complained of Turkish trade and business practices while Turks criticized the Iraqis' tendency to accumulate trade arrears. Iraqi concerns regarding the GAP project further accentuated the unease as Baghdad refused to extend Ankara the cooperation that had allowed Turkish troops to cross into northern Iraq in hot-pursuit operations against the PKK.[24] Because it abhors the "authority vacuum" in northern Iraq, Turkey has tried to get the Iraqi Kurds to negotiate with the regime in Baghdad. Nevertheless, Ankara's participation in U.S.-sponsored mediation talks in Ireland between the two warring Kurdish factions has unnerved the Iraqis. These were followed by active Turkish participation in the cease-fire negotiated between the warring parties by the U.S., which makes use of Iraqi Turcomans as monitors.

Convinced of the regional demonstration effect vis-à-vis the Kurds, Turkey is faced with difficult choices with respect to Iraq: On the one hand, while it ardently wishes that the Iraqis regain complete control of their territory, the continuation of the status quo increases doubts about the viability of a future Iraq.[26] Hence, Ankara's fears of the unknown are intensified. Driven by its concern to control the PKK, Ankara was being slowly drawn into the management of the enclave. It instituted a small aid package, $13 million worth, to the area, which provided it with some clout as well as a means of introducing its operatives to better scrutinize developments there. It actively encouraged a dialogue between the KDP and Baghdad. The continuous military operations into northern Iraq have resulted in the creation of a de facto 15-km-wide security zone; Ankara, in effect, has moved the international frontier.[27] Should there be a change in the regime in Baghdad, Turkey will find it difficult not to use its accumulated clout to influence the overall outcome in Iraq; in the process, it is also likely to antagonize not just Iraqis and Kurds but also other Arab states.

Meanwhile, the dramatic escalation in the conflict between the Kurdish rivals in September 1996, which initially resulted in Barzani's defeat of his rival Talabani and the PUK with the help of Saddam Hussein, further highlights Turkey's dilemma in northern Iraq. Despite the PUK's comeback, Saddam Hussein's alliance with Barzani, which has allowed his intelligence services to roam freely in KDP-controlled areas, has succeeded in greatly increasing his influence in the Kurdish enclave. He has also dealt a major setback to U.S. policy in the region by denying Washington a secure base of operations against the regime in Baghdad and by undermining one of its core premises, the protection of the Kurds from retribution. These events also endangered Operation Provide Comfort, which had to remove its small ground operation from northern Iraq. Still, Ankara, which has longed for the consolidation of Saddam's rule in the north, faces a situation in which the PKK is the third strongest military formation there; it is unlikely that the KDP will engage them on its own anytime soon, for fear of opening a second front when the cease-fire negotiated with the PUK remains fragile.[28] When the Turkish government announced that it would in the meantime seek to formalize a temporary "security belt" along its border with Iraq, it engendered a strong reaction in the Arab world.[29]

It is therefore possible that Ankara may be in for a rude awakening: A resolution of the Iraqi crisis may result in a federated state, or in the Kurds obtaining autonomy. Although hard-liners in Ankara have made it plain that this would be unacceptable, the fact remains that Iraq in the past had provided autonomy arrangements to the Kurds—even if Saddam sought every possible excuse to undermine them and has not hesitated to engage in genocide operations against the Kurdish population as a whole, including the use of poison gas. But from a legal and structural point of view, past deals between the Iraqi state and the Kurds did provide the latter many more rights than their counterparts in Turkey have enjoyed, including language rights, education, and the right of association. In short, their right to a distinct identity was recognized.[30] These sorts of arrangements represent precedents that Ankara will not be able to block or ignore in the future.

Iraqi compromises with their Kurdish population furthermore occurred at a time when the Turkish Kurds had not become strongly politicized; a replication of such autonomy arrangements in Iraq today, in the absence of a resolution on the Turkish side, would undoubtedly accelerate the mobilization of Kurds in Turkey. In the event that such arrangements are arrived at in Iraq, the comparisons between Iraq and Turkey that would be drawn internationally are likely to embarrass Ankara and multiply the pressures to change its policy.

There is yet another worry for the Turkish government: the realization that had Barzani succeeded in consolidating his gains in September 1996, the KDP leader would have achieved his declared goal of a federal arrangement within the confines of Iraq. A Barzani-controlled federal enclave with a potent PKK force entrenched in it would not have provided Ankara with the opportunities it now enjoys to cross the international boundary at will and hit the targets of its choice. Of greater likelihood is the probability that internecine fighting between the two Kurdish rivals will continue without either one of them achieving complete dominance over the other—and in the process further drag outside powers into the area.

In other words, Turkey's domestic Kurdish problem makes it difficult for Ankara to extricate itself from northern Iraq. Unable to determine events in northern Iraq and faced with increased pressure from domestic, regional, and international sources to alter its policy on the Kurds, Ankara may genuinely become isolated. Turkey fears two other possible scenarios in Iraq: the replacement of the Iraqi Ba'th by a Syrian Ba'th, or Baghdad's submission to Iranian influence, given the majority Shi'ite population in that country.[31] It is then that it would be in need of European and U.S. support.

Finally, Tehran too is fearful of growing Turkish clout among the Kurds of Iraq and of potential Turkish support for unity between the Azeris of northern Iran and the Republic of Azerbaijan; for this reason, it has used the PKK as a way of reminding Ankara of its own vulnerabilities. Iranian anxieties reached a peak with the ascendancy of Abulfaz Elchibey and his nationalist Popular Front in Baku. Elchibey, who did not hide his dream of unifying the Azeris of Iran with his own state, was enthusiastically backed by Ankara. The Iranians have since tried their best to undermine what they perceived to be growing Turkish, and indirectly U.S. influence in northern Iraq. Following the unsuccessful U.S.-sponsored talks in Dublin in September 1995, Iran has tried its hand at reconciling the two Kurdish factions, and it sent troops into the area to demonstrate that it too can move in and out at its leisure and therefore should not be taken for granted. And when the PKK unleashed its attack on the KDP following the Dublin talks, it was Iran that stepped in to arrange a cease-fire and put an end to the bloodshed, much to Washington's annoyance.

Increasing Iranian influence in northern Iraq has led one Turkish observer to argue that Turkey is losing control of northern Iraq. The Iranian presence is felt not only politically but also economically.[32] Iranian economic influence, especially in PUK-controlled areas of Sulaymaniyah, was also the result of the internecine Kurdish fighting and the double embargo imposed on the region by both the world community and Iraq. Iran's proximity and PUK's inability to access the Turkish border posts held by its KDP rival resulted in a natural rapprochement between the PUK and Tehran. Although the KDP would later use this as an excuse for calling in Saddam Hussein, the fact remained that the KDP too relied on Iran for both trade and political support when necessary. Iran, of course, has its own domestic reasons for being active in northern Iraq, where its own dissidents from the Iranian Kurdistan Democratic party (I-KDP) have found shelter. Iran would like to avoid what happened to Turkey: the growth of an insurgency with bases beyond its control.

Finally, Iran is also made deeply uncomfortable by the growing strategic rapprochement between Israel and Turkey. Tehran's rulers have for a while viewed Israel as a primary enemy in the region and suspect that the Turkish-Israeli military collaboration deals are aimed at them. During President Rafsanjani's December 1996 visit to Turkey, the Erbakan wing of the government hinted at the possibility of signing a military cooperation agreement with Tehran that would be similar to the one with Israel. The idea was immediately rejected by the Turkish military and Erbakan's coalition partners.

Relations with Russia and the Caucasus

The Kurdish question makes its impact felt significantly, but only indirectly, upon Turkey's relations with Russia and Russia's former republics. Turco-Russian relations have become increasingly embittered by Moscow's decision not to comply with CFE Treaty limitations in the Caucasus, relating to Russian troop strengths there. More important, the Kurdish insurrection provides the Russians, who have watched Turkey's economic and political moves to supplant them in Central Asia with great unease, with a card to exploit. Moscow has been particularly angered by Turkish moves to obtain international support for the construction of Azeri and Kazak pipelines that bypass Russian territory and empty in the Turkish port of Dörtyol in the Mediterranean.

Because of Turkey's perception of its own vulnerabilities over the Kurds, Moscow was successful in muting Ankara's criticisms over its attack against Chechens in Grozny (and Russian countercriticism regarding Turkey's initial handling of the Black Sea ferry carrying Russian citizens hijacked by Chechens or their sympathizers in Turkey).[33] Periodically, the Russians organize—or allow Kurds, including pro-PKK groups, to organize—Kurdish conferences on its territory in order to remind Ankara of Moscow's potential reach. The continued insurrection in the east and southeastern provinces casts a long shadow on the security, and to a lesser extent on the feasibility, of pipeline projects envisaged by Turkey to bring in Azeri and Kazak oil and Turkmen gas. An undefeated PKK could conceivably create severe problems for the long-run maintenance of such pipelines, although it could not altogether stop them from operating and transporting the oil and gas.[34] In short, Turkey's vulnerability to the Kurdish insurrection directly serves to crimp Turkey's hand from a more activist policy in support of Turkish interests in the Caucasus and Central Asia. Turkish nationalists who are strongly hostile to Kurdish political and cultural aspirations in Turkey are at the same time aware that failure to resolve the crisis prevents them from playing the more active role they seek in the Turkic republics of the former Soviet Union, in Chechnya, and even in Tatarstan.

Turkey in the Erbakan Era

How did Erbakan's assumption of power in a coalition with Çiller and her party alter the foreign policy matrix faced by Turkey? Erbakan campaigned on a pro-Islamic and anti-Western platform that included such proposals as the formation of an Islamic NATO and an Islamic common market to replace Turkey's relationships with the West. He also promised to do away with both Turkey's recently signed miliary exchange agreement with Israel and Operation Provide Comfort. He publicly questioned the long-held belief in Turkey that Syria and Iran had provided substantial support to the PKK. Blaming Turkey's excessively pro-Western policies for the deteriorating relations with Islamic countries, starting with Syria, Iran, and Iraq, he pledged to reverse the downward trend.

The coalition agreement allotted the main responsibility for foreign affairs and defense to Çiller and her party. This very quickly proved to be something of an illusion: Çiller, who was both deputy prime minister and foreign minister, appeared to be responsible only for relations with the West, whereas Erbakan has used the prime minister's office very effectively to arrange meetings with ambassadors and other envoys from the Muslim world—while excluding his coalition partner from them. For his first trip abroad he chose to go to Iran and other Islamic countries, demonstrating that he intended to live up to his long-held belief that Turkey ought to upgrade its relations with the Muslim world and make them coequal with those of the Western world. He also proposed a four-way summit, which was unlikely to occur, that would include Iran, Syria, Iraq, and Turkey, with the possible participation of northern Iraq's Kurdish leaders, to discuss the fate of the Kurdish enclave.

His opening to Iran, with which he signed a mammoth $23 billion natural gas agreement, his attempts to improve relations with Iraq—almost at the expense of violating U.N. sanctions on Baghdad—and entreaties to Syria are designed to be more than a charm offensive.[35] Erbakan believed in his own ability to accomplish a great deal more with these countries because of his known opposition to U.S. policy in the region, including the Arab-Israeli peace process. In the short run, Erbakan would have liked to obtain Syria's and Iran's cooperation in controlling the PKK. Had he succeeded in this early on, he would have improved his stature not just with the population but perhaps also with a very skeptical military high command. Because the coalition agreement called for a rotation of prime ministers after two years, Erbakan quickly engaged himself in efforts to improve Turkey's relations with Middle Eastern states.[36]

It was in the interests of both Syria and Iran to cooperate with Erbakan; any rise in Welfare's success represents a corresponding decrease in the potential Turkish-Israeli rapprochement and in U.S. prestige in the region as a whole. Despite such obvious reasons for cooperating with the Erbakan-led government, Syria and Iran made little effort in this direction. Syria, which could have muzzled Öcalan, and Iran, which could have reduced its cooperation with the PKK, stood idle. Erbakan's attempts notwithstanding, the differences that separate Turkey from its two neighbors are real and significant. As a result, Syria and Iran were unlikely to relinquish as important a card as the PKK completely, especially since no one could assure them that the Erbakan government in Ankara would survive, and any other administration could easily revert back to previous policies. Ironically, it was only when the Erbakan-led government was in serious trouble with the military that Arab voices were raised in his support.[37]

Before embarking on his first tour of Islamic countries, Erbakan made sure that Operation Provide Comfort was extended for another five months, a policy he had opposed vigorously over the years. While he has not undone the deal with Israel, which the Turkish military has supported, he did manage to symbolically delay the signing of a companion agreement between the two militaries, but has had to give in to the military's demands vis-à-vis Israel. He has also not interfered with the military's continued raids across the border into Iraq (or for that matter, with operations within Turkey). This is as much the result of a balancing act as it is derived from his own opposition to the PKK. On the other hand, the mixture of a temperate policy vis-à-vis Western interests and an opening toward the east is precisely what Erbakan and Welfare had hoped to be able to accomplish in the next few years.

Erbakan's foreign policy vision is decidedly Ottomanist in flavor. He and his party, as suggested earlier, envision Turkey as a leader of an Islamic world. This can only be accomplished in the longer run by gradually weaning Turkey away from the West. Erbakan also realizes that the Kurdish issue remains one of the most important stumbling blocks to the realization of his long-term wish. While he tried to deal with this issue early during his term in office, by and large he was unsuccessful. It is not clear that had he remained in office he would have fared any better.

Notes and References

1. See also Henri J. Barkey, "Under the Gun: Turkish Foreign Policy and the Kurds," in *The Kurdish Nationalist Movement in the 1990s,* ed. Robert Olson, 65–83.

2. For a bitter criticism of the present policy, see Mensur Akgün, "Türkiye Köseye Sikisiyor" (Turkey is being cornered), *Yeni Yüzyil,* June 11, 1996. Also, Philip Robins demonstrates how the fear of the Kurdish issue has forced Turkey to expend enormous energies to lobby all governments in Europe, large and small, in "More Apparent than Real? The Impact of the Kurdish Issue on Euro-Turkish Relations," in *The Kurdish Nationalist Movement in the 1990s,* ed. Olson, 119.

3. Eric Rouleau argues that Turkey's importance for the West actually increased with the end of the Cold War. "Turkey: Beyond Atatürk," *Foreign Policy* 103 (Summer 1996): 84.

4. For a discussion of both the creation and the controversies surrounding this force, see Kemal Kirisçi, *Provide Comfort or Trouble: Kurdish Ethnicity and Turkish Foreign Policy* (Istanbul: Bogaziçi Üniversitesi Arastirma Raporu ISS/POLS 94-2, 1994); and Oran, *"Kalkik Horoz:" Çekiç Güç ve Kürt Devleti.*

5. On the other hand, the Kurds of northern Iraq have been subjected to a double embargo: one imposed by the UN on all of Iraq and another by the regime in Baghdad. Hence, their ability to survive as long as they did can be viewed as a success in spite of the breakdown in communications between the two predominant factions led by strong-willed leaders.

6. Similarly, Washington's criticism of the May 1997 incursion was mild.

7. Turan Yavuz, *ABD'nin Kürt Kardi* (The U.S.'s Kurdish card) (Istanbul: Milliyet Yayinlari, 1993), 102–4.

8. *Yeni Yüzyil,* May 10, 1996.

9. Hasan Köni, "Yeni Uluslararasi Düzende Türk-Amerikan Iliskileri," (Turkish-U.S. relations in the New International Order) *Yeni Türkiye* 1, no. 3 (March–April 1995): 432.

10. In 1993, 59.1 percent of Turkish exports were destined for OECD markets, whereas 67.9 percent of imports came from those same markets. Europe's share of total exports and imports for the same year were 47.5 and 44 percent, respectively. TÜSIAD, *The Turkish Economy, 1994* (Istanbul: TÜSIAD, 1994), 159, 161.

11. That membership in the customs union will increase European vigilance over Turkey's human rights performance is also echoed by European diplomats. See Ilnur Çevik, "Lobbying: Left-wing Leaders in Britain and Germany Are Trying to Convince Their Parliamentarians to Vote Favorably," *Turkish Daily News,* November 15, 1995.

12. Similarly, Turkish leaders were mobilized to block the possible selection of the jailed Kurdish member of parliament Leyla Zana as the 1995 recipient of the Nobel Peace price. She did, however, win the European Parliament's Sakharov prize, embarrassing Turkish leaders.

13. Robins points to the "plethora of Kurdish expatriate organizations in Europe" and argues that compared with the diversity of opinion among Iraqi Kurdish groups, the Turkish-Kurdish ones tend to be dominated by the PKK ("More Apparent than Real?" 117).

14. The visit by the official from the Office for the Protection of the Constitution came in the immediate aftermath of a similar visit by a member of the German Parliament (*Reuters,* November 25, 1995). Both of these visits have predictably infuriated the Ankara government.

15. See Robert Olson, "The Kurdish Question and Turkey's Foreign Policy, 1991–1995: From the Gulf War to the Incursion into Iraq," *Journal of South Asian and Middle Eastern Studies* 29, no. 1 (Fall 1995): 1–30.

16. The Turkish chief of staff, Ismail Karadayi, accused Greece, and particularly its intelligence apparatus, of setting up numerous front organizations to provide logistical and financial support to the PKK (*Cumhuriyet,* February 18, 1996).

17. Hamit Bozarslan, "La régionalisation du problème kurde," in *La nouvelle dynamique au Moyen Orient: Les relations entre l'Orient Arabe et al Turquie,* ed. Elisabeth Picard (Paris: L'Harmattan, 1993), 184.

18. For an Arab reaction, see Rashad Abu-Shawer, who writes in *al-Quds al-Arabi* that "Turkey has also been wielding the water weapon, the key to life itself, against Syria and Iraq, drawing off the upstream waters of the Euphrates and leaving the Syrians to 'drink mud' . . ." (*Mideast Mirror,* May 21, 1996, 16). For a discussion of the Syrian role and the importance of water see Gün Kut, "Burning Waters: Hydropolitics of the Euphrates and Tigris," in *New Perspectives on Turkey* 9 (Fall 1993), and Muhammad Muslih, "Syria and Turkey: Uneasy Relations," and Murhah Jouejati, "Water Politics as High Politics: The Case of Turkey and Syria," *Reluctant Neighbor: Turkey's Role in the Middle East,* ed. Henri J. Barkey (Washington, DC: United States Institute of Peace Press, 1996).

19. Some of the Arab concern was provoked by a comment made by President

Demirel following the March/April 1995 military incursion into northern Iraq, when he was quoted as having called for border modifications between the two countries. His comments revived, at least in some Arab minds, the question of Mosul, which in 1926 Turkey conceded to England and, indirectly, to Iraqi sovereignty. See "Arabs Alarmed by Demirel's Call for Redrawing the Iraq-Turkey Border," *Mideast Mirror,* May 4, 1995, 14–19.

20. Arbuckle, "Stalemate in the Mountains," 50.

21. For details on the history of the PKK-KDP relationship, see Michael Gunter, "Kurdish Infighting: The PKK-KDP Conflict," in *The Kurdish Nationalist Movement in the 1990s,* ed. Olson, 50–62.

22. For a discussion of the burgeoning Turkish-Israeli ties see Allan Makovsky, "Israeli-Turkish Relations: A Turkish 'Periphery Strategy?' " in *Reluctant Neighbor: Turkey's Role in the Middle East,* ed. Henri J. Barkey, 147–170.

23. *Cumhuriyet,* November 9, 1995. Turkish-Syrian relations took a turn for the worse following an incursion by a large PKK contingent from Syria into Turkey and Syrian foreign minister Faruk al-Shaara's reported comments, which classified PKK activities as "resistance" and not "terrorist" (*Cumhuriyet,* November 28, 1995).

24. Ommar Salmon in *al-Ayyam,* reprinted in *Mideast Mirror,* May 6, 1997.

25. Even before the end of the Iran-Iraq War, the Iraqis made clear to visiting high-ranking Turkish officers their displeasure with Turkish air raids on their territory. Necip Torumtay, *Orgeneral Torumtay'in Anilari,* 86–87.

26. For a discussion of future possibilities in Iraq, see Graham E. Fuller, *Iraq in the Next Decade: Will Iraq Survive until 2002?,* RAND. N-3591-DAG, 1993.

27. Mehmet Ali Birand, "Türkiye, Kuzey Irak'ta Sinir Degisikligi Yapiyor . . ." (Turkey is implementing border changes in Northern Iraq) *Sabah,* June 25, 1996.

28. This way the KDP joined forces with the Turkish minority in May 1997 to dislodge the PKK. It is too early to tell whether this has been successful. The KDP may also have wanted to shore up its relations with Turkey at the expense of its archrival the PKK and also reduce its dependency on Saddam Hussein.

29. See, for instance, *Al-Sharq al-Awsat's* equating Turkey's attempts not just with the Israeli security belt in southern Lebanon but also with the Iraqi invasion of Kuwait in 1990. Reprinted in *Mideast Mirror,* September 10, 1996.

30. This was in the context of the March 11, 1970, peace accord, which collapsed. For details, see McDowall, *A Modern History of the Kurds,* 32–39.

31. While the Iraqi Shi'a will over time eventually gain dominant influence in Iraq as the majority of the population, fears that they will be dominated by Iran are largely without foundation. Iraqi Shi'a are keenly aware of their Arabness and, if anything, are rivals with Iran for voice over the international Shi'ite community.

32. Mehmet Ali Birand, "Kuzey Irak, Türkiye'nin Kontrolünden Kaçiyor" (Northern Iraq is escaping Turkish control) *Sabah,* June 26, 1996.

33. For the linkage between Turkey's Kurdish problems and how Moscow has sought to exploit them to limit if not silence Turkish criticism of its Chechen policy, see Robert Olson, "The Kurdish Question and Chechnya: Turkish and Russian

Foreign Policies since the Gulf War," *Middle East Policy* 4, no. 3 (March 1996); 106–18.

34. This is a fear that the military has taken seriously. According to *Cumhuriyet,* the Staff War Colleges published a report arguing that Russia has been offering the PKK logistical support to enable it to hit the pipeline project from Baku to the Mediterranean coast in Turkey (June 20, 1996).

35. Access to Iran is critical to any Turkish strategy that seeks to reduce dependence on Russia for gas and other such products.

36. To his dismay, Erbakan also found that the Kurdish question can rebound. During Erbakan's visit to Libya in October 1996, Colonel Kadaffi's intemperate public remarks regarding Turkish ill treatment of its Kurdish minority and his call for an independent Kurdistan created a furor back home for the Turkish prime minister, who had also managed to further alienate the U.S. by undertaking the trip.

37. The editors of two leading Saudi-owned publications, *al Hayat* and *Asharq al-Awsat,* came to the defense of Erbakan. *Al Hayat*'s Jihad Khazen went so far as to say that "the duty of Arabs and Moslems is to help [Erbakan] as much as they can." See *Mideast Mirror,* April 17, 1997. Also see Mohammed al-Hassan Ahmad in *Asharq al-Awsat* reprinted in *Mideast Mirror,* May 6, 1997.

7

Toward a Solution of the Kurdish Problem

The Nature of the Kurdish Problem

THE ESSENTIALS OF THE Kurdish problem can be reduced to four key elements in any search for a solution. First, while there are multiple aspects to the Kurdish problem, it is essential to recognize that the problem is fundamentally an ethnic one, thereby requiring an ethnic solution. The emergence of ethnic politics among the Kurds, as we described earlier, comes as a reaction to the official Turkish nationalism of the modern Turkish state and reflects a wider growth of ethnic consciousness on a global basis. The emergence of different ethnicities within one state does not, of course, imply automatic conflict. But historically, conflict has periodically arisen between Turks and Kurds.

The internal violence and virtual civil war or "anarchy" of the 1970s in Turkey mobilized many left-wing Kurds (as well as Turks) into ideological movements struggling to dismantle the existing state structure. It was out of this milieu that the PKK emerged, bringing by far the most serious Kurdish armed struggle into Turkish politics since the founding of the state. State violence in response against the PKK and the suffering this military campaign has visited upon the Kurds in the southeast have clearly exacerbated the problem and served to polarize the conflict. It is conceivable that the Kurdish search for official recognition of the Kurdish identity might not have taken military form if the PKK had not emerged when it did, and if, in response, the state had not taken such a hard line against Kurdish political and cultural aspirations.

While this kind of "what if" analysis is rather hypothetical, it does suggest that armed conflict between Turks and Kurds in Turkey was not predestined, even if rising Kurdish demands were. It also suggests that a political solution may yet be found if the quest for a polarizing military solution is abandoned. We do not believe that the Kurdish identity is likely to fade, since few other larger and unfulfilled nationalist movements elsewhere in the world are fading; furthermore, the political identity of the Kurds in Turkey is strengthened by the Kurdish struggle in both Iraq and Iran.

Major economic improvements and increased democratization in the southeast will help alleviate some symptoms of the crisis, but in the end a solution that addresses the ethnic character of the problem is required. At a minimum that means clear recognition of the existence of the Kurds as a culturally distinct identity, and recognition of the rights of Kurds to express their culture fully under a system of cultural autonomy. This would imply some degree of regional responsibility that permits Kurds to run many of their own local affairs—obviously excluding major national issues such as defense, currency, overall security, national economic policy, and foreign affairs.

It would be inappropriate, however, for this study to specify exact formulas; those can only come through a political process over time. In this context, Turks need to be aware that their problems are not unique; large numbers of other states in the world have faced and still face similar problems. The international community has accumulated much experience and developed a wide variety of formulas and mechanisms in other countries that might prove relevant to an eventual Turkish-Kurdish solution.

Second, the onus of responsibility for a solution lies with the Turkish state rather than with the Kurds as people. In Turkey the conflict is not, as it often is in other countries, between two mobilized and competing communities; here it is between a weak community attempting to mobilize and the state. The state is fundamentally responsible for the creation of the problem by its fateful decision in the 1920s to create a nation-state defined as consisting of Turks alone, compounded by several decades of enforced assimilation of Kurds—a decision that can no longer be sustained, imposed, or implemented. Continuing attempts to impose such a solution without formal acknowledgment of the existence of the Kurds will only lead to continued and perhaps even increased bloodshed and will only strengthen the possibility that the Kurds will indeed eventually insist on total independence.

Furthermore, the state holds virtually all the cards: The Kurds themselves have almost nothing to concede in negotiations, for they have nothing that the state wants except retreat from their demands. If a compromise is to be reached, the most the Kurds can offer is eventual peace, loyalty, and nonviolence. Even these Kurdish "concessions" will still entail demands upon the state that the state does not welcome, but they can come in the context of a retreat from some of the initially maximalist demands of the PKK for separatism and the establishment of a pan-Kurdish state.

Certainly, alternative Kurdish political parties inside Turkey can be more sensitive to Turkish public opinion so as not to exacerbate existing tensions, but with the state wielding most of the power, compromise depends more on the state than on any other factor. Only the PKK has offered the Kurds a genuine element of power vis-à-vis the state through military resistance and the costs it can impose on the state. Actual initiatives in negotiations can come only from the parties that hold the power. This does not mean that the PKK can be the only spokesman for the Kurds; the Kurds in fact have not yet had an opportunity to freely demonstrate just whom it is they do want to represent them.

Third, a critical part of the problem lies in the need to reformulate the very concept of the Turkish state as perceived by its citizens. Is the state a monolithic instrument, charged with the mission of forging a nation, preserving the state as it is known, and retaining a paternalistic hold over its development? Or is the state the instrument of its combined citizenry to attain the goals they seek? The former, statist concept, which emerges from nation-building concepts of an earlier era, was indeed relevant to Turkey in the Atatürkist period, when entirely new concepts were required to replace those of the collapsed imperial, multinational, and authoritarian Ottoman Empire. But today, it has become evident to all that the state has partially failed in its mission to homogenize the population: After more than seventy years, while some groups have been successfully integrated, the Kurdish question has not disappeared and indeed is growing. Thus, until the vision changes—in which the state is no longer the master but the servant of the people—it is unlikely that Turkey will be able to progress toward a solution to the Kurdish problem. This transformation of the role of the state does not pose a threat to the sovereignty of the state per se, but rather only to the role of the state over all of its citizens—Turk, Kurd, and others. The good news is that this transition is quite feasible for Turkey to manage, given its major progress toward democratization, liberalization, and the emergence of a strong civil society over the past decades. Other states facing such ethnic challenges are not so well off.

Fourth, there is a factor of time that cannot be ignored. Whatever military gains or losses are taking place on the ground, Kurdish self-awareness is expanding and will not go away. Changing global conditions—greater acceptance of nationalist movements in the aftermath of the collapse of the Soviet Union, the break-up of Yugoslavia, and any new political balances that might emerge in the Middle East following successful Israeli-PLO negotiations—will increasingly make it difficult for Turkey to ignore its own domestic diversity and pluralism. Thus the Turkish state does not have an indefinite amount of time to seek an equitable solution; the longer it takes to find resolution, the more radicalized the Kurds may become and the higher the cost of a settlement grows. The state deliberates over the issue as if time did not matter, but the clock is ticking, and certain realities are being created domestically and internationally that are not fully under the state's control.

The Kurdish factor in Iraq, for example, is also developing rapidly; Iraq cannot go back to the status quo ante of the 1960s, when the Iraqi Kurds had few political demands. Eventually, Iraq must move in the direction of some kind of federal state if the Iraqi state is ever to stay together. As argued earlier, Turkey would be wise to have settled its own Kurdish problem to the satisfaction of its Kurds by that time; Iraqi Kurds possessing a fair degree of autonomy will otherwise be a destabilizing model to Turkey's Kurds.

Conversely, satisfied Turkish Kurds can have major influence upon northern Iraq, possibly making Turkey the dominant free Kurdish voice in the region—the largest and freest body of Kurds in the Middle East. Turkey's Kurds, together with Turkey's own power, skills, and resources, can then become the leader and partner of all regional Kurds on many issues. At that point, Diyarbakir becomes a huge potential entrepôt for regional trade and communications, instead of an isolated city in a distant region near closed and militarized borders. If Turkey fails to satisfy the cultural aspirations of its own Kurds, it not only becomes permanent hostage to its own Kurds but also to events in the Kurdish regions of Iraq, Iran, and Syria—whose own internal political situations are very repressive, unstable, and doomed to face major upheaval. Nor can Ankara achieve its goals by pretending to ignore the Kurdish reality in Iraq, especially because it may not be able to influence it in the long run. Turkey's choices would thus seem to be clear—but that does not mean that the process of getting there is easy.

The Spectrum of Potential Solutions

Turkey possesses a broad spectrum of options in handling the Kurdish ethnic problem—ranging from totally repressing all ethnic expression of Kurds to granting the Kurds total independence. Both of these are undesirable extremes, with obviously a great range of choice in between. And while the problem is essentially an ethnic one, improvement of economic factors in the southeast will always have a beneficial influence on any situation, however bad. We review below the broad spectrum, in rough order of least change to greatest change. We believe that solutions to the Kurdish problem are to be found in some combination of solutions in the upper middle ranges of change, and not in the extremes of either repression or the foundation of an independent Kurdish state. In other words, realistic solutions are ones that satisfy Kurdish aspirations without truly threatening a modern democratic Turkey. This is a complex but quite achievable goal.

Repression and Enforced Assimilation

This study posits that the "solution" of repression is no longer realistic. Kurdish ethnic demands will have to be met to some extent, and they will grow more radical and extreme in expression as long as assimilation is the Kurds' only choice. Failure to acknowledge Kurdish ethnicity and cultural aspirations can only damage Turkey's economy, moral tone, stability, democratic order, and international standing. Some Kurds in Turkey have over time become assimilated—that is, turkified—but a significant number have not and are unlikely to become assimilated, especially during a period of conflict. In fact, it is more likely that the trend will be in the other direction—that is, toward assertion of the Kurdish identity. Today, precisely because so many within Turkey and outside have come to realize the mistakes of state policies in the past, it would be difficult to justify a new campaign of repression and forced assimilation. There is no ideological or even practical raison d'être for it. It is quite clear that such a policy would not only do severe damage to Turkey internationally, but it would also find many more detractors within Turkey itself. In effect, this would be a return to the 1920s and 1930s, which is unrealistic. There is no indication that the Ankara government is even seriously envisaging such a policy, although some may hope that by moving large numbers of Kurds to the West, they will lose their ethnic identity. There is no conclusive evidence that this is the case.

Maintaining the Status Quo

The status quo in Turkey is itself proving unstable and unsustainable—although it can be maintained for quite a number of years more if the cost is not calculated. Most of this study has focused on the future of the status quo option. Its primary policy basis is that the "terror must stop and then we can consider solutions." With massive use of military manpower and continuing evacuation of Kurdish villages—at a higher level than today—the army can probably reduce political violence in the region. But such a calm will be neither real nor permanent. It can be sustained only by military means, and violence and terror will reassert themselves once military forces start to withdraw.

As argued earlier, the process of politicization is difficult to reverse, especially with the degree to which international boundaries are rendered irrelevant with modern communications techniques. The Kurds in Turkey do not live in isolation anymore, cut off from the rest of the world, from their government, from their brothers and sisters in other cities and townships in Turkey. The Turkish government has, to quote Cem Boyner, bombed its own territory for more than ten years and it is no closer to resolving the issue than it was before the Gulf War. With the exception of Özal, there has been little effort expended at devising new ways to undermine the violence option. Violence can be undercut only when Kurds realize that they have clear reason for hope for progress using other means. In terms of public debate, which includes officials and politicians, most institutions and individuals acknowledge the need for change; for many it is only a question of when and how much. In short, in our view the status quo is not sustainable.

Cultural Concessions

The state can quickly make several cultural gestures to the Kurds, particularly in the areas of the Kurdish language. Language is one of the dearest and most emotional vehicles of any culture. Kurdish, despite its different dialects, is a distinct language, quite unrelated to Turkish. Among various cultural reforms, among the easiest to achieve and most effective are the freedom to publish and broadcast in Kurdish, the right to give Kurdish names to one's children and to offer private education to children in Kurdish, the reversion to original Kurdish place names in Kurdish regions, and tolerance for cultural activities of all types that celebrate Kurdish diversity. Above all, the state could explicitly and publicly recognize the existence of the Kurdish identity. Such steps would undoubtedly attract Kurdish attention and encourage a certain spectrum of Kurds to start looking to the state for further steps toward full acceptance of the Kurdish identity—via negotiations rather than by armed conflict. Such steps by the state would very likely begin to weaken support for the PKK if the arena of cultural and political progress for the Kurds were perceived to be shifting away from the battlefield to the state. These cultural steps are not likely to be sufficient in themselves over the longer run to satisfy the (growing) aspirations of most Kurds, but they will buy time and possibly force a change in the PKK's strategy and tactics, and they may even weaken it vis-à-vis other Kurdish organizations.

An important component of such cultural reform measures must include a toning down of the state's barrage of Kemalist discourse (statism and the mono-ethnic state, with all its slogans[1]) and with it its attempt to socialize all its citizens forcibly. In other words, it is not sufficient for the state to allow the private expressions of cultural plurality; the state must actually believe in it. Demirel, for instance, has argued that "you cannot forcibly call a Kurd a Turk,"[2] and yet he has refused to support education or TV broadcasts in Kurdish, or ease up on the other pressures. Similarly, as a response to the PKK-instigated celebrations at Nevruz, the Kurdish New Year, the Turkish government in 1994 declared Nevruz to be a Turkish holiday; but rather than trying to incorporate it, the new policy tried to deny the very Kurdishness of Nevruz and turkify it, in the process enraging many Kurds.

As simple as they may appear, these cultural reforms undermine one of the more fundamental principles of the Kemalist state: the notion of a unitary ethnic polity. It is worth remembering, however, that at present the challenge to the Kemalist state does not come exclusively from the Kurds. The Islamists seek a revision of the strict secularist ideology of the Kemalist project (which to many is not Western secularism but rather a state assault against all religious institutions.) The Islamists feel that their own Muslim identity is under assault. The Alevis too seek recognition of their own distinctness. These movements represent trends that also undermine the imposed essence of a uniform Turkish body politic. Still, the Kurdish assertions, because they contain the potential kernel of separatism, are the most dangerous ones for the state.[3]

The Kurds of the southeast also suffer from cultural, economic, and political exclusion. In other words, the southeast is not only the most economically disadvantaged region of the country, but in addition the cultural barriers and poor access to proper Turkish education have further deepened differences between Kurds and the rest of Turkish citizenry.[4] On the other hand, cultural concessions they seek should not be that significant to the state when considered within the context of an expanding, dynamic, and increasingly internationally integrated economy. Indeed, a number of Kurds, in and out of the southeast, have expressed the view that their children would be better off if they studied English or another international language instead of Kurdish.[5]

The important issue here is whether the state interprets the cultural changes as individual rights or as group rights. Allowing individuals to form cultural associations or publish or broadcast in Kurdish in a laissez-faire cultural atmosphere is very different from defining quotas and proportions. For example, by deciding a priori that if 20 percent of the population speaks Kurdish then only 20 percent of broadcast time can be devoted to Kurdish, the state is in effect establishing and delimiting group rights, and thus planting the seeds of separatist thinking.

Another often sought cultural reform regards the creation of institutes at universities for the study of Kurdish and Kurds. To Kurds this not only represents the official recognition of their existence but also provides the means to further develop a language that has suffered from neglect.[6] Already, independent Kurdish cultural associations exist with branches in different cities in the country, especially in Istanbul and Izmir. Among the better known ones is the Mesopotamia Cultural Association. Often harassed by the security services, such groups are not in fact associations per se but are incorporated business establishments, a necessary legal tactic to circumvent the rather restrictive association laws. A potentially positive development is the recent licensing of the Kurdish Foundation for Research and Culture.[7] We have already commented on the extreme shortsightedness of state policies that force Kurds to try to listen to PKK-sponsored TV programs in Kurdish by satellite, rather than permitting the state to broadcast in Kurdish.

Finally, acceptance of the cultural diversity of Turkey should not be taken as a reflection of the country's weakness. This said, the acknowledgment of diversity must be reflected in laws and regulation. Turkey had gone too far in trying to deny Kurds' existence by explicitly forbidding the use of the Kurdish language, by changing the names of villages from Kurdish to Turkish, and by not permitting parents to give Kurdish names to their offspring. Not only will these policies have to be reversed—as some have already been—but, more important, the Turkish public will have to be educated that these do not represent separatist or threatening activities.

Economic Programs

There is no question that decades of economic neglect have fueled the unhappiness of Turkey's Kurds. Major economic improvements are essential to a solution of the Kurdish problem but are not sufficient in themselves if they ignore the question of ethnic identity and cultural rights. It is economic hardship and underdevelopment that explain the large number of Kurds who have migrated to the cities in search of better opportunities—along with the razing of thousands of Kurdish villages in recent years of civil conflict in the southeast. However, those who end up in the cities, while doing better than in their places of origin, tend to occupy the lowest rungs of the economic ladder.

Hence any solution to the Kurdish problem will necessarily include an attempt at redressing the economic ills of the region. Since 1960, the southeastern and eastern provinces have been designated in State Planning Office documents and plans as disadvantaged areas in need of extra investments and incentives. Despite this categorization, investments to these re-

gions have not only failed to meet expectations, but in addition most have
been ghost investments: The state would initiate plans to build a factory,
but, more often than not, the investment would fail to materialize. By
1992, whereas GNP per capita for Turkey was $2,032, in the eastern prov-
inces this figure declined to $300.[8] Even Prime Minister Çiller's July 1995
announcement—executed with great fanfare amid a meeting of all the governors and security officials—that huge sums of money would be invested
in the southeast was greeted with a great deal of skepticism given the past
record, not to mention the sorry state, of Turkish public finances at the
time. Since then, other such programs announced by successive governments have met equal skepticism.

One of the critical problems for the southeast is the increasing bifurca-
tion that has occurred in the Turkish economy since January 1980. Then,
in a dramatic change, Turkey abandoned its inward-oriented economic
strategy in favor of a more open one. Almost immediately after the consolidation of this new strategy the Iran-Iraq War erupted, providing Turkey
with very large export markets to both belligerents. These were also the
neighboring states of the Kurdish areas, which allowed the Kurds to benefit extensively from the transit traffic. Unfortunately for this region, by the
mid to late 1980s the trade with these countries had slowed considerably.
But by then the qualitative difference between these less developed regions
and those that are more manufacturing-oriented had increased even more.
As western Turkey strove to export to Europe and OECD countries, it
attracted the lion's share of private and public investments. Turkish businessmen, who rarely considered investing in the southeast anyway, now
had even fewer reasons to do so. Kurdish businessmen have tended to
invest in the western provinces of Turkey, since the opportunities there
were so much more profitable. The emergence of the ethnic conflict in the
southeast, then, was simply the coup de grâce for the region.[9]

Yet no significant economic development can be attained in the southeast until the conflict is brought to an end. As long as the region is a
war zone—villages are being destroyed, crops and animals are being killed,
whole areas are being evacuated—the process of reconstruction is made
impossible. Forty-four percent of the rural population used to be engaged
in animal husbandry, an activity that has suffered severely from the hostilities;[10] the PKK has sought to kidnap flocks, and the state has imposed
severe restrictions on peasants' ability to take the flocks grazing. In large
areas security is insufficient for agriculture to be safely pursued. Any state

investments will become targets for the PKK. No private investors will dream of putting money into the region as long as it is threatened by military action or sabotage.[11]

Once a political agreement is reached with the Kurds, however, and the fighting comes to an end, the state can begin a process of reconstruction in the region, starting with rebuilding the villages so that villagers can return. Private investment can be encouraged at this point. Ironically, if the Turkish private sector is still reticent about investing in the southeast, there is a growing Kurdish bourgeoisie in the western cities that might be more willing to take risks unacceptable to others. One should not, however, underestimate the difficulty of this enterprise. For the reasons suggested above, the private sector will be reluctant to undertake projects in an area far away from the main trading routes. There have been many publicly heralded attempts by large industrial concerns to invest in the southeast. Most have not amounted to much. The latest such venture, called "Dogu Holding," is the brainchild of the president of the Istanbul Chamber of Commerce, Mehmet Yildirim. His idea is to have 400 large firms pool their resources by each investing some $60,000 into a common firm that will concentrate on animal husbandry and agriculture.[17]

Turkish officials have put a great deal of emphasis for the rehabilitation of the southeast on the Southeastern Anatolia Project, the GAP project. The GAP project, while not completely located in the Kurdish southeast, can potentially contribute a great deal to the region in general. It is designed to considerably augment electricity generation and the quantity of arable land through the development of a new irrigation network. The project emphasizes the development of more commercial forms of agriculture and an increase in the cultivation of cash crops. One such crop is cotton, whose cultivation is expected to increase by 200 percent, the gains coming at the expense of wheat; another such is tomatoes.[13] While these crops have higher market value, if they simply compete with other regions for a piece of a small pie in a shrinking export market their added value will not be of great significance. On the other hand, should the region's entrepreneurs succeed in opening Middle Eastern markets, then the prospects for the GAP project will be considerably enhanced.[14]

Yet with little industry in the southeast and the GAP region, much of the electricity generated will be channeled westward, as will the cotton crop. GAP's emphasis on electricity generation, driven by expected shortfalls in available electricity by the end of the century, can be seen in the fact that some 90 percent of the GAP's electricity generation targets have been completed, compared with only 5 percent of the irrigation targets.[15] Within the region, some provinces have done significantly better than others. Gaziantep and Sanliurfa have distanced the others as they have attracted investments from other regions. They have not been at the epicenter of the conflict either.

Another issue often overlooked with respect to this project is the skewed distribution of land: The southeast has one of the worst land distribution patterns in the country, a fact much aggravated by the conflict. This is one of the consequences of the decision of the state not to engage in land reform in the southeast, unlike other regions of the country, after 1945—a decision that was politically motivated because parties sought to capture the region's votes by engaging only the aghas and shaykhs. This has also retarded the development of a more enterprising peasantry.[16] Many people already complain that few individuals with good party connections have succeeded in getting the state to allocate large tracts of land to them. Nevertheless, the GAP project, once completed with care, will undoubtedly be a help to the region.

There is no doubt that economic advancement in the southeast is critically important to any state effort to win the Kurdish population in the region over to the benefits of association with Turkey.

It is imperative to slow down the exodus of large numbers of peasants from the southeast into western Turkey: They enter the big cities, increase unemployment, contribute to greater urban instability in overgrown cities, and are likely to be politically radicalized. Indeed it is also necessary to begin a process of reverse migration. It is unlikely that all those who migrated as a result of the conflict will return; nonetheless, the proposition that the state ought to encourage those who return has been well established, even though the conflict continues to claim more refugees. Improved economic conditions will reduce incentives for separatism, which at the moment are not yet high. An improved economy would give the Kurds a stake in a Turkey that has the potential of becoming a full-fledged member of the European Union, even if the target date for such an eventuality is decades away at this stage. In any case, a Turkey that is a member of the customs union is more attractive than one that is not.

Finally, Turkey needs to rethink the entire concept of a "Kurdistan." Bold reforms and institutional change over the longer run are far more likely to strengthen Turkey than weaken it. Turkey's Kurdistan will very likely forge natural and organic ties with the Iraqi Kurdistan to the south, and even with Iranian Kurdistan to the east, as well as deeper south into Baghdad and Tehran. Turkey is by far the most developed, most democratic, and strongest economy in the region, with deepening ties to Europe. This kind of a Turkey will potentially find its own Kurdish region—integrally linked with Turkey—as an economic and social magnet for all Kurds of the region. It is Iraq and Iran that need to be more concerned about the magnet affect reaching out of Turkey. Turkey stands to be the major beneficiary of an eventual opening of borders and an increase of ties among all Kurds of the region. Diyarbakir is the natural capital of the Kurdish region. Thus, while the development of these new relationships in the region involves the acceptance of a lot of new thinking by Turkey, the trend is inevitable and ultimately part of a global phenomenon of states that aspire to be part of the successful and functioning international order. Turkey over the longer run needs to face these developments with the confidence that its degree of development affords it.

Diminished Security Presence

State willingness to withdraw special teams from the region, lessen the presence of the gendarmarie and the regular army, reorganize or dismantle the village guard system, and lift the rule of emergency law would have major impact on the political situation. It would impress upon Kurds that new policies were underway and would stimulate a great deal of hope for the future, especially if combined with cultural concessions. It would clear the way for normalization of life and improve the conditions for commerce, trade, and investment in the region—and begin to allow the Kurds to return to a normal life, which they have not known for over a decade at least.

Reduction of the military presence in the southeast, however, represents a calculated risk for the state, and could only come as part of a broader commitment to move toward comprehensive political change in Turkey. Significant reduction or withdrawal opens the region to much increased political activity by many different groups—including both the PKK and those that might be rivals. The PKK would unquestionably take advantage of the withdrawal of military forces to extend its presence—although possibly without violence, particularly if a cease-fire were agreed to on both sides. The PKK would also be increasingly subjected to the realities of

Kurdish political life; the popularity of its programs and policies would be on trial with the Kurdish public. The PKK claims it is more than willing to take that risk by making the transition to peaceful politics rather than continue an armed struggle. If it were not willing to do so, and other representative Kurdish political organizations were to come into being, those organizations would bear the brunt of opposing the activities of the PKK if it were no longer popular among most Kurds, and probably it would be more ideologically effective at doing so than the state is now.

But continuation of the armed struggle by the PKK under these circumstances could not be completely ruled out, although a new dynamic would be at work in the region. The state would be attempting to demonstrate to Kurds that new state policies were moving toward satisfaction of most major Kurdish grievances. Even if a majority of Kurds were encouraged to cooperate with new state policies, it might take several years before hard-core PKK numbers might give up violence altogether. The state has almost no alternative, however, since continuation of the military pressure and repression creates conditions that push large numbers of Kurds toward the PKK as their only alternative. Cultural reforms for a period of time in advance of military withdrawal would definitely begin the process of moving numbers of Kurds away from active or passive support of PKK violence. Insistence that the state will make no reforms until all violence stops will not be trusted by Kurds, although it might bring about a mutual cease-fire, which the PKK has proclaimed itself ready for.

One issue that cannot be overlooked is the village guard system, which has, over the years, deepened the divisions within Kurdish society. Any dismantling or reconfiguration has to take into account the ill will that exists in the region between the guards and their local adversaries. These tensions provide the raw material for settling of scores and even blood feuds for some time to come.

Legalization of Kurdish Political Parties

Political parties in pluralistic and divided societies are not immune from the influences of class, regionalism, ethnicity, religion, and race. Turkey is no exception. Despite the proscription on appeals to religious and cultural differences, political parties in Turkey have surreptitiously made use of symbols and messages. The Alevis have traditionally voted en masse for the parties most identified with secularism, which has traditionally meant the Republican People's party (CHP). In the southeast, parties have proposed candidates with strong tribal ties to appeal to Kurdish votes. The Welfare party has never hidden its intentions while campaigning on a pro-Islamic platform.

The most cherished of the prohibitions, the ban on ethnic Kurdish parties, was not really broken until the emergence of the Kurdish HEP in an alliance with the SHP in the 1991 elections. This event has had a deeply unsettling impact on Turkish politics, as discussed above. HADEP, the last in the line of successors to the HEP, had been slowly inching its way into respectability. Legally, however, the Constitutional Court has the power to ban any party it deems threatening to the integrity of the state; that could yet include HADEP, although the foreign repercussions of its closure would be politically costly for Turkey.

HEP, DEP, and now HADEP have proven their ability to garner significant support, and they would probably have gained more if the state did not try to limit their appeal. The decision to permit ethnic parties to exist, however, is not a decision to be taken lightly. In a state that does not recognize the existence of ethnic minorities, ethnic-based parties are a source of potential friction. Political parties in a pluralistic society can be stabilizing institutions, but in divided ones they can have the opposite effect: They not only articulate existing grievances but also serve as a mobilizing and, therefore, polarizing influence. Such parties also make it difficult for nonconformist and smaller groups to exist independently, because they are forced into ethnic coalitions or engender ethnic countermobilization among rival ethnic communities. These are the concerns the Turkish authorities would advance in thinking about whether to acknowledge the existence of a Kurdish minority. It is an argument that has some foundation. The Turkish authorities can also point out that the Kurds are not the sole ethnic minority in Turkey: There are Circassians, Arabs, Laz, and so forth. With virtually every one of these other minorities, however, there is a Circassian, Laz, or Arab "homeland," whereas southeastern Turkey *is* the Kurdish homeland.

Ethnic parties are especially dangerous when the population of a state is evenly divided among two or more communities. It is then that their tendencies to destabilize the system and encourage intergroup conflict become pronounced. Parties then tend to become one-issue parties; they eschew moderation in favor of maximizing their vote potential by moving to the extreme, and their voters tend to remain loyal irrespective of outcomes.[17]

Yet Turkey in fact does not possess any of the problematic characteristics described above. The Kurdish community is not of an equal weight to the Turkish community, but rather constitutes a minority. Furthermore, Kurds in Turkey, whenever given an opportunity to vote for a distinctly ethnic party, have tended to split their votes among ethnic and nonethnic parties, indicating that, as a group, they behave in a more sophisticated manner than outsiders expect them to. Also, the level of polarization has not yet assumed extreme levels. And a Kurdish party faces many difficulties because, in a genuinely pluralistic system, as Turkey aspires to be, ethnicity may not be the most salient determinant of Kurdish voting behavior. In the 1995 elections, large numbers of potential HADEP voters in Istanbul appear to have cast their lot with the Welfare party because it had the ability to directly affect their daily lives.

Second, political parties have to produce results: A party representing a genuine minority cannot afford to alienate the majority perpetually, because it will then be shut out of the benefits the political system has to offer—even to those in opposition. Therefore, if such a party is completely incapable of delivering services to its potential voters, it will invite competitors. Any Kurdish party—including the PKK—might not automatically win a landslide of votes unless Kurdish voters were convinced that clear benefits would come from it. Ideally there might be not one but several Kurdish parties that would join in coalition with Turkish parties to work most efficiently for their own region.

On the other hand, there are many benefits to having one or more ethnic parties representing a community. They offer a means of political assimilation without compromising one's identity. Such parties—as long as they do not subscribe to violence—can consolidate the interests of a specific group that has hitherto been ignored and thus can provide an outlet for expressions of ethnic solidarity. As such, the Turkish establishment ought not fear such a party; on the contrary, it should welcome it at this stage because the state has otherwise failed to integrate the bulk of Kurds in the southeast through the old Kemalist model. And encouraging such parties to form alliances with other mainstream parties would help diffuse the process of polarization. One important Turkish politician who seems to think that not only ethnic parties but all other parties should have a fair chance to get their representatives into Parliament is Korkut Özal, the late president's brother. He even believes that the PKK ought to be legalized: "If their intention is not to kill but to seek some political and economic objectives, then the best way to achieve these is to enter into the political system. You cannot win by fighting in the mountains."[18]

This is not to say that such parties might not spawn more extremist ones or that they themselves might not be captured by their own extremists. No one can provide such a guarantee, but in a nontransparent system such as Turkey's, in which security officials enjoy tremendous judicial and extra-judicial powers, the process of ethnic polarization is already well under way even without such parties; the state therefore has little to lose by try-ing. This said, Turkish government and society have every reason to expect that such parties would not sanction or call for violence.

Devolution of Power and Decentralization

Just like any other country, Turkey is being buffeted by two contradictory global forces: the pull of the international economy and the localization of politics. In order to cope with these forces, the state structure needs to become more adaptable and flexible. It has to be able simultaneously to offer an integrated economic space and, at the same time, devolve power to local authorities; the central government can otherwise no longer cope with the complex impact of globalization upon these local communities.

Decreasing the Role of the Military

The task of decentralization of power and control begins with reduction of the lingering role of the Turkish army in politics. With the frequency of military interventions—1960, 1971, and 1980—the public has almost come to take the army for granted in its political calculations.[19]

The efforts initiated by President Özal to further civilian control and distance the military from daily politics ended abruptly with his death. Since then, both the prime minister and the president have continued to defer to—even abdicate responsibility to—the generals on major security issues, including the Kurdish question. The military's influence on politi-cians is not always direct: Very often, politicians will simply fail to act, or take an initiative precisely because they fear alienating the commanders, even if the latter have not expressed their preferences on a particular issue.[20] In February of 1994, the chief of staff at that time, General Dogan Güres, said in an interview that one ought not look for terrorists only in the mountains or in Lebanon's Bekaa Valley, but also in the Parliament. This set the stage for Prime Minister Çiller's successful maneuver to throw DEP members out of Parliament, remove their immunity, and then eventually try and sentence them.

Critical to the process of democratization is the separation of the civilian domain from military influence. The increased militarization of politics in the southeast was the predictable outcome of the insurrection. Not only has the conduct of the counterinsurgency campaign fallen to the purview of the military, but civil-military relations have also suffered as a result of the extension of the military's influence into domestic issues and foreign policymaking. The prominence of the National Security Council—in principle only an advisory body—and the deference shown to it obfuscate the distinction between the political leadership and the generals.[21] The ascendancy of military influence was also felt in the campaign that the generals conducted against the Erbakan-Çiller government in the spring of 1997, which eventually resulted in the resignation and defeat of that civilian leadership. The NSC's growing influence as a result of the insurrection has reversed the trend initiated by former president Özal. He had successfully capitalized on the military's heavy hand in the post-1980 coup to reduce some of their prerogatives. Since his death, however, political leaders have been more than willing to defer to the military in matters concerning the conduct of the counterinsurgency, in part because it indirectly absolves them from assuming responsibility for what generally is a failed policy. If this is failure, it does not seem to tarnish the armed forces: It is still the most respected institution in Turkey, as poll after poll has demonstrated.

No matter how severe its security aspects, the Kurdish problem in Turkey is fundamentally a political question, and it is about very difficult choices and decisions. The interference of the military serves to undermine the political process, creating incentives for politicians not to tackle what is an arduous process and also intimidating them, insofar as the problems present a moral challenge. How can a politician overrule people whose lives are perceived to be in harm's way? It is a classical dilemma faced in many countries at different times during their existence. For Turkey, it is one that has to be faced soon.

Decentralization

The process of democratization is not solely restricted to reducing the influence of the military. As argued earlier, the two contradictory forces of our time, the globalization of economic forces and the localization of politics, are quickly overwhelming the capabilities of the modern centralized state. Historically, the Turkish state has been overly centralized, primarily as a defense against centrifugal forces within the country. Ankara is at the center of all administrative decisions; it appoints all the regional administrators, save for mayors and municipal council members. The governors of the provinces, who exercise a great deal of power and have significant resources at their disposal, are also appointed by the center, as are the civil servants belonging to the various ministries, right down to the elementary school teacher in the smallest village. From the environment to housing, it is the state's "duty" to provide all services. Similarly, police officers and other security officials are posted from the center. While some circulation of administrative officers is necessary, such officials are often posted to regions not to their liking, as is the case for assignments in the east and southeast, and the relationship between the local population and the civil servants tends to suffer.

Municipalities have very limited means of raising revenues on their own and thus are dependent on the central government for almost all disbursements; this, in turn, creates opportunities for parties of opposing political persuasions to engage in mischief and the settling of scores. The municipalities are still governed by laws passed in the 1930s. Between 1986 and 1992 the share of investments earmarked for municipalities in Turkey has gone down from 1.1 percent of GNP to 0.5 percent.[22] Not surprisingly, in the absence of any attempt at devolution of powers to the provinces, a move is afoot to increase the number of provinces by dividing existing ones. This move is spurred on by residents of a provincial subregion who believe that they will receive better services from Ankara if they literally "secede" from the larger provincial administration. At sixty-seven, the number of Turkish provinces had been stable until the mid-1980s. Since then the number has increased to seventy-nine, with the most recent three being added only in 1995. This trend is likely to continue because it serves as a substitute—although a poor one—for more local autonomy.

The stifling centralization of the Turkish administrative state does not allow for the resolution of conflicts at the local level. This is as applicable to the southeast as it is to other parts of the country. Just as with other legacies of the earlier republican period, this degree of centralization may have been dictated by the requisites of that period. Metin Heper has argued that state elites, "who posed as guardians of Atatürkism as they themselves interpreted it," were intolerant of the periphery and tended to smother it.[23] In the end, the devolution of power to localities will play a significant role in helping defuse the Kurdish question, because then local Kurds—and not Ankara—would be seen as responsible to local community needs. Rule in the southeast thus becomes less "foreign" and more sensitive to local conditions. In fact, it is not just the Kurdish areas that would benefit from this devolution, but all localities in Turkey, including the large cities.

A reform of the administrative system governing Turkey has been debated for some time. The DYP-SHP coalition government had even come to some understanding regarding the limits and extent of this reform. With the exception of education, which it was thought would fall under the control of local Welfare officials, the coalition envisaged that health, cultural activities, road building, and so on would be devolved to the local authorities. The success of Welfare in the 1994 municipal elections doomed the project because it was feared that any devolution would transfer new resources to local Islamic officials.

Devolution of political power can assume many forms: At one end of the continuum it simply means the transfer of more authority to locally elected officials. At the other end, devolution can mean the creation of a federation. In between there are many different arrangements that can be devised that offer varying degrees of autonomy to localities. There is a qualitative difference between federation and some autonomy arrangements on the one hand, and simple devolution of power on the other. This, of course, has to do with the unitary character of the state. A federal arrangement differs structurally and politically in its conception of politics and the relationship between the center and the periphery. In a federal system, the state is composed of territorially defined autonomous units that relinquish important powers to the center, powers such as defense, foreign policy, national security, and the monetary system; in exchange, they keep the right to enact laws and share with the federal government the right to raise revenue.

There are three forms in which a significant amount of power can be devolved from the center: noncentralization, regional autonomy, and federation. That is not an exhaustive list, but it is intended to demonstrate, through three examples, what the implications of a formal attempt at rearranging the state's political structure are.

Under noncentralization, the center diffuses power to subunits and recognizes their right to make many decisions on their own. For example, Bretons in France, who constitute approximately 7 percent of the French population, began a militant series of protests and demands in the mid-sixties for economic, cultural, and political independence. A small group, the *Front pour la Libération de Bretagne,* carried out a sustained campaign of violence against private property. However, in 1981 the Mitterand government adopted a policy of regional decentralization and the promotion of regional languages and cultures. Brittany, along with 21 other regions, gained partial self-government the following year through a popularly elected regional council. By the early 1990s, the economic gap between Brittany and the center had virtually disappeared, and the extreme manifestations of Breton nationalism had vanished. Instead, their nationalist sentiments were directed into local political party activity.[24] As Ted Gurr points out, this policy was also successfully used with the French Basques. In the case of the Corsicans, however, the violent nationalists on the island have not disappeared altogether, even though they remain a small minority.[25]

Considering that France has been the archetypal case of extreme centralization, with a state tradition that dates back to Louis XIV, the creation of the regional assemblies has been well received there. Can the system of the Conseils Regionals work in Turkey, which claims to share a similar statist tradition? This is not a new idea for Turkey. In the optimistic atmosphere following the PKK ceasefire of 1993, the deputy prime minister, Erdal Inönü, suggested that the government was aware of the French model and its success in diminishing separatist sentiments everywhere save Corsica. The government, he said, was intent on increasing the power of localities.[26] But there are differences between the two cases. The French succeeded without undermining the basis of the unitary state. In the case of the Turkish Kurds, however, the level of violence, the economic differentiation, and the depth of the grievances appear to be far greater than in the case of the Bretons or the French Basques and even the Corsicans. In addition, French civil society and its political culture is far more advanced.

Cultural and Political Autonomy

The extension of formal autonomy to the Kurds in the cultural and political realm would represent a major step toward important change in state policy. Autonomy falls well short of any kind of federalism, and the exact terms would need to be devised among a great number of possible arrangements. What would be the political-administrative powers granted to the Kurdish region? As desirable as autonomy-based solutions appear, the correct determination of their exact details is essential to their success or failure.

The most significant example of the granting of regional autonomy is Spain. The Madrid government offered regional autonomy arrangements to all parts of Spain, but the aim was to defuse ethnic conflict primarily in the Basque and Catalan regions. Short of a federal solution, the autonomy arrangements provide for the regional assemblies to reorganize their own territory administratively, raise taxes, develop tourism and other infrastructure, and perhaps most important, to create local police forces. This last provision defuses conflict between a segment of the security forces and the local population by integrating the locals in the functioning of law and order. Spain has maintained Castillian Spanish as the only official language, although at the regional level it has granted a certain degree of leverage to local government, provided that Castillian speakers are not excluded. Catalan is widely used as the daily language of Catalonia, and public signs are written predominantly in Catalan. Catalonia often describes itself publicly as "a country in Spain," but its separatist leanings have largely disappeared.

Still, no such autonomy arrangement can do away with all forms of ethno-nationalism. The Basque terrorist group ETA (Basque Homeland and Freedom) continues to exist, though in much diminished form; it has lost most of its popular support but has not completely ended its use of political violence. Basque and Catalan nationalist parties have either pluralities or majorities in their respective regions, forcing the central government to deal with them. There are also continuous skirmishes between the center and these regions, which seek to maximize areas of functional autonomy and chip away at the powers of the center. (This is not an unnatural process, and it exists even where ethnic differences do not form the basis of local autonomous regions—such as in the United States.) On the other hand, these regions are integrated into the Spanish political system, as demonstrated by the political support offered by Catalonian parties to the minority government of the ruling socialists under Felipe Gonzales.

In comparison to Turkey, the Spanish case benefited from a number of advantages. Both Catalonia and the Basque country were economically well off and did not suffer from the neglect of Turkey's southeast. As a result, issues such as fiscal autonomy did not present the difficulties such an arrangement in Turkey would entail. Second, the level of violence and degree of polarization between the army and the security forces on the one hand and the local population on the other had not reached the magnitude it has in Turkey's southeast. Third, the institutional changes were introduced within the context of a broad, national transition to democracy following Franco's death and, therefore, were easier to implement. And finally, the change occurred in the context of a transition to membership in the European Community, providing incentives to remain within the Spanish union. While we are not necessarily suggesting at this stage that Ankara offer autonomy, the Basque and Catalan examples remain the most successful cases in their category.

In February 1996, the rebel Indian "Zapatista" movement in the Mexican state of Chiapas, after a two-year armed revolt, signed an agreement with the central government that recognized the "autonomy" of Mexico's Indians. That meant they were granted the right to adopt their own forms of government in their own communities or towns; the right to "multicultural education," including instruction in their own languages and "adequate" representation in national congresses; the right to have local courts and district attorneys' offices in Chiapas give Indians greater representation; and, in addition, the creation of a special office to monitor Indian human rights. The agreement does not, however, grant Indians special rights to local natural resources such as oil.[27] This case may bear closer resemblance to conditions in Turkey: The regions of Chiapas and the Turkish southeast have both been economically and socially underdeveloped, although the level of violence in Mexico has been much lower, and the Kurds are far more advanced in their sense of distinct ethnicity, literacy, and history than are the Maya.

A Federal Solution?

The degree of federalism implemented can differ markedly from country to country. By definition, federalism requires only two levels of government, one at the national level and the remainder as subunits. Both levels rule over the same territory, and each has at least one area of independent decision-making. In the case of Canada, the confederation agreement allowed the French-speaking Quebecois considerable latitude in maintaining their distinct culture, language, and Catholic traditions by giving the province of Quebec considerable legislative autonomy. In the process English speakers became a minority in Quebec, but even that did not manage to quell the nationalists' fears of being overwhelmed in an English-speaking Canada while they were instituting French-first policies throughout Quebec.

While a number of Kurds in Turkey speak readily of federalism, few actually envision the difficulties associated with such an arrangement. First, there is a debate over the question of whether Kurds consider themselves a "minority."[28] Unlike Ottoman Empire policies toward Christians and Jews, legally established minorities within Turkey, the Turkish state has never had provisions for Muslims as minorities, a hangover from the Ottoman concept. The state probably will eventually grant recognition to the Kurds as a minority within Turkey. But Turkish lawyers say that the Kurds reportedly are not willing to settle for such a "minority status." Kurds state that they are uncomfortable with minority status because they are not in fact a minority at all but a majority in large parts of Turkey. They seek the right to exercise their own local self-government as a majority in those regions. They fear that acceptance of the status of an "official minority" in Turkey would compromise that position. Is minority status in fact incompatible with self-government in predominantly Kurdish areas? Can Kurds have "minority rights" in those areas of Turkey in which they are in fact true minorities and yet enjoy majority status where they are a majority? Complex constitutional issues are involved.

One Turkish international lawyer expressed the view that Turkey could accommodate far more easily to the development of a Kurdish autonomous region inside Turkey once it had been accepted into the European Union. According to this rationale, without prior EU membership, any move toward regionalization could weaken the state vis-à-vis its regional opponents and would be out of keeping with the present unitary character of regional states. Once inside Europe, however, Turkey would need to face the new reality that the EU is not just a collection of European nations but rather a framework within which the nation-state is itself shriveling in favor of the emergence of more organic and natural economic regions;

these regions now ignore international boundaries in creating new international links among cities, or even among newly emergent "city-states."[29]

Acceptance of the concept of regionalization within Turkey would thus become far more acceptable in the EU context. While this thinking remains somewhat visionary for today's Turkey, it does suggest an intellectual framework in which Turkey will have to rethink entirely the concept of the state. Although federalism is designed to transform countrywide minorities into majorities in their own areas, the number of provinces in which Kurds are a majority is much lower than the number of provinces with a sizable Kurdish minority. Under the federal arrangement advocated by some, the regions of Turkey in which Kurds constitute a majority could potentially be granted federal status, with numerous regional powers granted to a Kurdish capital in Diyarbakir, powers roughly equal to those of Ankara.

But the federal solution gives rise to as many problems as it pretends to resolve. What regions would be considered Kurdish—merely those with a Kurdish majority? What would be the cultural rights and minority protections granted to Turks in the Kurdish regions of the country, and what would corresponding Kurdish cultural rights be in Turkish regions?

Especially considering the fact that by now nearly half of the Kurds in Turkey no longer live in their ancestral lands in the southeast but have moved to more western parts of the country, what are the implications of such an arrangement for those Kurds who have settled in places such as Istanbul and Izmir? It might further aggravate intercommunal tensions or create ones where none had existed before.

How many powers would be devolved to the Kurdish region? Some groups, notably the Kurdish parliament in exile, are on record demanding sweeping regional federal power. The same economic impediments associated with any kind of autonomy arrangement would be exacerbated under a federal option. The southeast is poor and underdeveloped, which is one of the primary reasons for the mass emigration to the western parts of Turkey and even to Europe of Kurds over the last decades.

Analyses of binational ethnic federations—especially in which there is considerable imbalance in the power and size of the regions—suggest that a federal arrangement can be unstable, possibly leading to a reassertion of power of the majority population and region over the minority, and thus encouraging a longer range trend toward total separation of the minority region. In fact, the "civilized" divorce between the Czechs and Slovaks has become an example, if not a banner, for many in such federal states as Belgium and Canada. Whereas federalism was supposed to cement the different groups around the idea of a common state, it has invariably became a stage in the process of dissolution.[30] Yet the federal solution is advocated by many Kurds, including the parliament in exile. Possible ways to prevent this include creation of several different federal regions, similar to the case in the United States, or—less felicitously—Canada.

For all the discussion among Kurds of alternative arrangements, the TOBB study by Dogu Ergil showed that while 13 percent of those Kurdish citizens interviewed in the southeast and south wanted independence, 42.5 percent preferred a federation, while those in favor of autonomy and noncentralization represented only 13 and 19.4 percent, respectively.[31] However, Ergil argues that those interviewed were not clear about the differences between federation, autonomy, and regional devolution of powers. In fact, to most respondents, they all signified a degree of independence from Ankara to conduct their own affairs. Such confusion also indicates the necessity of opening Turkey's press and civil society to debate the broad ramifications of these issues for both Kurds and Turks, so that all the advantages and disadvantages are clearly understood.

Independence and a Pan-Kurdish State

The principle of self-determination for individual nations, an idea that gained much credence with Woodrow Wilson after the end of World War I, is an idea that still mobilizes individuals and groups. The Kurds are no exception. Whether in Iraq or in Turkey, many Kurds volunteer their desire to see an independent Kurdistan on any part of the ancestral homeland. Kurds in Turkey who may genuinely not wish to secede from Turkey may still harbor the desire to see Kurds in northern Iraq become independent. It may represent a form of vicarious independence.

The fact remains that an independent Kurdistan on Turkish soil is both unrealistic and undesirable from an "objective" point of view. While satisfying the needs of die-hard nationalists, it does not reflect the preferred outcome of Kurds in Turkey. The same may not be said of Iraqi Kurds. Given the distribution of Kurds within Turkey and their level of integration in the economy and polity, even if a significant segment are still poorly adapted or unadapted, independence is unlikely to meet the needs of Kurds for whom nationalism is not necessarily of the first order of preference. Alongside cultural and human rights, Kurds do expect to benefit from the fruits of their labor, which has gone into making Turkey into the industrial powerhouse that it is. Therefore, independence is viewed as an unrealistic option by all Kurdish parties. Kurdish separation would destabilize the region and create new crises for Iraq, Iran, and Syria, in that it would produce pressures for a pan-Kurdish state. Almost everyone understands that Ankara could not accept such a "solution," thus resulting in a resurgence of warfare and bloodshed. A Kurdish state born under such circumstances would be quite isolated and unprepared for an independent existence, as even Öcalan himself has recognized.

Kurds in Turkey who discuss independence conceptualize the issue in very general terms. To many it is a right they ought to have, but they have no wish to exercise it. The TOBB report showed that those who favored the independence option were more heavily represented among Kurds forced to migrate as a result of the conflict,[32] indicating the polarizing aspect of the insurgency. The belief in secession results from the conviction that citizens will be better off under a new political arrangement, even though examples from history amply demonstrate that this is not necessarily the case. The desire for such an outcome is, therefore, a function of how the existing order serves a group of people. It is clear that, in Turkey, Kurdish desire for secession (as opposed to simple cultural rights) has ebbed and flowed with the political and economic performance of the state.

No Kurdish party in Turkey advocates a pan-Kurdish state at this point, although the PKK had spoken of it in its early years. This solution is, of course, not within the prerogatives of Turkey to grant, even if it wanted to, since it involves the territory of sovereign neighbors as well. Given the rise of ethnic separatism around the world and the high incidence of bad governance that often sparks such separatism, genuine questions exist as to whether Iran or Iraq will ever be able to settle their problems with dissatisfied Kurdish populations peacefully. Eventual separation of Kurds in either of those states thus cannot be ruled out, which would affect Turkey. But Turkey has the ability to meet the needs of most of its Kurds before the problem fully explodes. Thus the future of any pan-Kurdish state over the long run is uncertain; but preservation of the present Turkish state is still a possibility if the state deals positively with Kurdish needs now.

Process

How can the state reach a peaceful and permanent settlement that enables essential Kurdish aspirations to be fulfilled? Two basic things at least are required: a mechanism by which the Kurds can discuss with state officials their grievances and goals within Turkish society and the state; and a legitimate, legal means by which the state will permit Kurds to attain their goals. But is there a willingness on the part of the state to rethink the character of the problem? The discussion of potential avenues of solution discussed below may be unrealistic as long as the state apparatus is unmoved by a desire to alter the status quo. As long as the state still perceives Kurds as yet-to-be-assimilated Turks, present circumstances lack the elements of mutual willingness that, for example, at least began the Oslo process for an Israeli-PLO dialogue.

In general, one can conceive two kinds of instances in which one or both parties to a conflict are unwilling to pursue a resolution of their conflict. The first occurs when either one or both of the parties perceive the conflict as zero sum—that is, in which any degree of gain by one represents that degree of loss to the other. A zero-sum situation considerably increases tolerance for incurring costs, because any gain by one is perceived as a direct and unacceptable loss by the other. The second case of tolerance for protracted conflict arises when the costs of the conflict are not significant enough for one side to consider it worth contemplating a change in policy; as a result, maintenance of the status quo remains desirable for the stronger party. A conflict may inflict untold damage to one side, while requiring only a minimum effort and modest expenditure of economic and political resources for the other. Clearly, the latter actor has few incentives to seek remedies. Therefore, from the perspective of those directly involved in a conflict, an opportunity to resolve it can exist only if the conflict is not perceived as a zero sum, and if calculations of the future costs of a continued conflict are sufficiently high to warrant considering alternatives.

Calculations ought to reflect both estimates of the direct costs of continued conflict—such as economic, matériel, and even moral losses—as well as the tangible and intangible damage incurred in the international political arena in the form of loss of support, diplomatic damage, access to foreign exchange, investments, and the like.[33] At an estimated 3 percent of GNP,[34] the direct cost of the Kurdish insurgency has so far been bearable for the Turkish state. However, these costs can easily climb if the conflict were to spread into other sectors of the economy, including tourism. Already, businessmen blame the pursuit of the military solution for the high rate of inflation in the country. Continued costs—economic and political— together with diminished expectations that the insurgency will soon end is ultimately what will move the state to seek political solutions. Having shored up Turkish confidence by admitting it into the customs union, European allies too may now feel the time has come to press Turkey into a resolution of the Kurdish question.

The state can follow two broadly differing procedural approaches in dealing with the Kurds: unilateral solutions by the state, or democratic arbitration. Both have advantages and disadvantages.

Unilateral State-led Processes

A state-led unilateral initiative involves recognition by the state of certain needs within the Kurdish community and a unilateral move to fulfill them. For instance, the state could—on its own and without reference to the Kurdish community—officially recognize the existence of a Kurdish minority within the country and grant them certain cultural rights including media and private education. It could also unilaterally lessen the scope of military and security action in the southeast and assist in the reconstruction and economic development of the southeast. These measures would unquestionably have a powerful impact upon the Kurdish community and would weaken some of the appeal of the PKK. All of the above initiatives toward the Kurdish community would be made unilaterally by state executive organs without direct reference to the Kurdish population.

Such a move is typically the course of a state confident of its ability to maintain the struggle for a long period to come but yet averse to its mounting costs. The chief advantage for the state in this approach is that the state requires no Kurdish interlocutor, the process is entirely within state hands, no parliamentary process need complicate it, and the state could determine precisely just how far it would be willing to make unilateral "concessions"—although they would never be termed as such—to the Kurds. It would not (yet) require substantial change of philosophy on the part of the state. It would be based on the state's own interpretation of what the minimal needs of the Kurds are and would be presumably implemented at a time when it feels it has most if not all of the cards in its own hands. The state would simultaneously hope that such concessions might satisfy a large measure of Kurdish aspirations, thereby causing Kurds to abandon the costly armed struggle against the state and instead to cooperate with the state or seek new means to attain their goals.

From the state's perspective, another advantage of this approach is that it would seem far more preferable for Turkey to undertake unilateral actions in favor of the Kurds before engaging in dialogue with Kurdish interlocutors. Then such changes would not be perceived as responding to Kurdish demands, but rather to the demands for Turkey's conformity to European standards—part of the preconditions for close Turkish association with the European community in any case.

In short, the strategy would aim at preempting broader demands and co-opting the majority of the Kurdish population, most of whom are alienated today and who, at least passively, support the idea of PKK operations. We believe that the state is highly likely to select this option first, before introducing other major changes in policy, as both the safest and most controlled course, and as buying the state time. In fact, the state can at any time claim "victory" against the PKK—even if this is correct only in a military and not a political sense—and declare that the time had come to initiate reforms.

The chief disadvantage of the unilateral approach lies in its effort to avoid any empowerment of the Kurdish population by any official recognition, status, or dialogue. It is based on the calculation that the state's concessions would be sufficient to destroy the major source of PKK support. But what if it did not? What if most Kurds feel they still want formal recognition as an official ethnic component of the Turkish state? Whether or not the PKK's own ability to conduct guerrilla warfare would be fatally compromised, the PKK—or similar nationalist organizations—will almost surely continue the political struggle to raise the Kurdish national consciousness and to get explicit recognition by the state of Kurdish existence as a community with legal rights. Nor has the state's nearly exclusive focus on the PKK served Turkey well: While in the short run it highlights the activities and evils of a paramilitary organization, in the longer run it makes the PKK the only logical ultimate interlocutor.[35] Kurds could conceivably even be emboldened by these unilateral concessions and the PKK would take credit for having pressured the state into granting them; this is the greatest fear of Turkish authorities. This question is thus of exceptional importance: How many concessions and reforms are required before the armed struggle will lose most Kurdish support—passive or active? There is no obvious answer to this question; much will depend on the tenor of the approach taken by the state.

In addition, the Kurdish and PKK presence in Europe will remain a strong center from which any Kurdish movements can continue to influence the Kurdish population in Turkey, either if they feel they have been excluded from a settlement, or if serious reservations remain among Kurds in Turkey about the deal offered by the state. The political struggle could continue with a quest to establish Kurdish political parties (assuming there are none) and to use existing concessions to strengthen Kurdish unity and press for formal political gains. Other Turkish political parties could also criticize the government for either excessive or unwise concessions to the Kurds, threatening the party in power with the charge of "treason."

In short, this limited unilateral approach would undoubtedly have major impact upon the Kurdish situation, but whether or not it would put an end to the conflict depends on the extent of the reforms as well as other accompanying factors, such as the health of the economy, which would affect the resources available for investment in the southeast and compensation for victims. If these reforms were to fall short, at the very least this approach could buy time and possibly weaken the armed struggle in the interval. But the armed struggle will be difficult to contain without maintenance of the massive military and security presence in the region—that itself is one of the largest of Kurdish grievances. Removal of this security presence would lead to renewed political activity by the PKK and other nationalist organizations, even if political violence were dropped. Partial solutions thus leave critical dilemmas unresolved.

In a variation of the above unilateral approach, the state could seek a dialogue with Kurdish interlocutors of its own choosing, probably in private. The immediate problem, of course, would involve the selection of a credible interlocutor: whom to choose, and how? Would this be done openly or behind closed doors? The very act of anointing people interlocutors could automatically cast aspersions on their credibility with Kurdish nationalists, especially if the choice does not appear to them representative.

What most Kurdish nationalists would like to see is a genuine body of nationalist Kurdish interlocutors that does not exclude the PKK, the single largest Kurdish force. This option remains completely unacceptable to the state at present. There was, however, a precedent during the Özal period, when he used the DEP parliamentarians as an indirect conduit to the

PKK; this possibility cannot therefore be completely excluded. Alternatively, the state could appoint key Kurds from inside Turkey (and perhaps a few from outside Turkey as well) to represent Kurdish opinion and to serve as interlocutors—although they would have to be credible if the initiative were to go anywhere. These interlocutors would then "negotiate" unofficially with the state on Kurdish demands with the hope of reaching agreement. In view of the positions that have so far marked the state's stance, however, it is unlikely that it would engage in "negotiations," because that would suggest a kind of parity between the parties—even if it were with individuals of its own choosing.

In fact, what is really suggested here is a dialogue. If the state were uncomfortable that "dialogue" risks placing the Kurds on the same level as the state, it could alternatively appoint a commission that would include prominent Kurds as well as Turks to explore Kurdish grievances. The state would then have the liberty to accept as much of the commission's reservations as it wished.

The advantages of this approach lie in the fact that the Kurds would be represented by at least partially credible interlocutors. If a PKK-sanctioned group were selected, it would enjoy broad legitimacy as being representative of the Kurdish population. They could credibly engage themselves in a process of reform with the state that might prove durable. If the changes and reforms they obtained from the state were perceived by the Kurdish population as substantial and meaningful, their acceptance would markedly reduce Kurdish support for PKK operations in the region; popular support for the PKK would drop off sharply, and new recruits would be harder to come by. The PKK would be under pressure from the population to stop actions that were only complicating Kurdish daily life, now that hope for real improvement and new status was in sight. Indeed, if the PKK is politically astute, it will itself take the initiative in making a transition from paramilitary organization to political party.

This approach of unilaterally appointed interlocutors also contains several disadvantages. From the state's point of view, credible Kurdish interlocutors would probably demand more and greater concessions than would be required by a strictly unilateral approach. Second, non-PKK interlocutors could suffer from several potential disadvantages: unless the interlocutors were perceived as possessing strong nationalist credentials, they would stand vulnerable to the charge of a "sellout" at the expense of more nationalist forces. The PKK could act as a spoiler, reject the interlocutors, and attempt to continue the armed struggle in the hope that the Kurdish public would share their view that the interlocutors selected by the state were not credible. By this process, too, the result would create a more politically active Kurdish population. Even if they were quite willing to give up the armed struggle, they would seek to use the democratic process to seek more rights. In other words, the Kurdish struggle would not be entirely over. Finally, the Turkish party in power during the negotiations would remain vulnerable to potential charges of sellout by other political parties.

This is not to say that such a strategy, if it were adopted by the state, would necessarily fail. Obviously, the sooner a state engages in such action, the greater are its chances of success. Any unilateral move by the state can also be seen as a first step to a more engaged process, described below. More important, there is a need to build a majority coalition behind a peaceful political solution; any attempt by the government to seriously consider alternatives brings society closer to a search for a majority coalition. Özal, it is said, proposed to discuss the idea of a federation, not because he thought it viable but precisely because he wanted to demonstrate through a public argument how futile it was as a potential solution.

A Process of Democratic Arbitration

A process of democratic arbitration departs considerably from the unilateral approaches described above. Under unilateral state initiatives, the state either ignores the need for an interlocutor or appoints one itself. The question then arises, which interlocutor? Under a process of democratic arbitration, on the other hand, Kurdish interlocutors are chosen freely and democratically, outside the control of the state.

In addition, democratic arbitration would require the state to create the conditions whereby not only elections to select Kurdish representatives would result, but also an environment of openness, trust, national dialogue, and reconciliation that would facilitate discussions and negotiations. The role of the state indeed becomes that of facilitator rather than that of sole monopolizer of political developments.

The place for discussing the Kurdish question is the Parliament, and normal parliamentary elections would be the best vehicle for selection of Kurdish representatives. Kurds elected in Kurdish regions under free conditions would speak for the Kurdish people. Given the large number of potential delegates from the region, these Kurdish and non-Kurdish members of Parliament would then select from among themselves a much smaller representative body for dialogue with the state. In this way the question of specific party representation is avoided. But it would be imperative for the state to accept the legitimacy of all those chosen, regardless of political orientation. If many representatives chosen were close to the PKK, this would be a fact of life, democratically reflecting the strength (or weakness) of the PKK at elections.

The question of which Kurds are "representative" is a common theme in discussions with Turkish officials. The general working assumption held by many has been that while the PKK is vastly more radical than the majority of Kurds, it is imposing its ideas on the Kurdish population and pushing an agenda that most Kurds do not seek. Hence the PKK represent only a "small minority" of Kurdish thinking—and a "silent majority," in effect, does not follow them. Questions of "silent majorities" have always been a problem in politics. In reality, many big political movements in history, including the American Revolution, have not always represented the majority opinion, but rather the opinion of elites and leadership. These elites over time educate, persuade, or push nervous majorities into a course of political action. The PKK almost certainly does not represent a "majority" of Kurds, but does it represent a consensus among a politically active elite? The benefit of an electoral process is that it removes all question about "silent majorities." The state will need to deal with those whom the people select.

The Basque negotiations in the late 1970s and early 1980s were the most difficult ones because they were overshadowed not only by the violence coming from ETA but also by the intense pressure from the military, which adopted an uncompromising attitude toward nationalist demands. Critical to the process was the role played by the Basque Nationalist party, which assumed the role of the primary interlocutor with the Spanish state.[36] Because it had achieved a legitimacy in the eyes of the public, it could serve as a negotiating partner, although its previous positions on the issue had often displayed a great deal of ambivalence regarding its future goals and especially independence.

During any dialogue or negotiations, furthermore, the state would be wise to permit Kurdish representatives to consult with anyone, anywhere. If they wished to telephone to PKK headquarters in Damascus or the parliament in exile in Brussels, so be it. Any PKK support for the negotiations would only strengthen the legitimacy of the negotiations and ensure that the PKK would not then repudiate them later on.[37] Similarly, Kurds in jail or in exile abroad for nonviolent political "crimes" should be allowed to return home and participate in elections. Those involved in guerrilla activities might conceivably be allowed to return only after several years of peace, in the way that Israel is permitting radical Palestinian activists abroad to do. To ensure the democratic representation of all citizens of Turkey, Parliament could elect or select a commission representing all parties from their midst who would make recommendations on reforms and changes required to meet Kurdish needs.

A question still remains, however, on the legal status of the negotiations. On what legal basis would even a democratically elected body of Kurdish interlocutors then be negotiating with the state? Furthermore, many reforms are not within the purview of the executive alone: They require changes in Turkish security law, electoral law, the constitution, and the central structure of Turkish national administration, leading to greater decentralization. How could the state commit itself to these changes, which involve parliamentary approval? Or would a parliament, with all its public deliberations and grandstanding, be a better venue for tackling a deeply contentious issue like the Kurdish problem? And would changes in the Kurds' status be subject to ratification by the entire political system—remaining, in effect, hostage to the Turkish political electorate and party politics? In that case, the present one-third Kurdish membership in Parliament, currently almost totally silent—or intimidated—on the Kurdish issue, would be locked into bruising political confrontation with the majoritarian Turkish representatives—a likely source of intense national divisiveness. In short, there are a number of complex procedural issues that would need to be worked out—but nothing that creative statesmen could not do if the will exists.

Under any circumstances, it is imperative for the state to encourage the strong and active participation of civil society in search of a common agenda. The activities of civil society have the great virtue that they do not have to contend with the blinders the state has imposed upon itself. All elements of civil society—the press, intellectuals, professionals, trade unions—should freely engage in discussion of these issues in order to overcome the stereotypes and demonizations of the past, and to inform the broader public about the choices involved. Kurds too need to consider deeply not only their current grievances against Turkey but also the important potential benefits of continued association with Turkey—otherwise by far the most politically advanced and westernized state that Kurds are dealing with anywhere in the region. Debates must freely engage members of the Kurdish community, as well as Turkish communities, to create workable relationships. By opening the doors to discussion by civil society on this issue, the state can do a great deal to facilitate the transition to reformed relationships between Turks and Kurds.[38]

The business community has a vital role to play: As with Cem Boyner and Sakip Sabanci, members of this group tend to benefit from an immunity few others in society enjoy. Just as in South Africa, where the Anglo business establishment was very instrumental in changing the attitudes of many, though not all, with respect to apartheid, the Turkish business community has strong links with the West and also has a great many incentives to see the situation resolved for its positive impact on Turkey's economic fortunes. The Turkish public, like the bureaucratic establishment, needs to be educated on this issue; this is where the business elite can also play a role in changing some hardened attitudes. However, such activity must also be recognized for what it is: a small component of a larger-scale enterprise—one that would not succeed without changes at the level of the state. In the short run, the bureaucratic elite in Ankara is more likely to heed the discordant voices of its own business establishment than any other civil sector.

Getting the Process Moving

Large numbers of Turks have grave anxieties about moving toward an officially sanctioned multiethnic state. These anxieties are not without foundation. They represent a retreat from classic Kemalist visions about nation-building. They represent a calculated risk that the social glue of Turkish society and economy is sufficient to keep the nation together once the hands of the state have been lifted. We believe that Turkey as a society is in fact mature enough to face this new challenge and survive as a state—indeed, as a successful state. The process of national consciousness-building among the Kurds is irreversible; to attempt to arrest it is no longer possible and will lead only to increased violence and alienation—and it will ultimately guarantee the one outcome that Turkey fears the most, the separation of the Kurds altogether.

We do not believe that Kurdish independence is even on the Kurdish agenda today. It is not a realistic goal, even in the eyes of the PKK. But, Turks argue, may concessions not facilitate the independence of the Kurds down the road? This question cannot be answered one way or another with any certitude. Given the evolution of nationalist feelings in today's world, there is virtually no country in the world that is not threatened with ethnic division, potential conflict, and even separation over the longer run. Perhaps in fifty years the number of world states will have greatly multiplied. Or perhaps the concept of the state will have evolved into something much softer, in which the real meaning of national sovereignty will have been diminished, weakened from both above and below. If Europe is any model, vast processes of decentralization will make the concept of separation and independence far less urgent or even realistic. Any independent entity today must think very hard about how it will survive in tomorrow's economic world: Who will its trading partners be? What kind of links will it maintain with the world?

As in the case of Israel and the Palestinians, foreign encouragement can help in the process when governments sometimes get locked into frozen positions. While strong foreign pressure on Turkey can create a negative backlash, it is important for Turkey to know that the European Union—to whose membership Turkey aspires—has levels of expectations and standards of procedure that Turkey must eventually meet—for the benefit of all parties. Private, patient, and sensitive—but insistent—reminders to Ankara at all levels of the government of the need for progress on the Kurdish issue is essential to helping preserve Turkey's stability, democracy, and unity.

This persistent pressure and reminder is especially important at meetings at the highest levels of government. Unless Turkish leaders are personally convinced that the longer range success of Turkish cooperation and integration into Western institutions depends on progress toward resolution of the Kurdish problem, they may tend to avoid focus on this complex issue. U.S. policy in particular has so far not significantly changed Turkey's comfort level with the status quo—unlike the case with the more outspoken European contacts. Peaceful resolution of the issue is so important to the future stability of Turkey—a country of greatly increased geostrategic significance in the region—that everyone's interests, including Turkey's, are wrapped up in it. Western governments would be well advised to find some basic ways to index progress in Turkey with other goals that Turkey seeks from Western states, to ensure that the quest for a Kurdish settlement maintains forward momentum. Continued reminders to Turkey need not be public, but they need to be clear.

Entry into the customs union in 1995, for example, was an important milestone for Turkey—although the benefits to Europe too, must not be underestimated in the this context. This entry must be used to get the Turkish government to ease current restrictive policies. It is true that some liberalization concessions were extracted from Ankara, but these were largely symbolic. What the Turkish government has effectively managed to do is to reduce access to information, and it is here that Turkey's allies must take a very hard position. Harassment and imprisonment of reporters, Turkish or foreign, and banning of books and newspapers must not be allowed to continue. These are important values for the West, and since it is Turkey that wants to partake in that world, it must live up to these conventions and principles. While we recognize the importance of working through private channels, public positions are also important. Already, the U.S. State Department publishes an annual human rights report that is widely read. Armed with this document, Turkey's friends in the U.S. and Europe can be educated and asked to relay stern messages to Ankara.

The evolution of Turkish politics and society can also be promoted through encouragement of civil society and increased openness of debate. NGOs are in a position to help arrange meetings and seminars to discuss ways of moving forward. Such organizations have the best chance of altering the perception of the public. Organizations affiliated with the European Union and the U.S. have the access and the means to lend financial and logistical support to such civil society groups that include Turks and Kurds. International exchanges among professional associations, parliamentarians, lawyers, specialists on ethnic problems, businessmen, and so forth can include friendly discussions of the Kurdish problem.

The U.S. in particular has other means of influencing Turkey. The U.S. Department of Defense has access to many levels of the Turkish military. Because these contacts are generally of a technical nature and do not attract the political attention that other bilateral contacts do, the DOD is in a position to influence members of the Turkish military, who exercise a great deal of autonomy in the conduct of the campaign against the PKK and influence with the civilian leadership.

Turkish leaders are very sensitive to U.S. pressure. The most telling example came during Prime Minister Çiller's visit to Washington. Primed by her bureaucracy and entourage of journalists that she would be hearing a lot, especially from President Clinton, regarding human rights abuses in her country, she was surprised and perhaps relieved when the President did not bring up the issue. In fact, she told many on her plane ride back that she did not think the U.S. particularly cared about the issue and that the media and her bureaucracy had exaggerated the whole question.[39]

We realize that Turkey is an important strategic ally and that the policies of the U.S. and other governments will not be determined by human rights considerations alone. However, Turkey's long-term stability is in question, and it is in the interest of its allies to devise strategies that will be conducive to averting instability and chaos.

Traditional "second-track diplomacy" should also play an increasing role, as it did in settlement of the Arab-Israeli problem. Increased contacts between Kurds and Turks in informal, preferably isolated sessions over several days can have a major impact in bringing each side to appreciate the concerns of the other and to treat the other side as human beings, not as institutions, ideologies, or symbols. Turkey today is marked by a striking gap of awareness and understanding on both sides. Increased awareness will facilitate movement toward a settlement and lower the level of rhetoric as wiser voices come to prevail in both communities.

Finally, the governments of the U.S. and Europe must encourage an open and free debate in their own countries and especially encourage human rights organizations and NGOs to publicize and criticize both their own governments' attitudes toward Turkey and Ankara's practices. The reports published by these organizations, while dismissed out of hand by the Ankara government, if well done and documented, have an enormous impact on Turkish public opinion. They also help generate pressure from European or American political groups, whether concerned citizens or political parties, and in the process indirectly increase the pressure on the Turkish state.

Notes and References

1. Chief among them is the ubiquitous slogan "How happy is he who can say 'I am a Turk'" (*Ne mutlu Türküm diyene*) currently plastered all over the southeast. Defenders of this saying argue that the "Turk" is really a national composite and does not denote a specific ethnic group. Since the state was formed by as many as 20 different ethnic groups fighting in the early 1920s, the word *Turk* came to refer to all of them. See Toktamis Ates, "Anayasal Vatandaslik . . ." (constitutional

citizenship) *Cumhuriyet,* May 26, 1994. This, however, does not explain why the state went out of its way to deny that the Kurds ever existed.

2. *Milliyet,* March 23, 1994. He went on to say that "a citizen who calls himself a Kurd is a Kurd. . . . He has the same rights as someone who calls himself a Turk."

3. On the challenge posed by the multiplicity of anti–status quo identities, see, Bozarslan, "Political Crisis and the Kurdish Issue in Turkey."

4. In other multiethnic societies, while minorities may be disadvantaged in more than one respect, their loyalty may have been secured through other means. In Malaysia, for instance, despite the heavy emphasis on Malay culture and political, economic, and cultural preferences for the dominant Malay population, the primary ethnic minority, the Chinese, have traditionally done well economically. See Milton J. Esman, *Ethnic Politics* (Ithaca: Cornell University Press, 1994), 49–74. (Chinese minorities of course have other advantages going for them as well that the Kurds lack, such as traditionally high levels of education and commercial skills.)

5. In Morocco, where the Berbers constitute a significant segment of the population, the Berber language has survived mainly as a spoken language (although there are attempts underway to develop it in a written fashion) despite its different dialects. Yet many of the Berber citizens of Morocco have made tremendous efforts to learn French rather than simply "assimilate" through learning only Arabic.

6. This is not different from a proposal made by a former Turkish ambassador, Pulat Tacar. He suggests that Turkey adopt the French system that allows all local languages to be taught in regional schools and encourages the creation of institutes that help the development of these languages (*Milliyet,* July 3, 1996).

7. *Voice of America,* June 27, 1996.

8. Hamit Bozarslan, "Kurdistan: Économie de Guerre, Économie dans la Guerre," in *Économie des guerres civiles,* ed. François Jeans and Jean-Christophe Rufin (Paris: Hachette, 1996).

9. Even before the crisis in the southeast erupted, the regional distribution of Turkish private sector companies showed that in 1980, of the 421 largest companies, none were located in the southeast, east, or east-central Anatolia. By contrast, the Marmara region accounted for 67.2 percent of these firms. *Istanbul Sanayi Odasi Dergisi* 188 (October 15, 1981).

10. Seyhmus Diken, "Güneydogu'ya Bir Kez daha Lades mi?" *Yeni Yüzyil,* April 25, 1996.

11. Turkish businessmen are not unlike their counterparts elsewhere. Some of them have told us that they would rather invest in Central Asia, where the regimes are stable—read authoritarian—than in the southeast.

12. *Milliyet,* June 18, 1996; *Zaman,* June 23, 1996; and *Milliyet,* July 28, 1996.

13. Mustafa Sönmez, *Dogu Anadolu'nun Hikayesi* (The story of eastern Anatolia) (Ankara: Arkadas, 1990), 240.

14. The GAP project consists of the following provinces: Adiyaman, Diyarbakir, Gaziantep, Mardin, Şanliurfa, Siirt, Batman, and Şirnak.

15. Seyhmus Diken, "Güneydogu'ya Bir Kez daha Lades mi?"

16. Çaglar Keyder, "Toprak Reformu Bölgeyi Ülkeyle Bütünlestirebilirdi" (Land reform would have united the [southeastern] region with the rest of the country) *Milliyet,* February 21, 1995.

17. For an analysis of the ethnic parties, see, Donald Horowitz, *Ethnic Groups in Conflict* (Berkeley: University of California Press, 1985).

18. See Korkut Özal's interview in *Hürriyet,* June 21, 1996.

19. One voter interviewed during the 1995 elections summed up this psychology when he said that he would be voting for Welfare without worrying too much, since the military is always there to fix things if they get out of hand.

20. During the debate over the modification of Article 8 of the penal code, some political leaders openly suggested that the military opposed such an alteration and tried to use it to block the change.

21. The National Security Council debated, though to date has not accepted, a change in the law governing the displaying of the flag. It wants the flag to be displayed not only every day, instead of only on holidays, but also from mosques (*Hürriyet,* June 11, 1996). This is hardly a civil-military question on which officers need to be consulted, much less one they should initiate.

22. Ahmet Özer, "Yerel Yönetimlerin Yeniden Yapilanmasi" (The restructuring of local administrations) in *Yerel Yönetimler ve Demokrasi* (Local administrations and democracy), ed. Ercan Karakas et al. (Ankara: Sosyal Demokrasi Yayinlari, 1994), 106–7.

23. Metin Heper, "State and Society in Turkish Political Experience," in *State, Democracy and the Military,* ed. Heper and Evin, 5.

24. Ted Robert Gurr, *Minorities at Risk* (Washington, DC: US Institute of Press, 1993), 156.

25. *Ibid.,* 156–57.

26. *Milliyet,* April 7, 1993

27. Julia Preston, "Mexico and Insurgent Group Reach Pact on Indian Rights," *New York Times,* February 15, 1996.

28. For an excellent discussion of minority rights, see Kirişci and Winrow, op. cit. (See note 1, p. 17.)

29. The new triangle ties currently being forged between the three powerful cities of Lyons in France, Geneva in Switzerland, and Turin in Italy—all somewhat close to each other—are a key example of these new regional relationships, in which borders are irrelevant.

30. Jacques Rupnik, "Le Réveil des Nationalismes," in *Le Déchirement des Nations,* ed. Jacques Rupnik (Paris: Seuil, 1995), 32–36.

31. Türkiye Odalar Birligi, *Dogu Raporu: Teshisler ve Tespitler,* 38–39.

32. *Ibid.*

33. The Israeli government until 1993 also portrayed its fight with the PLO as zero sum; the PLO was defined only in terms of a "terrorist organization," pure and simple. The change of Israeli heart came about only after recalculation of the real cost of the Palestinian intifada and a growing awareness of Israeli isolation on

the issue—even vis-à-vis its close ally the U.S. Even now, a significant segment of Israeli public opinion (and Palestinian as well) refuses to accept the new calculation, preferring to continue to see the conflict as a zero-sum proposition.

34. Estimates of the cost of the insurgency vary widely: Eric Rouleau quotes a former minister of state's estimate for 1994 as being $8.2 billion ("Turkey: Beyond Atatürk," 81). Others have claimed that the amount of money allocated in the 1994 budget to fighting terror represented 5 percent of GNP. See TBMM, *Tutanak Dergisi,* October 18, 1994, 383. If the trend is maintained through 1996, this would put the expenditure at around $10 billion. The fact remains that a real estimate of the cost of the conflict is elusive: In Turkey, military budgets are not examined and there are numerous nonpublic off-budget accounts that can be used to supplement any effort. On the other hand, the 3 percent of GNP estimate suggested in this study, or approximately $4.5 billion, is a rough calculation that takes into account the fact that the Turkish army is largely a conscript army, and Western estimates of troop deployment may not translate well in the Turkish context. The Turkish General Staff has gone on record saying that the total cost of maintenance and operation of all security services is $4 million a day, or $1.5 billion a year (*Hürriyet,* April 30, 1997). This figure, at the very least, does not include damage estimates to the villages, countryside, and infrastructure, or indirect costs such as loss of production.

35. If you don't negotiate with the enemy, with whom do you make peace?" as liberal Israelis used to ask when arguing in favor of direct negotiations with the PLO.

36. Juan Diez Medrano, *Divided Nations: Class, Politics, and Nationalism in the Basque Country and Catalonia* (Ithaca: Cornell University Press, 1995), 117, 146–47.

37. In the later phase of negotiations with the Palestinians prior to the first Arafat-Rabin meeting in Washington, the Israelis permitted Palestinian negotiators to remain in regular touch with PLO headquarters in Tunis, even though Israel had not yet recognized the PLO. Israel felt this was wise, because it meant that their Palestinian interlocutors gained in legitimacy through consultation with the PLO, strengthening the solidity of any agreements eventually reached.

38. In Israel, the difference between the Likud and Labor parties in their attitudes to the Palestinians in many ways originated from a simple fact: Many Labor party members, while not espousing the ideas of the Palestinians, over the years had had much contact with the other side, sometimes even at the risk of breaking Israeli laws that forbade contact with the PLO.

39. Many people who have recounted this incident also claim that the Turkish government would have been more inclined to initiate some changes had the president pushed. The president did not because the meeting had gone so well until then that he did not want to mar its results.

Conclusion

The end of the Cold War, the weakening of the left, and the process of globalization have unleashed new forces in many countries. Of these, the return of nationalism, almost with a vengeance, is probably the most notable. Turkey is no exception. Although it predates the dissolution of the Soviet Empire and the ensuing nationalist scramble in Europe and elsewhere, the Kurdish crisis in Turkey gained further momentum from these events.

The forces of nationalism buffeting Turkey do not originate simply from a resurgent Kurdish identity, but also from the discovery of the multicultural character of Turkish society. The primordial essence of nationalism aside, the problem confronting Turkey is the longer term repercussions of the conflict in the southeast. In discussing the case of Bosnia, Jacques Rupnik argues that "it is not 'ancient' hatreds that are at the root of the war in Bosnia. Rather, it is the war which created the hate."[1] The conflict in the southeast is particularly challenging because it is in the process of sowing the seeds of future hatreds.

As William Zartman points out, "internal conflicts seem to have the ability to continue for decades and arrive neither at victorious resolution for one side nor satisfactory reconciliation for both." Zartman also argues that "ethnic conflicts are best handled early, before they get out of hand, and they are best handled through an increased role in their own general affairs and an elimination of blockages and discrimination."[2] In the case of Turkey, the Kurdish issue, while having lasted since the beginnings of the republic according to some, or since 1984 according to others, is still in its relatively early stages. It is not a civil war, but an insurrection. As such, the cost to the Turkish government and military establishment may be tolerable. The cost calculations that tend to focus on tangible items omit other indirect costs. Chief among them is the damage to institutions of state and society.

It is not surprising, therefore, that democracy in Turkey has been one of the primary victims of the conflict in the southeast. Whether it is the use of emergency rule in the region, which puts severe restrictions on individual liberties, or the growth and proliferation of security agencies and services, or the use of repressive laws to ban newspapers and jail dissidents, Turkish democracy has not given a good accounting of itself in recent years. No matter how true the Turkish officials' refrain about terrorism being a fundamental violation of human rights, a state's behavior is not comparable to that of an illegal organization. Turkey has always prided itself on being a society that respects and lives by its laws; it cannot afford not to apply them or be perceived as selectively interpreting them.

In the seventy-odd years since independence, the Turkish state has not managed to trust its citizens; it has cajoled and nurtured them, but it has never entrusted civil society with real power. The tutelary democracy into which the Turkish system has evolved has learned to tolerate dissent, but only within certain very prescribed bounds. Whether because of the watchful eyes of the National Security Council or threats of military intervention or interference by other state institutions, there have been many excuses for the lack of determined political leadership. It is not just with respect to the Kurds and the southeast that there has been resistance to change, but also on issues relating to religion or the transfer of assets from the state to the private realm—by this we mean not just the privatization of state companies and their transfer to a burgeoning capitalist sector but also the transfer of assets to private individuals. The conditions that necessitated the restrictions of the early republican period have all but disappeared, and, to the extent that some exist, they are the products of state policy. In the words of one Turkish observer, it is the societal paranoia over the prospect of the division of the country that hampers the prospects for democracy.[3]

But democracy is precisely what is necessary to the emergence of a leadership that does not have to look over its shoulder. This is not a new insight, since many observers, especially Turkish ones, have advocated it. On the Kurdish question per se, Sahin Alpay argues that there is no guarantee that democratization will completely eliminate the violence instigated by separatist forces, and it may, in the short run, even increase that violence. In the longer run, however, it is the only means by which those in favor of violence and separation will be isolated.[4]

In the end, we remain optimistic about Turkey's prospects for settlement of its agonizing Kurdish problem. The basic democratic structures are in place, and Turkish society is strikingly mature in the regional context. But these structures also need improvement, reform, and modernization. Indeed, this process of political modernization is a global dilemma and never easy. Turkey's future success is linked to continued political and social evolution, and not just for the sake of the Kurdish problem alone. For all its opportunism and obscurantist views, the Welfare party was not, in the final analysis, blocked from assuming power in the summer of 1996. This represents a major watershed in Turkish politics even though the military forced this government out. It may also augur well for the future of the Kurdish problem, not because Welfare is capable of resolving or even willing to resolve the problem, but because it pushes the limits of Turkish democracy.[5]

It is important that Turkey not feel uniquely singled out for criticism in this area, but rather made to realize that its problems are typical of ethnic problems around the world in which a variety of potential solutions are available for consideration, discussion, and examination. Turkey's friends and allies around the world can also be made more alert to the urgency of a solution to the Kurdish problem, before it drags Turkey in dangerous directions of broadened civil war, economic weakness, domestic terror, polarization, chauvinism, and curtailment of democratic liberties.

Notes and References

1. Jacques Rupnik, "Le Réveil des Nationalismes," in *Le Déchirement des Nations,* ed. Jacques Rupnik (Paris: Seuil, 1995), 24.

2. I. William Zartman, "The Unfinished Agenda: Negotiating Internal Conflicts," in *Stopping the Killing: How Civil Wars End,* ed. Roy Licklider (New York: New York University Press, 1993), 20, 32.

3. Enver Sezgin, "Kürt Sorununda Çüzümün Anahtari Diyalog (The key to the solution of the Kurdish problem is dialogue), *Yeni Yüzyil,* June 27, 1996.

4. Sahin Alpay, "Kürt Sorunu Nasil Asilabilir?" (How can the Kurdish problem be overcome?) in Seyfettin Gürsel et al., *Türkiye'nin Kürt Sorunu,* 161.

5. From another perspective, this represents one fewer taboo left to combat. Hüseyin Çakir, "Bir tabu daha bitti, simdi sira Kürt sorununda" (Another taboo has disappeared, now it is the turn of the Kurdish question), *Yeni Yüzyil.* July 11, 1996.

Index

About the Authors

Henri J. Barkey is associate professor of international relations at Lehigh University and has published extensively on Turkish affairs. He is the author of *The State and the Industrialization Crisis in Turkey* (Westview Press, 1990), and he edited *The Politics of Economic Reform in the Middle East* (St. Martin's, 1992) and *The Reluctant Neighbor: Turkey's Role in the Middle East* (USIP Press, 1996).

Graham E. Fuller is a senior political analyst at RAND and former vice chairman of the National Intelligence Council at the CIA. Mr. Fuller lived in Turkey for many years. He is a coauthor of *Turkey's New Geopolitics* (Westview Press, 1994), and his article "The Fate of the Kurds" appeared in *Foreign Affairs* (Spring 1993).